D0375849

Crime:
Emerging Issues

edited by

James A. Inciardi
University of Delaware

and

Harvey A. Siegal
Wright State University

PRAEGER PUBLISHERS
New York

Published in the United States of America in 1977
by Praeger Publishers, Inc.
200 Park Avenue, New York, N.Y. 10017

©1977 Praeger Publishers, Inc.

All rights reserved

Library of Congress Cataloging in Publication Data

Main entry under title:
Crime: Emerging Issues.

    CONTENTS: The rediscovery of violence in America:
Frantz, J. B. The frontier tradition, an invitation to
violence. Bettelheim, B. Violence, a neglected mode
of behavior.--Geis, G. Violence in American society.
Glaser, D. Violence and the city. [etc.]
    1. Crime and criminals--United States--Addresses,
essays, lectures. 2. Violence--United States--Addresses,
essays, lectures. 3. Crime prevention--United States--
Addresses, essays, lectures. I. Siegal, Harvey A.
II. Inciardi, James A.
HV6789.E4   364'.973   76-15244

ISBN 0-275-64320-4

Printed in the United States of America

Crime:
Emerging
Issues

To the memory of
Ibn Khaldún

Contents

Introduction
The Nature and Heritage of Criminology

Criminology, in its broadest sense, is the entire body of knowledge society possesses regarding crime, and the efforts it makes to both control and prevent it. Thus, the substance and method of criminology is drawn from all areas of society—science, medicine, law, religion, sociology, social work, education, political science, economics, and public administration. Traditionally, however, criminology has been specifically concerned with the scientific study of crime and criminals, and in this sense, it has extended its inquiries in a number of directions. First, it analyzes the causes of crimes and the characteristics of offenders; second, it investigates the varying conditions under which behavior becomes recognized and defined as criminal; third, it attempts to measure the extent and distribution of crime; and fourth, it experiments with the control and prevention of crime, and the rehabilitation of offenders. Within each of these areas, and during any given period in its history, the discipline or science of criminology reflects various theoretical and substantive orientations and focal concerns.

THE SEARCH FOR CAUSES

A visit to the historical repository of criminology reveals that the first of its scientific medley of hypotheses, generalizations, concepts, theories, and conclusions circumscribed a concept of causation. This focus has endured through many generations of criminologists, and in its variant forms has been generally based on the doctrine of *determinism*. The assertions of scientific determinism in relation to criminal behavior denied the existence of freedom and claimed that the choice of alternatives to action was an illusion. The determinists negated the concept of criminal responsibility based on free will.

> Suddenly, one morning, on a gloomy day in December, I found in the skull of a brigand a very long series of atavistic abnormalities. . . analogous to those that are found in inferior vertebrates. At the sight of these strange abnormalities—as an extensive plain is lit up by a glowing horizon—I realized that the problem of the nature and generation of criminals was resolved for me.[1]

With this proclamation made more than a century ago, Italian criminologist Cesare Lombroso, who is credited with having been the "father of modern criminology," gave substance to the *anthropological* study of criminals. As a positivist, Lombroso had observed the prevalence of tatoos on criminals, as well as a high frequency of such physical "stigmata" as low forehead, receding chin, more than the normal number of fingers, abundance of wrinkles, atypical head size or shape, and eye peculiarities. Since such physical peculiarities had also been observed as those of the primitive savage, he concluded that the criminal was an *atavism*—a throwback to an earlier stage in the evolution of man.

As the discipline of criminology matured, the Lombrosian ethos came to be viewed with less favor, but many theorists nevertheless continued to embrace the deterministic model. In time, the search for the causes of crime focused not only on the individual but also on the offender's social milieu and wider cultural environment. The basic methodologies that guided the studies of causation were characterized by both raw *empiricism*, a faith in the senses and the power of observation and a willingness to be ruled by observable evidence, and *rationalism*, which assumes the universality of natural laws.

The deterministic position was also grounded in a definition of misconduct in society. Men set down rules of conduct and behavior, and departures from these rules constituted deviance. Most of the rules were interpreted as being intrinsic to a natural order and were "given" as a natural reality. As such, the inquiries of the determinists were straightforward: Who are the deviants? Why do they behave in such a manner? How can they be best controlled?

The search for the causes of crime went beyond the anthropological position of Lombroso and his followers. A *medical* approach sought to study the influence of physical disease on crime; a *biological* approach attempted to relate crime to heredity; a *physiological* and *biochemical* approach correlated crime with both normal and abnormal physiological functions and types; a *psychological* approach analyzed motivation and diagnosed personality deviations; a *psychiatric* approach specialized in mental disease; a *psychoanalytic* approach traced behavior deviations to the repression of basic drives; a *geographical* approach attempted to demonstrate the influences of climate, topography, natural resources, and geographical location on crime; an *ecological* approach investigated the impact of the spatial distribution of men and institutions

upon behavior patterns; an *economic* approach looked for relationships between various economic conditions and crime; a *social* approach considered
educational, religious, recreational, occupational, and status factors as they
related to crime; a *cultural* approach examined the influence of various institutions and social values that characterized groups, and the conflicts between
the cultures of different groups, on crime; and a *sociological* approach was
concerned with the nature and effects of social attitudes and relationships
on behavior.[2]

CRIMINOLOGY AND THE SOCIOLOGY OF DEVIANCE

During recent decades, new approaches to the study of crime have emerged.
Circumscribed by the notion of *nominalism*—that realities are achieved only
when they can be imagined and labeled—misconduct, deviance, and crime are
viewed as subjectively problematic. Nominalism is characterized by a conception
of deviance and crime as having *no* meaning until they are given meaning.
Inquiries are directed to the processes of social interaction which define behaviors as deviant or criminal.   More specifically, the approach views crime
as one of many forms of deviant behavior, and examines the genesis and definition of deviance as an interactive process, with three major themes: the definition of deviance; the labeling of deviants; and the reactions to deviation.

In tracing the various schools of thought that have contributed to this "sociology of deviant behavior," it can be readily observed how its alternative perspective and method have given new direction and utility to the discipline of criminology.   According to this point of view, deviance is a human construct, and
the definition of behavior as deviant involves a process, a status transformation
that may take place over a long period of time.

Becker indicated in 1963 that "social groups create deviance by making
the rules whose infraction constitutes deviance."[3]   But the rules that are trans-
gressed do not occur automatically, and they are not brought to bear on specific
behaviors without some reason.   Rules are directed toward behaviors that are
perceived to be "harmful" to a group, for as Erikson described it in 1966,
"the term, deviance, refers to conduct which the people of a group consider
so dangerous or embarrassing or irritating that they bring special sanctions to
bear against the persons who exhibit it."[4]   What may be harmful to a group,
or "dangerous or embarrassing or irritating," is of a relative nature, and must
be discovered and pointed out.   Becker suggested that the process of discovery
and designation is the enterprise of the crusading reformer.[5]   Such a crusader,
or "moral entrepreneur," is "fervent and righteous" and operates with an
absolute ethic.   The crusader views certain elements in society as truly, totally,
and unconditionally evil, and feels that nothing can be right in the world until
rules are made to remove or correct such wickedness.   The crusader's mission

is a holy war, for the perfidy that has been perceived represents a potential breach in the stability of society, and its eradication will ensure a better way of life.

The new perspective offered by the study of deviance resulted in multidisciplinary approaches to the study of crime. Sociologists and criminologists of divergent orientations began to examine the language of deviance and criminality, looking to history as a laboratory for the testing of propositions, hypotheses, and theories. Gusfield, for example, studied Prohibition and the temperance movement,[6] Erikson investigated crime in Puritan society,[7] and Becker examined early narcotics legislation.[8] Inquiries of this kind suggested that the efforts of many "crusading reformers" and their supporters were not necessarily or entirely humanitarian, with the result that criminological thought had still further directions to explore.

In this respect, Quinney suggested in 1970 that criminal definitions are descriptive of behaviors that conflict with the interests of those segments of society that have the power to shape public policy.[9] Modern society, he argued, is characterized by an organization of differences, with varied interests distributed among the socially differentiated positions. These interests, furthermore, are organized around the activities pursued by each segment, usually of a political, economic, religious, kinship, educational, or civic nature. Since there is a structured inequality in society characterized by an unequal distribution of power and conflict among its various divisions, combined with a differentiated interest structure (as determined by the respective classes, statuses, sexes, ages, occupations, races, religions, political orientations, and general attitudinal and value systems), the segments tend to compete with each other in terms of the priority of their respective interests.

The Prohibition movement, for example, reflected numerous "interest structures" on the part of the reformers and their supporters as well. The movement was seemingly an assertion of a rural Protestant value against that of the urban culture emerging at the end of the nineteenth century: Drinking and the liquor trade were seen as key-signatures of an urban morality and of urbanism in general, which were diametrically opposed to the more fundamental rural creeds, which emphasized individual human toil, total abstinence, and faith in the Bible. The new urban centers with their commercialization and specialization were destroying the self-sufficiency of the farm and village, creating a situation of unwanted dependence.[10] Urbanism was perceived as the real sin in society, and the reform movement was an organization of rural interests against the "wicked city" and its impending dominance. In general, the reform group was typically composed of, and probably dominated by, people in middle and upper positions in the social structure, and their efforts were directed at providing "salvation" for the less privileged. But this provision of the means of salvation was a legitimation of the reformers' own moral posture—a segment of their complex of interests—and of the power they derived from their superior position in society. More specific interests were also at stake. Frances E. Willard of the Women's Christian Temperance Union (WCTU), for example, saw the movement as a means of uplifting the position of women in society. Conscious of the censure the women of America had received for their general lack of *esprit de corps*, she used the WCTU as a way of developing feelings of mutuality and consensus among women.[11] And from their point of view, industrialists felt that Prohibition would provide a more manageable, productive labor force.[12]

The deviance perspective also suggested that the efforts of the moral crusader were generally ended soon after they aroused the makers of public opinion and public policy. Actual formulation of laws was left to those charged with the duty of constructing legislation that typically supported the crusaders' interests. As such, the definition of behavior as deviant, and, finally, as criminal, emerged as the end-product of a long-term enterprise. Ultimately, the given law was a creation and interpretation of specialized rules generated by the interest structures of those groups who had sufficient power to translate their interests into policies.[13]

CRIMINOLOGY AND THE LABELING PERSPECTIVE

Although the sociology of deviance offered a fresh perspective on how crime could "come into being" as a social construction, the discipline of criminology quickly recognized that while a criminal definition might be *absolute* for a given society, the application of such a definition was *relative* to different segments and populations within that same society. In its efforts to understand this phenomenon, the criminological enterprise not only expanded its boundaries of inquiry; in addition, it generated fresh interpretations from many of the sophisticated, yet forgotten or ignored, contributions of earlier periods.

Becker's initial discussion of the genesis and definition of deviance had indicated that "one who cannot be trusted to live by the rules agreed on by the group . . . is regarded as an *outsider*."[14] The process that labels an individual an outsider or deviant or criminal, however, is not a simple one. In this respect, Quinney suggested that the probability that the deviant or criminal label will be applied tends to vary according to the extent to which the behaviors of the powerless conflict with the interests of the powerful.[15] As such, the application of deviant and criminal definitions would appear to be a type of *political enterprise*.

In 1938, years before the sociology of deviance took shape as an integrated approach to the study of crime, Tannenbaum studied those issues that ultimately led to the conceptualization of the criminal process in a political perspective. In his discussion of societal reaction to deviant behavior, or, more appropriately, the "dramatization of evil," he suggested that one's reputation is a type of public definition, and that the process of making a criminal is one of "tagging, defining, identifying, segregating, describing, emphasizing [and], making conscious and self-conscious . . . ."[16] Lemert, a decade later, introduced the idea of *politicality* when he viewed societal reaction in terms of the rivalry of groups struggling to maintain their position in a hegemony of power relations. Innovation in behavior, he suggested, represented a departure from recognized patterns of social action and tended to be viewed as unfavorable since it upset a system of reciprocity between groups; the reaction of society to these innovative behaviors involved the triad of awareness, policy determination, and reform.[17] A further explanation of this theoretical construct was offered by Vold, who suggested that crime may indeed be "political behavior, and the criminal becomes in fact a member of a 'minority group' without sufficient public support to dominate the control of the police power of the state."[18]

The conception of the application of criminal definitions as the political process described by Tannenbaum, Lemert, Vold, and Quinney had its foundations in the writings of the economic determinists as well as in the later criminological discussions of conflict and "criminogenesis." Karl Marx, in his *A Contribution to the Critique of Political Economy* (1859), discussed the power-conflict view of society and argued that the mode of production determined the character of social, political, and spiritual existence. Society, in Marx's view, was organized around the pursuit of human needs, and the essential nature of social interaction was the facilitation of such need-acquisitions through a division of labor. In the course of history, classes arose which seized the primary modes of production and exploited the subordinate classes for their own acquisitive purposes. These classes not only dominated the social structure, but through their possession of economic strength they also controlled the primary determinants of political power. Power, in turn, was used as the vehicle for the maintenance of both the class structure and the prevailing economic order. Thus, capitalist and working-class interests were polar and tended to conflict for dominance. In this framework, Marx claimed, law was a tool employed by the capitalists for the maintenance of their position through the exploitation of workers; as such, law represented a means for the institutionalization of conflict.[19]

"Criminogenesis," in the words of Taft, described modern industrial society as being characterized by materialism, growing impersonality, political democracy, individualism, insistence upon the importance of status, group loyalties, lack of scientific orientation in the study of society, racial discrimination, survival of frontier traditions, tolerance of political corruption, general faith in the law, disrespect for some law, and acceptance of quasicriminal exploitation. Further, these values are subscribed to by the majority of the segments of the highly stratified society whose materialistic orientation places a high value on the acquisition of wealth and power.[20] The ensuing competitive struggle for these favorable goals was described by Merton, who recognized such aspirations as common to all.[21]

The criminological interpretation of these views drawn from the school of economic determinism suggested that the structured inequality that exists in society tends to produce conflict among its various segments, with each segment attempting to foster its common interests. And as noted earlier, those groups with the greatest power have greater ability to translate their interests into public policy, and hence, are more capable of shaping the nature and direction of law enforcement and administration. Quinney carried this interpretation further by demonstrating how groups whose interests were in conflict with those represented in prevailing law were highly vulnerable to having their behavior defined as criminal. He argued, however, that the probability of such labeling taking place would depend heavily on prevailing criminal conceptions, community expectations of law enforcement, and the organizational and ideological structure of the criminal justice system.[22]

The labeling perspective carried its efforts still further by studying how criminal conceptions were constructed and diffused throughout society, through both personal and mass communications, and how society reacted to given types of crime. In addition, researchers and theorists investigated the nature of varying criminal conceptions, how these were related to community expectations of law enforcement, and consequently, their impact on differential law enforcement.

THE STUDY OF OFFENDER TYPES

Criminology has not limited itself to studying the causes of crime, the genesis and definition of deviance, and the criminalization process as generalized areas of inquiry. Simultaneously, it has attempted to understand and analyze specific forms of behavior. Even Lombroso was sensitive to the fact that there were alternative offender types, and that the explanation of one pattern of behavior would not necessarily apply to other types. While a number of practitioners in the discipline examined different kinds of criminals in the institutionalized setting, others went directly to the front lines of the underworld, to observe and attempt to understand crime and criminals in their native habitat. The methods of inquiry were both quantitative and qualitative, and the number of significant contributions was almost limitless.

Among those who had a profound impact on criminology was Edwin H. Sutherland. During the 1930s, Sutherland intensively studied the professional thief, a highly specialized career criminal who engaged in crime as a way of life. With the publication of his *The Professional Thief* in 1937,[23] the first systematic analysis of a criminal behavior system that heretofore had remained unstudied from the perspective of social science became available. It revealed the details of a "profession" that was not typically recognized as such at that time, making manifest the nature and complexity of a criminal career. Further,

The Professional Thief was a contribution to general sociology and history, since Sutherland's effort demonstrated the relationships between the culture of the underworld and general social institutions. He pointed out how the profession of theft had originated and was perpetuated in social disorganization, and why it would continue to persist in the absence of modifications in the basic social order.

But as important as Sutherland's effort was, it represented only a prelude to a theoretical perspective that continues to serve a major role in contemporary criminological thinking. Two years later, in an attempt to provide an understanding of crime that would replace the multiple-factor approaches of his day and go beyond the simple enculturation explanations, Sutherland offered his theory of *differential association*.[24]   In its final form, the theory contained the following propositions: (1) criminal behavior is learned; (2) criminal behavior is learned in interaction with other persons in a process of communication; (3) the principal part of the learning of criminal behavior occurs within intimate personal groups; (4) when criminal behavior is learned, the learning includes (a) techniques of committing the crime, which are sometimes quite complicated, sometimes quite simple, and (b) the specific direction of motives, drives, rationalizations, and attitudes; (5) the specific direction of motives and drives is learned from definitions of the legal codes as favorable or unfavorable; (6) a person becomes delinquent because of an excess of definitions favorable to violation of law; (7) differential associations may vary in frequency, duration, priority, and intensity; (8) the process of learning criminal behavior by association with criminal and anticriminal patterns involves all of the mechanisms that are involved in any other learning; (9) while criminal behavior is an expression of general needs and value, it is not explained by those general needs and values since noncriminal behavior is an expression of the same needs and values.

Although the differential association theory has some serious weaknesses and has been severely attacked, it called attention to the importance of many social factors, and to the similarity between the process of learning criminal behavior and that of learning lawful behavior. It provided an integrative theory for criminology, one which assumed that the many diverse factors and correlates of crime were important to the extent that they affected an individual's associations and learning experiences. And finally, Sutherland's work provided criminolgy with a stimulus which has resulted in many elaborate studies of various offender types, categories of crime, and criminal behavior systems.

THE MEASUREMENT OF CRIME

Empirical analysis of the magnitude and trends of crime enjoyed a level of interest even before the onset of criminology as a scientific pursuit. The initial impetus for the study of criminal statistics began in 1827, when France became the first country in the world to gather statistical data on crime in the modern sense.   Lambert-Adolphe-Jacques Quetelet, a mathematician and astronomer, and André-Michel Guerry, an attorney, were quick to seize upon the records of crime newly available in their country as raw material for analytical explorations into the distribution of crime in society and assessments of its significance. Quetelet's *Recherches statistiques sur le Royaume de Pays-Bas,* published in 1833, represented energetic investigations of crime in relation to age, sex, profession, education, economic conditions, climate, and ethnicity.   Their calculations clearly suggested the existence of phenomena in the social order that had far-reaching implications for criminology and criminal justice—that the annual totals of recorded crimes and the main classes of crime remained essentially the same from year to year.[25] These notions were later elaborated in the nineteenth century by French sociologist Émile Durkheim, who is credited with having given both method and direction to twentieth-century sociology. Durkheim's observations of the regularities and persistence of crime led him to the conclusion that the extent of crime in a society was a function of the machinery available to recognize and control it.   He further indicated that crime was a "normal" part of the social order, and that its complete eradication was impossible.[26]

The United States was not graced with the wealth of data on crime that was available in France during the 1800s, and although judicial criminal statistics were available in some states as early as 1829, these were generally incomplete and of little value to the criminologist.[27] The collection of criminal statistics at the national level began with enumerations of criminals, referred to as "statistics of crime," in the census volumes from 1850 through the turn of the century. But these too were of limited utility to the serious investigator.   They were, in actuality, prison statistics, relating to individuals found in prisons on a certain day of the year or to those committed during the year preceding the census inquiries.[28]

The uniform collection of crime statistics on a national basis began in 1930, when Congress authorized the Federal Bureau of Investigation to collect and compile nationwide data on crime.   Known as the *Uniform Crime Reports (UCR),* these data are now published annually, and are divided into "crimes known to the police" and "arrests." Sharp criticisms have been leveled at the *Uniform Crime Reports,* because of the limited scope and incomplete nature of their data.   There shortcomings, in fact, have been the general criticisms of all criminal statistics, including those collected by local police agencies, courts, and correctional facilities, since so many criminal acts go unreported to the police.   It must be emphasized, however, that even with the restricted scope of these statistics, there is nevertheless more empirical data on crime available for study than there exists for any other social phenomenon.   Criminologists have both complained and taken delight in this reality, and they have also made concerted efforts to improve the state of criminal statistics.

A major contribution to criminological research was the development of victim survey research. To determine the extent of unreported crime and gain insights into public attitudes toward police, crime, and criminals, the President's Commission on Law Enforcement and Administration of Justice initiated the first national survey of crime victimization.[29]   In 1965, the University of Chicago's National Opinion Research Center (NORC) questioned ten thousand households, asking whether any member of a household had been a victim of crime during the previous year and whether the crime had been reported. More detailed surveys of high and medium crime-rate precincts were made in Boston, Washington, and Chicago.   The surveys suggested that the amount of crime in the United States was several times that reported in the *Uniform Crime Reports.*   The NORC survey suggested, for example, that forcible rapes were three-and-a-half times the reported rate, burglaries three times greater, aggravated assaults and larcenies of fifty dollars and over more than double, and robbery 50 percent greater than the reported rate.   The overall number of personal injury crimes reported to NORC was almost twice the *UCR* rate and the amount of property crimes more than twice as much.   For certain specific offenses the Washington survey showed from three to ten times as many crimes as the number indicated by police statistics.   Even these rates were believed to understate the actual amounts of crime partly because, as Biderman pointed out, "most incidents of victimization, even many that are 'serious' legally, are not highly salient experiences in a person's life."[30]

During January 1971, surveys were conducted in a representative sample of homes and businesses in Montgomery County, Ohio (Dayton), and Santa Clara County, California (San Jose).[31]   The subject of these surveys was the extent to which citizens and businesses in the two counties had been victims of crime in the preceding year.   These surveys again suggested that the incidence of crime was significantly higher in both cities than had been apparent in official statistics. More recently, a survey by the Law Enforcement Assistance Administration (LEAA) of the incidence and characteristics of crime in thirteen major cities across the United States pointed out that unreported crime was twice as high as reported crime in eleven of the thirteen cities studied.[32]

In sum, victimization studies, although only in their infancy, offer unlimited potential for the discipline as a whole.   For in addition to providing more complete information on the statistics of crime, these surveys also offer significant data on the characteristics of victims and offenders, victim-offender relationships, and the circumstances under which the offenses occur.   Furthermore, since much of this research is undertaken on an in-depth basis, reliable data are obtained on citizen's attitudes and perceptions relative to the fear of crime, personal safety, police effectiveness, and the quality and functions of the criminal justice system.   And finally, the technology of the victim survey method continues to improve, so that the technique as a whole can be reliably used for estimating the "actual" incidence of crime in a given area.[33]

CORRECTIONS AND THE SOCIAL CONTROL SYSTEM

"Corrections" is one part of a set of institutional arrangements, activities, and processes which are collectively referred to as the "criminal justice system." Corrections, along with law enforcement and the judicial process, is a sub-system of the criminal justice system; it includes the country's prisons, jails, juvenile training schools, probation and parole machinery, and the programs implemented within these institutions and agencies for the purposes of rehabilitating the offender and protecting the community. Traditionally, corrections, or "penology," has also been a subfield or branch of criminology dealing specifically with the operation of correctional agencies. Within the academic setting, criminology and penology were invariably the subject matter of one course of study, and many of the earlier texts reflect this approach.[34]

More recently, however, with the increased specialization in all of the social and behavioral sciences, corrections is emerging as a discipline separate from the field of criminology and is becoming a part of the wider field of social control and the administration of justice. Practitioners of the new specialization are less often criminologists and more often from the disciplines of law, public administration, organizational management, and social work. In fact, the field of corrections has now grown to the extent that schools of criminal justice throughout the nation are now offering specialized degree programs in various aspects of the correctional process. Criminologists, nevertheless, continue to concern themselves with a number of areas which are decidedly "correctional" such as follow-up studies of given types of offenders, studies of deterrence and capital punishment, and research into the social order of the prison.

Law enforcement and the judicial process, on the other hand, are viewed along with corrections as part of the total criminal justice process, and, as such, reflect only a minimal amount of criminological effort. The majority of the criminologcal research in these areas has generally been limited to police behavior, the victims of crime, and the prevention of crime. These subjects have remained with the criminologist since they relate directly to the empirical substance of criminology—the necessary data descriptive of the changing nature, magnitude, and trends of crime.

EMERGING ISSUES IN THE STUDY OF CRIME

The preceding overview has attempted to provide a brief survey of the heritage and substance of criminological thought and inquiry. Without question, the *total* subject matter of the sociology of crime has not been reviewed, and numerous significant contributions to the archives of criminology have been left unmentioned. In addition to the major forces that have shaped the direction and scope of this science over the last century—causation, theories of deviance, criminal statistics, offender typologies—many topics of a more specific nature have captured the attention of students of crime in any given time period. During the 1950s, for example, the major concerns included the structure and behavior of the delinquent subculture and the violent gang. During the 1960s, criminologists turned their inquiries to political violence, the police, drug use, and organized crime. As such, the substance of criminology at any given time is shaped not only by the overriding theoretical, methodological, and intellectual interests which will contribute to its growth and maturity as a science but also by the more topical and pragmatic issues that reflect contemporary crime problems in American society. It is to the latter position that this collection of essays will address itself.

The forthcoming decade will undoubtedly witness any number of issues of importance to criminology, decidedly too numerous for discussion in any single volume. The topics examined here, however, have been isolated for discussion for two notable reasons: first, they are of current interest and have significant implications for contemporary society; second, they are emerging (or reemerging) as critical problems that will endure for some time to come.

Violence, as it relates to the personal safety of individual citizens, is not a problem new to American society. Yet with the political terrorism and collective violence that became so prominent during the 1960s and early 1970s, citizens became more aware of themselves as potential victims of individual violence. Contemporary society now reflects levels of violent personal crime that are even higher than those of only a few short years ago. As a result, the fear of crime has forced large segments of the population to adjust their life styles, for example, the changing of time schedules and travel routes, the acquisition of security and protective devices, and the like.

In response to the growing epidemic of violence and predatory crimes, *crime prevention* suddenly emerged as a major activity among police, citizens' groups, and for researchers in many professional fields, as well as a primary economic burden in terms of both governmental spending and personal self-protection. Since the kind of social change necessary for effectively preventing and reducing crime stands in contradiction to prevailing social patterns and governmental interests, crime prevention as a critical path will necessarily endure for years to come.

History has suggested that complex societies are continually evolving, and that in any given period in that evolution numerous aspects and segments of such societies will undergo some form of change. And typically, changes in a society's technology, political philosophy, social awareness, and economic concerns result in the generation, recognition, or discovery of *new types of offenders* and *new types of crimes*. As we noted earlier, the Prohibition movement had suddenly applied deviant and criminal labels to behaviors that had previously fallen outside the arena of antisocial conduct. In the contemporary setting we have observed the rise of the new female criminal, governmental lawlessness, and crimes by agents of the law. Much of this will persist. The increasing crime rates among women stem, in part, from the more equal status in society that they have now attained. Governmental lawlessness and criminal politics are the result of the institutionalized symbiotic alliance between the criminal, political, and economic realms. Crimes by agents of the law, and those governmental crimes that violate constitutional rights, are the result of institutionalized corruption as well as the war on crime which seeks, by any means, to implement the impossible contradiction of "order—under the rule of law."

Within this context, violence, crime prevention, female criminality, and governmental lawlessness represent criminological issues and problems that are emerging (or reemerging) in the United States today. The articles that follow relate to these critical, central, unresolved, and emerging issues, and are crucial to the contemporary study of crime.

NOTES

1. See Cesare Lombroso's opening address in the *Comptes—Rendus du VI-e Congrés International D'Anthropologie Criminelle* (Turin, 1906), cited in Leon Radzinowicz, *Ideology and Crime* (New York: Columbia University Press, 1966), p. 29.
2. For an expanded analysis and interpretation of the many theories of crime causation, see George B. Vold, *Theoretical Criminology* (New York: Oxford University Press, 1958), and Stephen Schafer, *Theories in Criminology* (New York: Random House, 1969).
3. Howard S. Becker, *Outsiders: Studies in the Sociology of Deviance* (New York: Free Press, 1963), p. 9.
4. Kai T. Erikson, *Wayward Puritans: A Study in the Sociology of Deviance* (New York: Wiley, 1966), p. 6.
5. Becker, op. cit., pp. 147-63.
6. Joseph R. Gusfield, "Social Structure and Moral Reform: A Study of the Women's Christian Temperance Union," *American Journal of Sociology* 61 (November 1955): 223-30.
7. Erikson, op. cit.
8. Becker, op. cit., pp. 121-46.
9. Richard Quinney, *The Social Reality of Crime* (Boston: Little, Brown, 1970), p. 16.
10. See Andrew Sinclair, *Era of Excess: A Social History of the Prohibition Movement* (New York: Harper & Row, 1962), pp. 9-22.
11. Frances E. Willard, *Woman and Temperance: or, the Work and Workers of the Women's Christian Temperance Movement* (Hartford, Conn.: Park Publishing Co., 1883).
12. Becker, op. cit., p. 149.
13. Richard Quinney, *Crime and Justice in Society* (Boston: Little, Brown, 1969), pp. 26-30.

14. Becker, op. cit., p. 1.
15. Quinney, *The Social Reality of Crime*, pp. 15-25.
16. Frank Tannenbaum, *Crime and the Community* (New York: Columbia University Press, 1938), pp. 19-20.
17. Edwin M. Lemert, *Social Pathology* (New York: McGraw-Hill, 1951), pp. 56-59.
18. Vold, op. cit., p. 202.
19. For a discussion and analysis of the Marxian view of society, see Rolf Dahrendorf, *Class and Class Conflict in Industrial Society* (Stanford, Calif.: Stanford University Press, 1959), pp. 3-35.
20. Donald R. Taft, *Criminology* (New York: Macmillan, 1956), pp. 337-39.
21. Robert K. Merton, *Social Theory and Social Structure* (New York: Basic Books, 1957), pp. 166-76.
22. Quinney, *The Social Reality of Crime*, p. 18.
23. Edwin H. Sutherland, *The Professional Thief* (Chicago: University of Chicago Press, 1937).
24. Edwin H. Sutherland, *Principles of Criminology* (Philadelphia: Lippincott, 1939), pp. 4-9.
25. For a concise discussion of the contributions of Quetelet and Guerry, see Radzinowicz, op. cit., pp. 29-42.
26. Émile Durkheim, *The Rules of Sociological Method*, 8th ed., trans. Sarah A. Solvag and John H. Mueller (Glencoe, Ill.: Free Press, 1950). The first French version appeared in 1895.
27. Louis Newton Robinson, *History and Organization of Criminal Statistics in the United States* (New York: Hart, Schaffner & Marx, 1911), p. 40.
28. Social Science Research Council, *The Statistical History of the United States from Colonial Times to the Present* (Stanford, Calif.: Fairfield Publishers, 1965), p. 215.
29. Philip H. Ennis, *Criminal Victimization in the United States: A Report of a National Survey* (Washington, D.C.: U.S. Government Printing Office, 1967).
30. Albert D. Biderman, "An Overview of Victim Survey Research." Paper presented at the annual meeting of the American Sociological Association, Washington, D.C., 1967.
31. U.S. Department of Justice, Law Enforcement Assistance Administration, *Crimes and Victims: A Report on the Dayton–San Jose Pilot Survey of Victimization* (Washington, D.C.: U.S. Government Printing Office, 1974).
32. LEAA News Release, April 1974.
33. E.L. Willoughby and James A. Inciardi, "Estimating the Incidence of Crime: A Survey of Crime Victimization in Pueblo, Colorado," *The Police Chief* 62 (August 1975): 69-70.
34. For example, John Lewis Gillin, *Criminology and Penology* (New York: Appleton-Century-Crofts, 1945); Richard R. Korn and Lloyd McCorkle, *Criminology and Penology* (New York: Holt, 1959); Elmer Hubert Johnson, *Crime, Correction, and Society* (Homewood, Ill.: Dorsey Press, 1964); and Paul W. Tappan, *Crime, Justice, and Correction* (New York: McGraw-Hill, 1960).

Part I
The Rediscovery of
Violence in America

The 1960s occupy a unique place in our jagged images of violence in the United States. The decade began with the assassination of John Fitzgerald Kennedy, the fourth President in our history to die by such means. But Kennedy's death was only the beginning. His alleged assassin, Lee Harvey Oswald, was shot to death within thirty-six hours of the President. A year later, Black Muslim leader Malcolm X died violently in New York City. In 1967 American Nazi George Lincoln Rockwell was shot to death by one of his followers. The next year the lives of civil rights leader Martin Luther King and Senator Robert Kennedy were taken by assassination. And of less political renown, the sixties also saw the cold-blooded murders of three young civil-rights workers by members of the Ku Klux Klan in Mississippi, with the connivance of local law enforcement officers; the fire-bombing of the "freedom riders" in Alabama; the bloody battles at Kent State, Ole Miss, and many other campuses across the nation.

Then there was the protest rally at the Democratic National Convention in Chicago, in August 1968. Anger over the war in Vietnam had led numerous antiwar groups, radicals, Yippies, supporters of Senator Eugene McCarthy, non-radicals, and thousands of others to that city to denounce the war, the Democratic Party, and Vice President Hubert Humphrey. Mayor Daley's decision not to allow peace marches was backed by his force of 6,000 police, 6,000 Illinois National Guardsmen, and 6,000 regular army troops armed with rifles, flame throwers, and bazookas. The final conflict resulted in tear gas attacks and the clubbing of hundreds of protesters, journalists, news photographers, and bystanders.

Not to be forgotten are the ghetto riots of the decade. The first to occur were New York City's Brownsville, Bedford-Styvesant, and Harlem riots in the early

15

years, followed by California's Watts riot in August 1965. The conflict in Watts began with an incident of alleged police brutality against a black man, and after six days of rioting, it ended with 34 persons killed and 1,032 injured, $40 million in property destroyed, 600 buildings damaged or demolished, and 4,000 adults and juveniles arrested. By 1967 ghetto uprisings had erupted throughout the country. During the first nine months of that year there were 164 disorders and 83 deaths, capped by major outbreaks in Newark, New Jersey, and Detroit, Michigan.

Finally, violence in the more traditional sense—murder, mugging, robbery, and rape—had increased at an accelerated rate during the decade. In the ten-year period ending in 1970, murder had increased by 76 percent, aggravated assault by 117 percent, forcible rape by 121 percent, and robbery by 224 percent. In all, violent crimes had increased by 156 percent with the *rate* of violent criminal victimization increasing by 126 percent.

The 1960s was indeed a violent era, and will remain conspicuously so in our history books. Yet with the close of the decade and the onset of the seventies, concerns over the epidemic of violence began to decline. Protest demonstrations had diminished, campus unrest had dwindled, civil rights marches had come to an end, urban ghettos had become quiet, and political assassinations had ceased, all to a degree that suggested that America had solved many of its problems. And with the waning of these more gregarious forms of violent conduct, the collective American mind also turned its thoughts away from the traditional forms of violence in the streets. The 1970s had new sets of issues to be addressed and honored—Watergate, political corruption, the CIA, and the energy crisis. Yet violent crimes were still accelerating; by the end of 1971, they had increased by an additional 10.5 percent over the previous year, followed by still another 7 percent during the next two years. In all, by the end of 1973, violent crime rates were 32 percent higher than they had been at the close of the violent era of the sixties. And the critical issue here is that the United States has a long history of violence, and a remarkable lack of memory where violence is concerned. Much of our violence remains buried in a long and crowded history, and the 1960s represent only another peak moment in that history. Each decade and generation tends to shrug off the memories of previous periods and looks away from its contemporary violent patterns until directly confronted with them.

There are many indicators that suggest that violence is again beginning to occupy the attention of the American people. Public opinion polls and victimization surveys reflect increased concerns over personal safety; there have been renewed attempts to initiate interest in strict gun control legislation; public agencies across the nation have instituted crime prevention programs that stress self-protection; and there is increased interest and activity in the development of public-oriented nonlethal weapons.

Within this context of growing concern, the selections that follow address a broad spectrum of violence. Rather than focusing on specific patterns or on particular instances of violent behavior, the selections chosen for inclusion here are essentially of a more timeless nature. Written in response to the violence of the sixties, they are applicable to the *general* nature of violence in American society.

In recognition of the growing level of violence that occurred during the 1960s, the National Commision on the Causes and Prevention of Violence was formed on June 10, 1968, to accomplish the task of analyzing the many facets of this type of behavior in America. Among the Commission's many tasks were the summarization of our present state of knowledge about violence and identification of the gaps where more or new research might be encouraged, acceleration of known on-going research, and the undertaking of new research projects within the limits of available funds and time. The end-result was hundreds of thousands of words, staggering man-hours of investigation, learned research and painstaking analysis, and historical parallels. Yet with all this effort, the answer was not even close at hand, but in summarizing our state of knowledge, the Commission did generate some of the more definitive essays on the subject. Significant in this respect was Hugh Davis Graham and Ted Robert Gurr's compilation, *The History of Violence in America* , from which the first selection in this Part has been taken. In "The Frontier Tradition: An Invitation to Violence," Joe B. Frantz demonstrates how deeply ingrained in American life is the tradition, even the love, of violence. He points out that in some ways the American frontier was Elizabethan in its quality—simple, childlike, and savage. It was a wilderness to be approached afoot, on horseback, in barges, or by wagon by only the most durable persons with a readiness for adventure. It was a land of riches where swift and easy fortunes were sought by the crude, the lawless, and the aggressive, and where written law lacked form and cohesion. Frantz illustrates how the tradition of violence grew from the pioneer spirit of the American frontier, a spirit both attracting and engendering strength, self-sufficiency, and rugged individualism.

Switching from the historical to a more psychological point of view, Bruno Bettelheim, in "Violence: A Neglected Mode of Behavior," views such behavior as a normal form of conduct. He suggests that by ignoring the existence of violence as a normal mode of human behavior and acceding it the status of a taboo topic of thought and conversation, society has prevented its members from discovering alternative methods of dealing with situations creating violent emotional actions and reactions. Bettelheim feels that certain forms of aggression can be directly attributed to the prevailing suppression of the existence of violence as a natural behavior and the concomitant suppression of its acceptable substitutes.

Gilbert Geis' "Violence in American Society" addresses a series of themes. First, he points to the fact that there are numerous forms of violent behavior, some of which are sanctioned and praised while others are deplored and defined by legal codes as murder, assault, rape, and robbery, The crucial issue that surrounds this diversity is the different parts of a violent act that can be viewed and interpreted. Do we simply look at the inherent nature of the act itself, at its overt manifestation, at its social or legal definition, and/or its consequences? Geis also offers a discussion of violence versus cunning, and how human beings would be affected if there was no threat of violence, and he comments on the issues relative to violence and the mass media. In his treatment of specific crimes against the person, he attempts to give us some insight into the changing level of violence in the United States.

Daniel Glaser's "Violence and the City" views the acceleration of violence in urban areas and offers some interpretation of the phenomenon in terms of population growth, the increased proportion of persons living in a "subculture of violence," the increasing numbers of alienated youth, and the breakdown of the criminal justice system. In addition, Glaser offers a series of measures that could reduce violence, indicating, however, that such solutions would require a long period of time, as opposed to the more desirable "quick fix" approaches.

The Frontier Tradition: An Invitation to Violence

Joe B. Frantz

On September 26, 1872, three mounted men rode up to the gate of the Kansas City fair, which was enjoying a huge crowd of perhaps 10,000 people. The bandits shot at the ticket seller, hit a small girl in the leg, and made off for the woods with something less than a thousand dollars. It was highhanded, and it endangered the lives of a whole host of holiday-minded people for comparatively little reward.

What makes the robbery and the violence notable is not the crime itself but the way it was reported in the Kansas City *Times* by one John N. Edwards. In his front-page story he branded the robbery "so diabolically daring and so utterly in contempt of fear that we are bound to admire it and revere its perpetrators."

Two days later the outlaws were being compared by the *Times* with the knights of King Arthur's Round Table:

It was as though three bandits had come to us from storied Odenwald, with the halo of medieval chivalry upon their garments and shown us how the things were done that poets sing of. Nowhere else in the United States or in the civilized world, probably, could this thing have been done.[1]

Quite likely this deed was perpetrated by the James brothers: Jesse and Frank, and a confederate. The details really do not matter. What pertains is the attitude of the innocent toward the uncertainly identified guilty. The act had been perpetrated by violent, lawless men. If the *Times* is any indication, a respectable

SOURCE: Hugh Davis Graham and Ted Robert Gurr, *Violence in America: Historical and Comparative Perspectives* (A Report Submitted to the National Commission on the Causes and Prevention of Violence) (New York: Bantam Books, 1970), pp. 127-54.

section of the people approved of their action. No one, of course, thought to ask the little girl with the shattered leg how she felt about such courage. Nearly 17 months later, Edwards was quoted in the St. Louis *Dispatch* as preferring the Western highwayman to the Eastern, for "he has more qualities that attract admiration and win respect. . . .This come from locality . . . which breeds strong, hardy men—men who risk much, who have friends in high places, and who go riding over the land, taking all chances that come in the way." The purpose here is not to belabor one reasonably anonymous newspaperman of nearly a century ago, but merely to point up a fact—and a problem—of the American frontier.

The frontier placed a premium on independent action and individual reliance. The whole history of the American frontier is a narrative of taking what was there to be taken. The timid never gathered the riches, the polite nearly never. The men who first carved the wilderness into land claims and town lots were the men who moved in the face of dangers, gathering as they progressed. The emphasis naturally came to be placed on gathering and not on procedures. Great tales of gigantic attainments abound in this frontier story; equally adventurous tales of creative plundering mark the march from Jamestown to the Pacific. It was a period peopled by giants, towers of audacity with insatiable appetites. The heroes are not the men of moderate attitudes, not the town planners and commercial builders, not the farmers nor the ministers nor the teachers. The heroes of the period, handed along to us with all the luster of a golden baton, are the mighty runners from Mt. Olympus who ran without looking back, without concern about social values or anywhere they might be going except onward.

We revere these heroes because they were men of vast imagination and daring. We also have inherited their blindness and their excesses.

Just by being here, the frontier promised the spice of danger. And danger, to paraphrase Samuel Johnson, carries its own dignity. Danger therefore was the negotiable coin of the American frontier, and the man who captured his share of danger was a man of riches, beholden only to himself.

To live with danger means to be dependent to a considerable degree on one's own resources, and those resources in turn must be many and varied. Courage and self-reliance, while not exclusive with the frontiersman, take on an enlarged dimension because so many instances of their use can be recalled. Whereas the town neighbor or the corporate manager may need a type of moral courage that exceeds the physical in its wear and tear on the human soul, such downtown courage is hardly recountable and seldom even identifiable. But when the frontiersman has faced down an adversary, he usually has a fixed moment in his life when he can regale an audience or when others can recall admiringly his dauntlessness. Even a foolhardy adventure brings applause. To the human actor no reward is more desirable.

The fact that back East, which meant from ten miles behind the cutting edge of civilization all the way to more sophisticated capitals of Europe, men were daily facing monumental problems of planning, and sometimes even of surviving, meant nothing to the frontiersman. Nothing in the frontiersman's way of life gave him any sympathy for the man who made his decisions on paper or in the vacuum of an office or stall. Decision was made on the spot, face to face. The questions were simple; the solutions, equally simple. Today that heritage of the frontier continues in more remote areas. The subtleties of law and order escape the isolated mountain man, for instance, whether he be in Wyoming or in eastern Kentucky. If a man does wrong, you chastise him. Chastisement can take any form that you think is necessary to hold him in line. One of the acceptable forms is murder, which means that lesser violence visited upon the offending person is even more acceptable. Such behavior has the advantage of being swift and certain, without the agony of deciding what is comparatively just and without the expense of trials and jails and sociologists and welfare workers.

Of course, one reason that this simplistic attitude toward settlement of problems prevailed on the frontier was a physical one of lack of jails. Where do you put a man when you possibly have no place to put yourself? To be neat and economical, you must put him away. This may mean tying him to a tree and leaving him to starve or be stung to death; if he has been real mean, you might like to wrap him in rawhide and then let the sun shrink the rawhide slowly around him until he is gradually strangled. Or you might find it more economical to find a convenient tree with a branch a sufficient height off the ground. The scarcity of jails then, either nonexistent or inadequate, often left the frontiersman with little choice, insofar as he was concerned except to hang, lynch, or ignore the offender.[2]

What do you do with a man whose crime may not really warrant execution? Either you execute him anyway, stifling your doubts, or you let him go. If you let him go, as happened frequently, then you may have set a killer at large to roam. In Arkansas in the generation during which Judge Isaac C. Parker ran his notorious Federal court, more than 13,000 cases were docketed, of which 9,500 were either convicted by jury trial or entered pleas of guilty. During a 25-year period at Fort Smith, 344 persons were tried for offenses punishable by death, 174 were convicted, and 168 were sentenced to hang. Actually 88 of these were hanged, and six others died either in prison or while attempting to escape.

By current standards the hangings themselves would have been invitations to violence. One contemporary of the judge tells of the hanging of John Childers, a halfblood Cherokee Indian charged with killing a peddler for his horse. A thunderstorm had come up, and a bolt of lightning struck nearby just as the death trap was sprung. "A moment later the ghastly work was done, the cloud had vanished and all that was mortal of John Childers hung limp and quivering," the reporter writes. "The entire proceeding, the grim service of the law ... filled the spectators with awe."

Standing next to Judge Parker in local fame was George Maledon, a smallish Bavarian celebrated as "the prince of hangmen" for having executed more than

60 criminals and shooting two to death during 22 years prior to 1894. Twice he executed six men at one time and on three other occasions he hanged five together. As for Maledon, when he was once asked by a lady whether he had qualms of conscience, he replied in his soft way, "No, I have never hanged a man who came back to have the job done over." This same reporter describes Judge Parker as "gentle, kind, familiar and easily approached."[3]

The truth is, the lawman was as closely associated with violence as the outlaw. The greatest gunfighters frequently played both sides of the law, shooting equally well. Bill Hickok comes down as a great lawman in Kansas. He also shared a good many of the qualities of a mad dog. Hickok first came to public notoriety near Rock Creek, Nebraska, where from behind a curtain in the Russell, Majors, and Waddell station he put a single rifle bullet through the heart of one David McCanles, who had come with a hired hand and his 12-year-old son to protest nonpayment of a debt. Hickok was acquitted on a plea of self-defense. For this dubious bit of law tending, Hickok became a national hero, although it took a half-dozen years for his notoriety to become nationwide. He filled in that time by doing creditable work for the Union Army, and pursuing a postwar career as a gambler in Missouri and Kansas. This stretch of social service was punctuated by a town square gun duel which left Hickok standing and his adversary forever departed.

In his long hair and deerskin suit, Hickok could have joined any police confrontation in Chicago or Berkeley a century later. Nonetheless he became a deputy U.S. marshal out of Fort Riley, and helped rescue 34 men besieged by redskins 50 miles south of Denver. With this background he was elected sheriff of Ellis County, Kansas, in August 1869. He killed only two men, which is not meant as an apologia, for he was credited with many more. His fame as a stanchion of the law brought him to Abilene as city marshal in the spring of 1871. Whereas his successor, the revered Tom Smith, had operated from the mayor's office, Hickok utilized the Alamo Saloon, where he could fill in his time playing poker and drinking the whiskey for which he also had a storied appetite. He ran a tight, two-fisted town, especially aimed at keeping undisciplined Texas cowboys in hand. When 6 months later he killed Phil Coe, as well as (by mistake) his own policeman, he was soon sent packing by the town. Naturally enough, he left this life as the result of a shot in the back while playing poker in a Black Hills gambling joint.[4] This violent man is the hero who is supposed to have quelled violence on the frontier and to have brought the blessings of organized law and order to our Western civilization. But he was ever ready to kill, on either side of the law.

One writer, detailing the lives of the bad men of the West, has put together an appendix consisting of the bad men and another one of the peace officers. Among the bad men he lists are Judge Roy Bean, who dispensed the "Law West of the Pecos."[5] Hickok is also listed with the bad men. Ben Thompson shot up Kansas and almost crossed with Hickok, and wound up as a city marshal of Austin, Texas. Bill Longley was a deputy sheriff and one of the more notorious killers in the business. Doc Holliday was a lawman in both Kansas and Arizona under Wyatt Earp. And Arizona remains split to this day whether Earp belongs with the bad men or the good. Certainly the frontier story is replete with men of peace who were equally men of violence.

Undoubtedly a lot of the violence spawned on the frontier emanated from the restlessness engendered by successive wars. The American Revolution, the War of 1812, the Mexican War, and the Civil War all disgorged some men who had tasted action and could not return to the discipline of the settled world. Consequently they stayed on the frontier, where their training and penchant for direct action held some value. Undoubtedly this was more true of the survivors of Civil War action than of any of the other major wars. The men who fought in the Western areas of the Civil War, both North and South, enjoyed more than a little activity as guerrillas. But what does a guerrilla do when he has no more excuse for hit-and-run tactics? Either he settles down on a Missouri farm or he continues to hit and run against targets of his own devising. The most notorious of such men would have to be the James brothers, though their company is entirely too large. The Jameses could rob and kill almost with impunity if they selected their target well. Since the James boys had been on the Southern side, they were cheered by their Southern fellows, embittered by the outcome of the war, who felt a bit of reflected glory in the harassment of the cold-blooded Yankees. Reputedly, Ben Thompson tried to get John Wesley Hardin to kill Wild Bill Hickok because Hickok shot only Southern boys. For once Hardin, the most prolific killer of them all, turned down an opportunity to notch his gun again. Had he shot the Yankee Hickok, he might have become a true Southern hero instead of just another killer—well, not just another killer— who needed to be put away. All across the West the antagonisms of the late conflict continued, and were justified really in the name of the war. It did not matter that you killed, so much as whom you killed.

Running parallel with this tendency for a strong individual to range himself actively on one side or the other of the law is the tendency throughout history of men and groups to take the law into their own hands, sometimes with reasonably lofty motives. As John Walton Caughey has written, "to gang up and discipline an alleged wrongdoer is an ancient and deep-seated impulse."[6] Whether such impulses run counter to a belief in the orderly pursuit of government is not debatable here. The fact is that throughout history societies, both frontier and long fixed, have moved through phases of private settlement of what should be public disputes. The operation of the Ku Klux Klan in a settled South with its centuries-old civilization is a case in point. Vigilantism is a disease or a manifestation of a society that feels a portion of its people are out of joint and must be put back in place whether the niceties of legal procedure are observed or not. That the end justifies the means is the authorizing cliché.

Not unmixed with vigilantism is frequently a fair share of racism, which has its own curious history on the American frontier. In some ways the frontier was the freest of places, in which a man was judged on the quality of his work and his possession of such abstractions as honesty, bravery, and shrewdness. The Chinese merchant, the Negro cowboy, the Indian rider—all were admired because of what they could do within the frontier community and not because of their pigmentation. On the other hand, the only good Indian was a dead Indian, "shines" could seldom rise above the worker level, and "coolies" were something to take potshots at without fear of retribution, either civic or conscience. Just as lynching a Negro in parts of the South was no crime, so shooting an Indian or beating an Oriental or a Mexican was equally acceptable. Like all societies, the frontier had its built-in contradictions.

In Kansas cowtowns, shooting Texas cowboys was a defensible act per se; popular agreement in that area was that although there might here and there be a decent cowboy, nonetheless most cowboys were sinister characters who were likely to ruin your daughter or your town. In other words, cowboys and Texans were in the same class as snakes—the garter snake can be a friendly reptile in your garden, but stomp him anyway in case he grows into a dangerous rattler.

But then, cowboys, whether Texan or Montanan, had a notoriously brazen unconcern toward nesters and grangers as Wyoming's Johnson County war will attest. How could the cattleman believe in legal law enforcement if, as one stockman put, no jury of "Methodist, Grangers and Anti-Stock" would convict the most blatant cattle thief? A.S. Mercer, who felt that cattlemen were a menace to his Wyoming, nonetheless concluded that "as a matter of fact, less stealing and less lawlessness [occur] on the plains of the West than in any other part of the world."[7] Backing himself, Mercer quotes the Federal census report of 1890, which points out that the Northeastern states, "which are supposed to be most civilized," had 1,600 criminals to the million people while Wyoming ran 25 percent less, or 1,200 to the million. However, the real cattleman dislike was for the sheepherder, who was lower than a nester, rustler, or even a cowboy who had married a squaw. As one scotsman who emigrated opined, when he brought his flock down from the hills in Scotland, people would exclaim,"here comes the noble shepherd and his flock." Out west, however, they said "here comes that damned sheepherder and his bunch of woolies!"[8]

Certainly the cowboy treatment of the sheepman showed something less than the normal extension of dignity due a fellowman. Cattlemen tried intimidation, and if that failed, they tried violence. If mere violence were not enough, next came murder, either for the sheepman or his flocks. As public sympathy was generally with the cattlemen, the sheepman had no recourse at law if his herder were killed or his sheep driven off the range. As a general rule, as in most vigilante situations, the cowboy always tried to outnumber his sheepherding adversay by five or ten to one, preferably all on horseback to the one herder on foot.

Nowhere was the sense of vigilante violence more noticeable than in the cattleman-sheepman feud. It was vigilantism, for the cowman looked on the sheepman's mere presence as immoral and illegal, an intrusion on his frontier life as he knew it. Along the upper reaches of Wyoming's Green River, for instance, a masked group, organized by the cattlemen, attacked four sheep camps simultaneously. The group blindfolded the herders, tied them to trees, and spent the remainder of the night clubbing to death 8,000 head of sheep. From wholesale dispatch of sheep to wholesale dispatch of men is really but a short, sanguine jump.

The coming of barbed wire into the cattle country led to another outburst of vigilantism. Violence alone was insufficient against barbed wire because it was an inanimate object that did not directly pit man against man. Like the men it fenced in and fenced out, barbed wire was savage, unrefined, cruel, and hard. And in a sense, like the men whose ranges it controlled, it helped make the Great Plains finally fit for settlement.

As fence-cutting skirmishes broke out from Texas all the way north to Montana, people were killed, property destroyed, business crippled, and otherwise peaceful citizens alienated from one another. Men cut fences because their cattle were thirsty and their tanks were enclosed, or because they desired the good grass now out of bounds, or because the large ranching syndicates had fenced in whole counties. The XIT Ranch in Texas enclosed within wire grasslands approximately the size of the State of Connecticut. To fence in the XIT required 6,000 miles of single-strand wire. The Spur Ranch, also in Texas, erected a drift fence in 1884–85 that strung out for 57 miles, while an old Two Circle Bar cowboy told of seeing 10 wagonloads of barbed wire in the middle 1880's in transit from Colorado City, Texas, to the Matador Ranch. Again, men gunned down fence builders, violated enclosed land, and otherwise took the law into their own hands in resisting the coming of a new order. But legality eventually prevailed, and many men who had fought the new orderliness came to embrace it.

In effect, vigilantism was nothing more than lynching. Despite the fact that the South has been internationally damned for its lynching proclivities, it must share some of the tradition with other parts of the world, most notably with the frontier. Nowhere was lynch justice more swift, certain, or flourishing than on the frontier. Human life simply was not as valuable on the frontier as property. Taking a human life was almost as casual as our killing 50,000 people a year now by automobile murder. The fact that Colt's revolver and the repeating rifle were present and the courtroom was frequently absent undoubtedly aided such an attitude. Mitigating or extenuating circumstances for the transgressor were virtually unknown. Either he done it or he didn't.

The truth is that vigilantism, or "group action in lieu of regular justice," as Caughey calls it, reflects the thinking of a substantial body of local sentiment. The community sits in judgment. It condones because it believes. However, a vital difference exists between vigilantism of the frontier and the vigilantism of the latter twentieth century. The pioneer was beyond the reach of regular justice; he had to fill the vacuum. Sometimes he filled it with grave concern for the decencies of human relations. More often he moved in a state of emotion, even as modern society would like to have done following the deaths of the two Kennedys, when the identities of the assassins were suspected.

The difficulty with frontier vigilantism is that it has no stopping place. Men accustomed to taking law into their hands continue to take law into their hands even after regular judicial processes are constituted. They continue to take the law into their hands right into these days of the 1960's. They do not approve of a man or a situation, and they cannot wait for the regular processes to assist their realizations. They might not know a frontier if they saw one, and they certainly are not aware of the extension of the frontier spirit down to themselves. But they do know that they must get rid of the offending member or section of civilization. So they burn down a ghetto, they loot and pillage, they bury three civil rights workers beneath a dam, or they shoot a man in a caravan in Dallas or on a motel balcony in Memphis. True, to them the law and the other civilized processes may be available, but like the frontierman they cannot wait. But whereas some frontiersmen had an excuse, these people merely operate in a spirit which does violence even to the memory of the frontier.

So much of vigilantism of the frontier had no place at all in a legally constituted society. The vigilantes of San Francisco in the 1850's were operating after legal redress had been properly constituted. The Mexican, Juanita, "a very comely, quiet, gentle creature apparently, [who] behaved herself with a great deal of propriety," was visited in Downieville on the night of July 4, 1851, by a Joseph Cannon. When he literally fell through the door, Juanita sprang out of bed and stabbed the drunken intruder. She was seized, the cry went out that she had stabbed a popular citizen, a court was formed in the Downieville plaza, and a jury of 12 men was selected from the crowd that gathered.

Towards night they found the woman guilty and sentenced her to be hung at sundown . . . they gave her half an hour to get ready to die. She was finally taken down to the bridge, about four feet high from the bridge, and a rope put up over the crossbeam, with a noose attached to the end of it . . . . this woman walked up the ladder, unsupported, and stood on the scantling, under the rope, with the hungriest, craziest, wildest mob standing around that ever I saw anywhere.

The woman adjusted the rope around her own neck, pulling out her braid of hair, and at the firing of a pistol, two men with hatchets, at each end, cut the rope which held the scantling, and down everything went, woman and all. The mob then turned upon Dr. Aiken, who was still a resident of that city, because he had tried to defend the woman; and they drove the gambler with whom the woman was living out of town, and also some other friends of the woman, showing from first to last the utter irresponsibility of mobs.

The hanging of the woman was murder. No jury in the world, on any principle of self-defense or protection of life and property, would ever have convicted the woman . . . there was considerable ill feeling toward Mexican gamblers and women generally, and there was no other way but to hang her. During the trial of the woman, ropes had to be brought into requisition to keep the mob back; they would once in a while make a rush for her, and the conductors of the prosecution would have to appeal to them, calling on them to remember their wives, mothers and daughters, to give this woman a fair trial; and in that way they were kept quiet until this woman was executed.

The truth is, every frontier state went through its period of lawlessness and its corresponding period of mobocracy designed to bring the lawless element under control. Further, the reformers did not cease imposing their personal ideas of reform with the coming of judicial processes. The truth is also that a century later, with or without our frontier background as justification, groups of citizens still make charges outside the law, and some even insist on enforcing those charges. A proper frontier tradition is great and effective, a true heritage for a people who must have heroes to point directions. But a frontier heritage misstated and misapplied is a disservice to the true cause of heritage and a negation of the freedom for which many frontiersmen gave their lives.

Invariably we return to a continuing, fundamental problem of race hatred. Nowadays it is dramatized as between black and white. Once it was between red and white. The hatred may not have been endemic, but the incursions of the white men on the Indian land drove the red man again and again to desperate, savage, and invariably futile war. The missionary loved the red man, from the days of the Spaniard clustered around the Texas and California missions down to the Quakers preaching brotherly love during the Indian massacres of President Grant's days. The fur trader also found the Indian a friend, and particularly found great comfort in the Indian woman. The Indian accepted both occupational groups.

But the one man who could neither assimilate the Indian nor be accepted by his red brother was the farmer. As the farmer moved westward, cutting back the forests, muddying up the streams, and beating back the game, the Indian's enmity toward him grew deadly. As for the frontiersmen, the Indian ranked somewhere below the dog. Certainly the Indian was well below the Negro slave, for the latter had function and utility. How do you handle an element for which there is no positive use? You exterminate it, especially if in your eyes it has murderous propensities. And so the inevitable, as virtually all the world knows, happened. The conflict between the two races, in the words of Ralph Gabriel, "like a forest fire, burned its way westward across the continent."[10] The noble savage was not noble at all in the sight of his adversary but a beast who bashed babies' heads up against trees and tore skin bit by bit from women's bodies. Each atrocity on either side evoked an equal retaliation. The list is long and painful, and no credit to either side.

From the standpoint of twentieth-century society, however, the white-Indian conflict for 300 years has important implications. For one thing, during the periodic lapses into peace which the young American nation enjoyed, these vacations from war did not by any means allow only for dull consolidation of the nation's politics and economics; instead they offered prime time for violent internal action. Almost always an Indian war was going on somewhere. On some wing of the frontier the white man was being menaced by the Indian, or he was menacing the Indian. He was running the Indian out of the woods, he was running him off the grasslands, he was running him across the desert and over the mountains to the west. With an insatiable earth hunger he was destroying the Indians' hunting grounds, until eventually he destroyed the game itself. This is not to discount those sincere Americans who had an interest in Indian culture and a desire for the two races to live side by side, but merely to point out that if any young man, full of the rising sap of the springtime of life, wanted to flex his muscles and pick a fight, he could find some Indian to fight against. The fact that the frontier also attracted the rootless and the drifters, and that these were often desperate men, added to the conflict and the inability to maintain peaceful Indian relations.

A mere listing of the battles with Indians would cover hundreds of pages in 6-point type. Take the Pequot War, King Philip's War, the French and Indian War, the Natchez War, the Fox War, Pontiac's Rebellion, Lord Dunmore's War, the problems of George Rogers Clark and at a later day William Henry Harrison, the Creek War, the Blackhawk War (which enlisted the attention of young frontiersman Abraham Lincoln), the Seminole War, all the raids by the Comanches and Apaches and Kiowas against the Texans and all the raids by the Texans against the Comanches, the Apaches, and the Kiowas, the Cheyenne-Arapaho War, the Sioux War, the Washita War, the Red River War, and the Ghost Dance Wars—these go on and on, seemingly without end. Where do you want to fight? When do you want to fight?

And if you get home from a war or a skirmish, you have instant hero status if you have halfway behaved yourself. There is a premium on killing Indians, a premium whose dividends continue through life. Men who came in after the end of Indian wars falsely delegated themselves as Indian fighters as they grew older and no one could prove them wrong. Often, criminal acts against other white men could be forgiven because a man had distinguished himself in combat against the Indians. Thus the retreating Indians constituted a kind of omnipresent safety valve for those people who liked to dance with danger, vitalize themselves with violence, and renew themselves with revenge.

Actually, although the only good Indian might be a dead one, there were two types of Indian. There were the peaceful ones, like California's 150,000 "Digger" Indians, a tranquil people who lived off the product of the land. There were also the warrior Indians, like the Sioux and the Apache. The white frontiersman generally looked on both with suspicion and distaste. California's miners murdered the Diggers as though they were endangered by them. On the other hand, murdering the warrior Indian was often a question of killing before you got killed, which simplified the problem. Skilled horsemen, these Indians, largely from the Great Plains, hit and ran with tactics that would have brought admiration from such mounted generals as Phil Sheridan, Jeb Stuart, or Erwin Rommel. Theirs was lightning warfare, and at full run they could loose twenty arrows while their longer-shooting foes were trying to reload. The wars themselves are reasonably straightforward, and could perhaps be condoned as inexorable conflicts. But the individual atrocities have no justification, even though at the time the perpetrators were often saluted as heroes. This latter statement holds true for both sides.

Nowhere has a lust for blood been more deeply etched than in the infamous Sand Creek massacre. Shortly after sundown on November 28, 1864, Col. J.M. Chivington and his men left Fort Lyon, Colorado, to surround the followers of Chief Black Kettle. At dawn Chivington's militia charged through the camp of 500 peaceful Indians, despite Black Kettle's raising an American and then a white flag. Not just warriors were killed. Women and children were dragged out, shot, knifed, scalped, clubbed, mutilated, their brains knocked out, bosoms ripped open. Four hundred and fifty Indians in varying stages of insensate slaughter lay about the campground. There is no defense whatsoever for the action. It was bloodier than Chicago or Detroit or Harlem ever thought of being. Chivington and his cohorts were widely hailed as heroes by many of their fellow Americans.

.   .   .   .   .

If during this essay it seems as if the frontier heritage is predominantly negative and directed toward violence, such a conclusion is misleading. The purpose here has been to examine a facet of the frontier heritage, that surface which not only condoned but actually encouraged the idea and practice of violence but which undoubtedly plays a role in shaping twentieth-century American attitudes. The examination could go into as much detail as the danger, the frontier heritage established the idea of the individual's arming himself. This activity is almost unique with the United States frontier. Instead of a central armory to which men could go to gather their arms, each man bore his own. He thus had it always at the ready. When danger arose, he could get together with another man, and another and another, until an armed mob was on its way. It might be a mob in the best posse sense, or it might be an extra-legal group which felt that its private preserves and attitudes were threatened. But it was always a mob.

The prevalence of arms over the fireplace of every frontier cabin or stacked by the sod-house door endures in the defense which groups like the National Rifle Association membership carry on today against attempts to register arms and control the sale of guns and ammunition. A man had to have a gun, not solely for game to feed his family but because he had to be ready to defend. This heritage continues. As of this writing, it still prevails in most parts of the nation. Almost no other country permits such widespread individual ownership, but the United States through its frontier experience has historical justification. In pioneer days a frontier boy came of age when his father presented him his own gun as surely as a town boy became of age by putting on long pants or his sister became a woman by putting up her hair. In many areas of the United States in A.D. 1969 a boy still becomes a man, usually on his birthday or at Christmas, when his father gives him a gun. A generally accepted age is twelve, although it may come even a half-dozen years sooner. The gun may be nothing more than a target weapon, but the boy is shown how to use it and how to take care of it, and he is a gun owner and user, probably for the next 60 years of his expected life on this earth. Whether he shoots sparrows out of the eaves of the house, quail and deer in season, or his fellowman with or without provocation remains for his personal history to unfold. The fact is that in his gun ownership he is following a tradition that goes back to John Smith and Jamestown and has persisted ever since.

And yet, as every schoolboy knows, the frontier has given us other traits which also mark us and often improve us. The frontier made us materialistic, because we needed things to survive. The frontier, by the very act of its being there for the taking and taming, gave us an optimistic belief in progress which again has marked the nation for greatness. The frontier fostered individualism as in no other region of the world. It gave us mobility; a man could move up and down the social, economic, and political scale without regard to what he had been before. The frontiersman could remold institutions to make them work. The frontiersman did not necessarily believe in individual freedom, except for himself, for he turned to his constituted government for every kind of help, particularly economic. The frontier also made him physically mobile long before the mechanics of transportation made such mobility easy. The frontier made him generous, even prodigal and extravagant, particularly where national resources were concerned. The frontier undoubtedly made the American nationalistic.

Thus we see a blending of a man's qualities that is both good and bad. If the good could somehow be retained, while those qualities which have outlived their usefulness could be eschewed or dismissed forever, the human material which constitutes this nation could develop in the direction of an improved society. To argue which facets of the frontier experience have outlived their utility can be argued interminably, but certainly the wistful look backwards which Americans, informed and uninformed, cast toward the violence associated with the frontier has no place in a nation whose frontier has worn away. The time for everyone, from scenario writers to political breast beaters to economic and social individualists, to proclaim the virtues of the frontiersman and his reliance on simple solutions and direct action does not befit a nation whose problems are corporate, community, and complex.

REFERENCES

1. William A. Settle Jr., *Jesse James Was His Name* (Columbia, Mo.: University of Missouri Press, 1966), pp. 44ff.
2. William Ransom Hogan, *The Texas Republic* (Norman: University of Oklahoma Press, 1946), pp. 261ff., relates several accounts of decisions engendered in early Texas by a lack of prison facilities.
3. Frank L. Van Eaton, *Hell on the Border* (Fort Smith, Ark.: Hell on the Border Publishing Co., 1953), pp. 72, 32ff. Glenn Shirley, whose *Law West of Fort Smith* (New York: Henry Holt & Co., 1957) is the best book on Judge Parker, puts the figure at 160 men sentenced to die and 97 hanged, p. ix.
4. Kent Ladd Steckmesser, *The Western History in History Legend* (Norman: University of Oklahoma Press, 1965), pp. 106ff.
5. George D. Hendricks, *The Bad Man of the West* (San Antonio: The Naylor Co., 1941), p. 272.
6. John Walton Caughey, *Their Majesties the Mob* (Chicago: University of Chicago Press, 1960), p. vii.
7. A. S. Mercer, *The Banditti of the Plains* (San Francisco: The Grabhorn Press, 1935), pp. 6-7.
8. Quoted in Charles Wayland Towne and Edward Norris Wentworth, *Shepherds' Empire* (Norman: University of Oklahoma Press, 1943), p. 256.
9. David P. Barstow, Statement 1878, from the H. H. Bancroft Collection, University of California, Berkeley, quoted in Caughey, pp. 47-50.
10. Ralph Henry Gabriel, *The Lure of the Frontier: A Story of Race Conflict* (New Haven: Yale University Press, 1929), pp. 4-6.

Violence: A Neglected Mode of Behavior
Bruno Bettelheim

These violent delights have violent ends. *Romeo and Juliet*

Aggression is by now a respectable object of study among students of human behavior. But in this paper I should like to refer to violence, which the same scholars tend to ignore or else treat with contempt. I may even share their contempt. But simply agreeing that violence is bad resolves nothing. To study aggression in detail while we close our eyes to its source is like wishing to clean out all filth without soiling our hands. If we are serious about understanding agression and its role in society, we have to start with a good look at the desire to do violence. Robert Ardrey, whose *African Genesis* found deservedly widespread attention,[1] makes the important point that Cain, and not Abel, is the father of man. If we are children of Cain it behooves us to know Cain well, to examine carefully his behavior and what causes it, and not to look away in disgust. The good friar of Verona knew that violent delights have violent ends. But if they were not delights, would we not shun them, since we all know they lead to disaster?

Man and society were born out of both: violence and gentle cooperation. To neglect either wellspring of life in our efforts to better human relations will be fruitless. In this paper I use aggression and violence as terms so closely related as to be interchangeable. I intend it as an invitation to study violence seriously, and not to stop short at its milder form, aggression.

SOURCE: *The Annals of The American Academy of Political and Social Science* 364 (1966): 50–59. Copyright © 1966 by The American Academy of Political and Social Science. Reprinted by permission.

VIOLENCE AND HEROES

One of our best literary critics, Robert Warshow, wrote a defense of the Western movie, in particular of the gunfighter as a moral hero.[2] This assertion is startling since few of us would accept the cowboy in the Western as our moral hero, or gunfighting as an ideal way to solve moral problems. But let us remember that the sword-bearing Achilles stands as *the* moral hero at the beginning of Western civilization. Because of distance in time, the vast difference in settings, and our veneration of *The Iliad*, it is often difficult to recognize what Simone Weil was the first to point out—the *The Iliad* is a poem of violence.[3] Violence there was before Homer. But with him appears the new civilizing Greek spirit, and this he casts into his poems. The new attitude he represents is that violence is the central problem to be dealt with in a world striving to be civilized, and that nothing good ever comes of violent means. Paris, who broke violently the peace of Menelaus' home, has to perish. So does the greatest hero, Achilles, who tried to join the avenging party, not to speak of the fate of Agamemnon.

The human race, in *The Iliad*, is not divided into victorious heroes and victims. If there were conquering heroes, violence might even seem justified, at least to the victors. But in the course of *The Iliad*, if the Greeks win one day, the Trojans do the next, and in the end all of them perish. In this poem there is not a single man who does not, at one time or another, have to bow his neck to force. That the use of violence leads to retribution, with almost geometric rigor—this was a main subject of Greek thought; it is the soul of *The Iliad*. Therefore, our first great epic impresses on us that we have to think seriously of what our inner and outer attitudes to violence should be. It may also explain the gunfighter of the Western film as a moral hero—why he has taken such hold of our imagination, and not only among youngsters but also among grownups.

This condition exists, Warshow thinks, chiefly because the Western

> offers a serious orientation to the problem of violence such as can be found almost nowhere else in our culture. One of the well-known peculiarities of modern civilized opinion is its refusal to acknowledge the value of violence. . . . We train ourselves to be shocked or bored by cultural images of violence, and our very concept of heroism tends to be a passive one: we are less drawn to the brave young men who kill large numbers of our enemies than to the heroic prisoners who endure torture without capitulating.

What we do seek in the Western is

> the image of a single man who wears a gun on his thigh. The gun tells us that he lives in a world of violence, and even that he "believes in violence." But the drama is one of self-restraint: the moment of violence must come in its own time and according to its special laws, or else it is valueless.

There is little cruelty in Western movies, and little sentimentality; our eyes are not focused on the sufferings of the defeated but on the deportment of the hero.

Really, it is not violence at all which is the "point" of the Western movie, but a certain image of man, a style, which expresses itself most clearly in violence.

He is there to "suggest that even in killing or being killed we are not freed from the necessity of establishing satisfactory modes of behavior."

This, then, is our problem: to establish "satisfactory modes of behavior" though we live in a society where violence is rampant. The gunfighter in the Western has found his solution to the problem. Obviously, it cannot be ours, but he at least, as Warshow has shown, takes the problem seriously, and we ought to do the same.

VIOLENCE AND CHILD-REARING

Nowadays, parents receive a great deal of help in accepting their children's instinctual desires, as far as intake and elimination are concerned. Even about sexual behavior we tend to be more understanding, more accepting in our emotional attitudes. But as far as violence is concerned, Freud might never have written *Civilization and its Discontents*, or have concluded it by saying:

> The fateful question for the human species seems to me to be whether and to what extent their cultural development will succeed in mastering the disturbance of their communal life by the human instinct of aggression and self-destruction.

If this is the fateful question, and I certainly agree that it is, what measures are we taking to help our children do a better job of mastering the disturbance of their communal life that comes from the instinct of aggression? Freud certainly did not mean denial or suppression to be the answer, any more than he meant it for our sexual instincts. About these drives we have followed his teaching and try to be reasonable. We try to satisfy them within acceptable limits, so that they do not generate so much pressure as to cause explosive outbreaks or a crippling of the total personality. In regard to violence I find no such reasonable efforts.

Children are supposed neither to hit nor to swear at their playmates. They are supposed to refrain from destroying their toys or other property—so far, so good. But what outlets for violence do we provide for them? As a matter of fact, in regard to violence, we are so unreasonable that here is where the parent is apt to resort to violence himself. Few children of the educated middle class are slapped for masturbating any more, though they are not exactly raised in sexual freedom. But let the same parent meet with violence in his youngster, and as likely as not he will slap the child or thunder at him, thus demonstrating that violence is all right if one is older and stronger, and makes use of it under the guise of suppressing it. So we end by using violence to suppress violence, and in doing so teach our children that, in our opinion, there is just no other reasonable or intelligent way to deal with it. Yet the same parents, at another moment, would agree that suppression is the worst way to deal with the instincts.

Unlike Wertham, who pleads for the suppression of vicious comics, I am convinced that neither comics nor television seduce the innocent.[4] It is high time that both the myth of original sin and its opposite—that of original innocence—be dispatched to the land of the unicorns. Innocence is neither an inborn characteristic nor a useful weapon; most of the time it is little more than an anxious clinging to ignorance.

Particularly in matters of violence, there is no protection in ignorance. Elsewhere I have tried to point out that one's ignorance of the nature of violence, as during the Nazi regime, did not lead to bliss but to death.[5] Those under Hitler who wished to believe that all men are good, and that violence exists only in a few perverted men, took no realistic steps to protect themselves and soon perished. Violence exists, surely, and each of us is born with his potential for it. But we are also born with opposite tendencies, and these must be carefully nurtured if they are to counterbalance the violence. To nurture them, however, one must know the nature of the enemy, and this is not achieved by denying its existence.

What concerns me here is that, contrary to good therapy, Wertham attacks the symptom instead of the underlying disease. This error he did not make in *The Show of Violence,*[6] where he made exactly the opposite case: namely, that in the treatment of criminals it will not do to legislate against crime; that the only intelligent way to do away with crime is to do away with what breeds it. Comic books are apt to reinforce delinquent tendencies and to teach new and better ways of being delinquent. But then the basic issue is the delinquent tendencies, not the comics. And the case of the children merely reflects the pattern among adults.

Violence as Normal Behavior

We have abolished the red-light districts and outlawed prostitution. I am all for such progress, mainly because it offers the girls more protection from being exploited. But for those who cannot afford the call girl, we have closed off an easy way to discharge both sexual and violent tendencies. Worse, by asserting that there is no place for sex outside of marriage, and none for violence in our society, we force each individual to suppress his violent tendencies till they build up to a pitch where he can no longer deny them or control them. Then they suddenly erupt in isolated acts of explosive violence.

These outbursts are conspicuous. By their spectacular nature they even give the impression that ours is an age of violence. So we clamor for still greater suppression of even small eruptions of violence that could act as safety valves, draining off small amounts and leaving a balance that the individual could assimilate. Even among psychoanalysts, Freud's death instinct is not quite respectable, because we decree that what is supposed not to exist cannot and does not exist; all evidence to the contrary is simply disregarded as nonexistent.

What I believe is needed, instead, is an intelligent recognition of "the nature of the beast." We shall not be able to deal intelligently with violence unless we are first ready to see it as part of human nature, until we have gotten so well acquainted with it, by learning to live with it, that through a slow and tenuous process we may one day domesticate it successfully. In short, we cannot say that because violence should not exist, we might as well proceed as if it did not.

Violence is, of course, a short cut toward gaining an objective. It is so primitive in nature that it is generically unsuitable to get for us those more subtle satisfactions we want. That is why it stands at the very beginning of man's becoming a socialized human being. It is not only the heroic sagas, marking man's entry into the modern world, that are so dominated by themes of love and violence; it is true of our own entrance to life. The temper tantrum, so characteristic of the child about to become a complex human being, shows how the violent and destructive outburst heralds our coming ability to master inner drives and the external world.

Though we do not wish to acknowledge how normal this really is, many a birthday party of happy, normal children should teach us better. The birthday child, in his natural eagerness to get at the enticing present, will tear off the wrappings to get at the toy. And if the box he is ripping should be part of the game, so much the worse for the game. Thus desire begets violence, and violence may destroy the object desired. In this sense, as in many others, violence is both natural and ineffective. It rarely reaches its goal or else, in getting at it, destroys it. True, discharge itself is a goal. But then we discharge the anger, and there is no further need to find out what caused it; it does nothing to prevent what enraged us from happening again.

To recount the evils of violence here is unnecessary. Having shown in my simple example that violence is a normal mode of human behavior, I shall say no more of its nature. Instead I shall consider whether our attitudes toward violence are reasonable, given our goal to contain it, and what might better serve our ends.

Gang Warfare

Let me begin with the obvious, which is too often neglected when we think about violence. Whether or not it will be used or avoided depends entirely on what alternative solutions are known to a person facing a problem. Thus, violence is the behavior of someone who cannot visualize any other solution to a problem that besets him. It shows up most clearly in gang warfare.

Today we are constantly bombarded by images of a life of ownership and consumption, but for a great number of people the means to consumership are slim. This is particularly true of many young people before they find a sure place in our economic system, and even more so for those from marginal or submarginal backgrounds. Yet they are told that without such things they cannot have a satisfying life. They feel helpless to provide themselves with what they feel is even a minimal satisfaction of the demands we create in them. But they see no alternative to reaching their goals except through violence, while the pressures of frustration only tempt them more to use it. Nothing in their education—and I shall return to this later—has equipped them to deal with violence, because in their whole educational life we have denied its existence.

Lewis Yablonsky, in an excellent analysis of what makes for the violent gang,[7] remarks with irony that their views and outlook, as in a nightmarish mirror, merely reflect back the official ethos. The purpose of violence for the gang member is to achieve precisely what are the major values of respectable society: success and prestige in the eyes of one's peers. He quotes one homicidal youngster who explains his actions as follows: "I'm not going to let anybody be better than me and steal my 'rep' [reputation] . . . . When I go to a gangfight I punch, stomp and stab harder than anyone."

Yablonsky has correctly described what the violent act does for the doer. He says that the very fact that senseless, not premeditated, violence is most respected by the gang shows the function that violence has for them. Despairing of alternative solutions, or, perhaps more correctly, convinced that for them no alternatives exist, they seek a quick, almost magical way to power and prestige. In a single act of unpremeditated intensity, they at once establish a sense of their own existence and forcefully impress this now valid existence on others.

Frustration and Anxiety

Unfortunately, gang youth is merely one extreme of a situation that breeds violence, not only among gangs but among normal, decent human beings. While similar situations exist all over the United States, I found the best account of it in Oscar Lewis' *Children of Sánchez*, the scene of which is laid in highly urban Mexico City. To understand fully what I mean, it will have to be read.[8]

Suffice it here to say that Jesús Sánchez, tied deep within himself to the communal ways of his old village life but wishing desperately to make a go of life in twentieth-century industraial society, is defeated again and again in his aspirations. Yet he is kept going, even driving himself beyond endurance, to see, at least, his children succeed in this world that is so alluring while it frustrates at every turn. Bewildering frustration and the fact that he can see no way out lead both him and his children to be violent, simply because they know of no alternative solution.

Nor is it only the lower-class world of the gang or the children of Sánchez who share the feeling that no alternatives exist, no ways out. The whole of our society seems caught in a spirit of believing that we lack alternatives. "Red or dead" seems to be the slogan—either preparing for violence by creating weapons that are ever more destructive, or turning violence against the self: being ready to surrender without resistance to communism if it should knock at our door. And this anxiety about world affairs trickles down to college boards and grades and so on through the fabric of our lives.

In the face of such persistent anxieties about success and survival, and by denying that violence is one way out, we fail to provide any safe or constructive channels for draining it off. Ours is by no means an age of greater violence than others—on the contrary. But the chances for discharging violent tendencies are now so severely curtailed that their regular and safe draining off is not possible any more. So the essential questions then are: How can violence be husbanded? How can it be discharged in ways that are socially useful? Rural life before farming was mechanized offered the child at least a chance for vicarious discharge of violence. In my native Austria, slaughtering the pig was a distinct highlight in the lives of peasant children. But so were chopping wood and other forms of aggressive manipulation of nature which at least provided outlets that were socially useful and contributed to the well-being of the family. Moreover, such a discharge was safe; it aroused no counteraggression in the target.

Our competitive or spectator sports are no real substitute, because, in the first place, they raise the aggressive feelings of competition to the boiling point. And, secondly, for every time that one wins, one is likely to lose, and every lost game builds up more aggression than the player may have discharged in playing.

VIOLENCE AND EDUCATION

Having said this much, I must admit that I am at a loss to suggest what we should do. Maybe we should not go so far in suppressing violence in our children. Maybe we should let them experience—within safe limits—how damaging violence is, thus not denying them acquaintance with a tendency they must learn to control. But it is not the only way. If our experience at the Orthogenic School may serve as an example, children seem to want to learn *about* aggression, and not just to discharge it, though they want that too. Right now, the stories we teach them in class never contain any incidents of aggression. No child ever hits, becomes angry, or destroys things in an outburst. The worst they do is to tease or to pout. All of them live on Pleasant Street, in Friendly Town.

Maybe if our educational procedures were to acknowledge aggression, our children would not have to be glued to the television screen to see a bit of violence. Maybe there was some psychological wisdom to those old-fashioned readers where the child was told over and over what cruel fate befalls the evil-doer. While these stories scared the children, they allowed for some vicarious discharge of hostility, and, having discharged it, the children's positive tendencies could be freed for the learning process. We can do even better. We can tell children through stories that people are sometimes angry at each other and quarrel, but that they can make up, and that if they do they will have a better life together.

It is peculiar to our culture that, in pushing the competitive spirit to a pitch, we stress those aggressive emotions that power competition, though aggression itself is tabooed. In a way we commit a parallel folly in our schools. But certainly one way to deal with anger is not to arouse it in the first place. Yet for quite a few children, our nice teaching materials do exactly that. Seeing pictures of the nice houses that other children have, when they themselves are living in slums, makes them angry.

How angry this makes some unfortunate children, so angry that they cannot learn, is taught us over and over by our children. One such child, who grew up in a variety of foster homes, was unable to learn and repeated first grade three times. While at the Orthogenic School, he finally was able to learn to read and print words as complicated as *soldier, submarine, fireman,* and *fighting*—all terms that were in line with his dominant feelings of hostility. But he still could not learn to read simple words like "come here," because no one had ever wanted him to come or had lovingly called out to him.

Considering the number of adopted children who feel strongly about their natural parents having given them up, and considering also the number of children who have severe emotional difficulties with their parents, I wonder if the time has not come to add neutral stories to our primers. I mean stories where family relations are not touched upon, so that children who find them upsetting can learn to read more enjoyably without anger being aroused.

Once we do offer our children a chance to learn what is foremost in their minds, or I should say what is most deeply buried there, then they learn fast and furiously,[9] like the Maori children in Sylvia Ashton-Warner's novel *Spinster.*[10] The heroine, a teacher, realized that these children wrote exciting stories of their own, only the titles of their stories were less apt to be "Fun with Dick and Jane" than "I Want You" or "I'm scared." One of these Maori children, Tame, wrote:

> I ran away from my
> mother and I hid
> away from my mother
> I hid in the Shed and
> I went home and
> got a hiding.

Having just read this, the teacher goes to the standard primer and turns curiously to the page from which this child was supposed to learn to read. There she finds the following story:

Mother went to a shop.
I want a cap, she said.
I want a cap for John.
She saw a brown cap.
She saw a blue cap.
I like the blue cap, she said.

Irini, a six-year-old, asks the teacher to spell several words, and then writes with concentration. Finally she brings the teacher what she has written:

Mummie said to Daddy
give me that money else
I will give you a hiding.
Daddy swear ta Mummie
Daddy gave the money
to Mummie. We had
a party. My father
drank all the beer by
hisself. He was drunk.

The teacher turns again to the primer and finds a story about parents:

Look at the green house.
Father is in it.
It is father's home too.

There is Mother.
She is in the green house.
She can see us.
Let us run to mother.

Compare the matter-of-fact acquaintance with aggression in these Maori tales with those in primers of the British dominions or our own up-to-date efforts.

Mrs. Ashton-Warner describes how she had to find what she calls "key words" in order to get her Maori children interested in reading and writing. Long before her, our children at the Orthogenic School forced us to similar conclusions. If we wanted them to learn, we too had to convince them that reading, writing, and spelling would help them with what concerned them most deeply. When we did that, children who for years had resisted learning even the simplest words, had been unable to learn to read from primers that pictured life in a single color—as all sweetness and light when their world was just as often drab and unhappy—these children were suddenly eager to read. Some of them who for years had not learned to read a single word then learned to recognize, read, and spell a hundred words or more in a couple of weeks' time.

When we felt they were ready for it—that is, when we felt that the resentment of learning built up through previous school experience had waned—we introduced to them certain ideas, in a short talk, in language they could understand. We told them that what is hardest to do—and the biggest problem in learning and living, but at the same time the most important one—is to master one's own scary ideas; that to learn words that help us separate the event of which we are afraid from what we only think about this event is greatly helpful. Because, while scary events that really happen are overpowering, our only thinking about them, or talking and reading about them, need not be. And in this way we come to understand them and learn to deal with them.

After such an explanation, three of our children picked as the first words they wanted to learn, *scary, fire,* and *hit.* To me it seems that in these three words our children, without knowing it, outlined a course on how to deal with aggression, at least in the classroom-learning situation. One word, *hit,* deals with animate aggression; the second, *fire,* with inanimate destruction; and the third, *scary,* with the outcome of aggression and destruction. If we permit them to state their aggressive tendencies, they can also come to recognize their scary character, and only this kind of recognition can lead to something better than denial and suppression. It can bring the conviction that in self-protection, and to avoid scary experiences, one must deal in constructive ways with the tendency to violence, both one's own and that of others.

A small sample of the emotionally charged words our children usually learn to read after seeing them once, and learn to spell and write after a few repetitions, are the following: *fire, knife, cut, crash, shoot, kill, hit, bite, teeth, cry, fight, jail, scream, yell.* Consider how much aggression they reveal, and the desire to learn about it. And compare these with what are generally considered easy words to learn.

It is just as enlightening to see how closely the words selected by our emotionally disturbed children compare with what Mrs. Ashton-Warner tells of her normal Maori children who were learning to read:

> Rangi, who lives on love and kisses and thrashings and fights and fear of the police and who took four months to learn "come," "look," and "and," takes four minutes to learn: butcher-knife; goal; police; sing; cry; kiss; Daddy; Mummie; Rangi; haka (a native word); fight.

Each of our children selected different words because what was emotionally significant to one was not so to the others. The interesting thing is that all children learned emotionally charged words, even ones not too meaningful to them, when they saw that they were charged words for another child. They shared not only learning but each other's emotions.

As we developed our method we realized that charged or scary words some-times aroused too much emotion. We then devised many categories, only five of which I shall mention: scary words, not-nice words, nice words, warm words, and cold words. Maybe I should mention some of the nice words the children selected. They include things like *orange juice, milk, play,* and *hot dog.* And they tell us what experiences the children think are needed to counterbalance violence. In view of the fact that most primers concentrate on what we would call nice words, it might also be of interest that the children learn the not-nice and scary words much faster and more permanently than the nice words.

To make some comparison with "normal" learning: though our children do not, like Rangi in *The Spinster,* learn eleven words in four minutes, one of our boys who learned four nice words in one day, learned ten angry ones on the same day, including ones as difficult as *witch, tornado,* and *fighting.* Which shows how the wish to master what is important to us is a powerful motivating force for learning to read, whether important things happen to be pleasant or not. And that learning about violence makes for learning in general. Because learning what the world is really like means learning about emotions—and that includes violence and what it is really like. Mastery through understanding is still the best way to equip our children for dealing with their own tendencies to violence.

For this reason the heated discussions about Viet Nam and related issues, pro and con, in public and at the dinner table, are a heartening sign. First, it brings into the open the ineffectiveness of violence as a way of ending our anxiety about nuclear war. And, second, it brings widespread attention to possible positive alternatives. In place of "red or dead," either one a defeat, it offers peace through compromise. And it documents how self-defeating a solu-tion is force, since it can only bring a war in which nobody wins. "Thought," said a living British physicist,

is born of failure. Only when action fails to satisfy human needs is there ground for thought. To devote attention to any problem is to confess a lack of adjustment which we must stop to consider. And the greater the failure the more searching is the kind of thought which is necessary.[11]

NOTES

1. Robert Ardrey, *African Genesis* (New York: Atheneum, 1961).
2. Robert Warshow, *The Immediate Experience* (Garden City, N.Y.: Double-day, 1962).
3. Simone Weil, "The Iliad, or the Poem of Force," *Politics* (November 1945).
4. F. Wertham, *Seduction of the Innocent* (New York: Rinehart, 1953).
5. Bruno Bettelheim, *The Informed Heart* (New York: Free Press, 1960).
6. F. Wertham, *The Show of Violence* (Garden City, N.Y.: Doubleday, 1949).
7. Lewis Yablonsky, "The Violent Gang," *Commentary* (August 1960), pp. 125-130.

8. Oscar Lewis, *The Children of Sánchez* (New York: Random House, 1961).
9. This familiar construction, "learning fast and furiously," tells how well-known (though neglected) is the fact that we learn fast and well if, through the act of learning, we can also discharge fury, or "attack the problem," as we say.
10. Sylvia Ashton-Warner, *The Spinster, A Novel* (London: Secker & Warburg, 1958).
11. L. L. Whyte, *The Next Development in Man* (New York: New American Library, 1950).

Violence in American Society

Gilbert Geis

On Easter Sunday, 1967—as on other days in recent times—thousands of young persons gathered at points spanning the country to participate in a contemporary version of Christian ritual. In Los Angeles' Elysian Park an estimated six thousand "hippies," many of them carrying flutes and tambourines, came together for a "love-in," the men wearing East Indian robes or American Indian blankets, the girls dressed in miniskirts, their legs painted psychedelic colors. Children and oldsters, according to a local newspaper, "danced on the grass like Pans in a rite of spring." In New York City, on the same day, some ten thousand young persons gathered in Central Park for what they called a "be-in." An observer commented: "They sang love, shouted love, and lettered love on their foreheads in pink paint."

Meanwhile, other persons were attending more traditional Easter services. Both the "hippie" and the "square" gatherings, tranquil and almost transcendental in nature, were counterpointed by events which provide a fundamental key to the ambiguous role of violence in contemporary American society. At the Easter religious services in Los Angeles, for instance, pickets paraded the circumference of the Hollywood Bowl, bearing signs with messages such as "Would Christ Drop Napalm?" Near Elysian Park, where the younger generation was romping, one of their number, wandering from the main body, was set upon by a gang of children aged ten to twelve. The gang boys threw rocks and bottles and flailed the "hippie" youth with clubs, sending him to the hospital in critical condition, with a threatened loss of his right eye.

The duality between peacefulness and passivity, on the one hand, and aggression and violence, on the other, is one that has continuously permeated Ameri-

SOURCE: *Current History* (1967): 354–58. Reprinted by permission.

can life. Both forms of behavior are at times rewarded, both are encouraged, and both at different times are denigrated and denounced. It has been said that it is cowardly not to fight, that if you *don't* throw your weight around people will ignore you, that subtlety is more effective than force, that women may be weak and "nice" but that boys should be strong and aggressive. These, with similar bits of folk wisdom, constitute the variegated and confusing indoctrination regarding violence that is transmitted in the United States. From it emerge diverse amalgams of violent behavior, some of them sanctioned and praised, others of them deplored and interdicted by the criminal codes under names such as murder, manslaughter, assault and battery, rape, and robbery.

It is important to keep clearly in mind which element of an act of violence is being stressed in discussions of the subject. Is it the inherent nature of the act itself, is it its overt manifestation, is it its social or legal definition, or is it its consequences?

Take, for instance, the matter of consequences. It is evident that unprovoked physical attacks by gang members on passers-by are deplorable because innocent people are unreasonably maimed or killed; fear of similar attacks impairs the freedom of movement and sense of well-being of an untold number of other citizens. It seems obvious that street violence of this kind should be outlawed and that persons who commit it should be put out of circulation or otherwise convinced that they must behave in a fashion acceptable to society.

There are, however, many other things which also maim and kill innocent people that are tolerated and even approved. If, for instance, governors were placed on automobiles, permitting them to travel at speeds not greater than forty or fifty miles an hour, perhaps ten thousand fewer persons would be killed in highway accidents each year and untold numbers of others would be spared injury. Fast driving, within speed limits, is perfectly permissible, however, and persons who bring about accidents under these conditions normally are not considered to be "violent." Their victims are written off as sacrifices to an ethos that prefers to move rapidly from one place to another rather than to keep alive thousands of driving casualties. It cannot, therefore, be only the lethal consequences of violence which make it abhorrent.

Infringement of freedom of movement, another outcome of unchecked street violence, may also be produced by numerous other situations. It is sadly true that residents in cities such as New York are likely to be fearful about venturing forth after dark, particularly in certain neighborhoods. But it is equally true that a much greater number of persons are much more seriously circumscribed in the freedom of their movement by actions bearing upon them that, while less direct and physical in their manifestation, are equally efficient. Lack of money and absence of adequate transportation, for instance, are but two such circumstances. It cannot, therefore, be only the restrictive consequences of violence which make it abhorrent.

It would seem, in such terms, that it is only in part the results of violence which contribute to concern regarding it. More important probably is the degree of directness involved—the fact that we may readily identify the perpetrator, and thus blame him, and that we may easily view and pinpoint the immediate wounds brought about by the particular violent act. It is much less easy to maintain with certainty that quietly vicious parents have produced a mentally ill, frightened child, or that a remote landlord, charging exploitative rents in a slum district, has produced a defeatist, alienated member of a minority group. It is quick, direct violence that we primarily attend to, undoubtedly in large measure because it is so much easier to do so.

VIOLENCE VERSUS CUNNING

Physical violence need not be the most devastating form of aggression. Stab wounds heal and victims of beatings recover. Violence directed against enemies may prevent greater social and personal harm, though the remoter effects of recourse to force to combat force is an arguable—and much argued—proposition. Violence in the form of athletic contests may tend to inculcate self-reliance and a will-to-succeed which in their turn can be personally and socially enabling. Without threat of violence, human beings may succumb to apathy and inertia, making them vulnerable to more overwhelming assaults, though perhaps, given the proper conditions, they will use energy no longer considered necessary for self-protection for more constructive ends.

Each of these propositions requires a much more careful delineation and appraisal before a flat declaration of the value of violence for a social system and for an individual can be reached. They merely indicate that violence is not necessarily despicable.

Many early societies, weighing the matter, placed more severe penalties upon offenses involving guile than upon those involving physical aggression. A citizen, they reasoned, had some possibility of protecting himself from direct attack, but few resources with which to cope with superior cunning. Today, covert and wily forms of aggression may be replacing frontal expressions of anger and hostility as self-control becomes a more valued trait. It is moot, however, whether this change is an improvement.

Consider, for example, the pattern of child-rearing that is said to be fairly characteristic of middle-class American families. Themselves perhaps resentful of their own upbringing, contemporary parents tend to eschew spanking and similar physical attacks on their offspring in favor of tactics of deprivation. Deprivation generally involves a delicate determination of precisely those things which a child cherishes, such as a particular television show. Then, in the face of misbehavior, the parents cut off the treasured "privilege."

The outcome of deprivation may be much less desirable than the consequences of violence by parents against children. For one thing, hitting has a certain cathartic effect for parents. They will, despite their infuriating (to the child) claim that it hurts them more than its hurts the child, usually feel a good deal better afterwards. For another, the matter usually ends there, the air much purified. The difficulty is the same as with any expression of physical violence; it conveys to its recipient the vivid lesson that physical strength is the fundamental resource to be employed to resolve difficulties, especially when a weaker object can be found. In its extreme form, parental maltreatment has been found to be the most significant experience of murders for whom "remorseful physical brutality at the hands of parents had been a common experience. Brutality far beyond the ordinary excuses of discipline had been perpetrated on them; often, it was so extreme as to compel neighbors to intercede. . . . "[1]

Deprivation punishment, for its part, may bring in its wake equally formidable difficulties. For one thing, the clever child soon learns to conceal his pleasures from the parent, knowing that otherwise they may be taken away in the event of misbehavior. Finally, as the contest of wills proceeds, the insecure child, with few other resources to sustain him, may find that his only protection lies in developing no attachment to or fondness for anything. Failing this, he is apt to be desperately hurt by the withdrawal of valued things. As an adult, such a child is likely to become a flat, emotionless individual, often particularly liable to exploit others because he has developed no fellow feeling for them or for anything else.

In such terms, it must be stressed that single-minded ideas about violence being good or bad, desirable or undesirable, preferable or outrageous, all must be carefully reviewed in regard to the available alternatives and *their* consequences and in regard to the total context in which the violence occurs.

THE CRIMES OF VIOLENCE

Little enlightenment on the amount of violence involved in the categories proscribed by the criminal law is apt to be gained from scrutiny of official tabulations. Fashions play altogether too great a role in compilations of official crime statistics to allow them to be taken very seriously. For one thing, public confidence in a police department will condition the amount of crime reported to it. For another, the efficiency of a department will itself influence the volume of crime coming to its attention so that, paradoxically, a very good police department may look quite bad in terms of the amount of crime in its jurisdiction when compared to a poorer department which neither discovers nor solves most crimes within its realm. For a third thing, intramural recording procedures may vary from year to year, conditioning the level of crime reported by the police. For instance, a 72 per cent increase in crime in New York City was recorded in 1966—virtually all of it traceable to changes in the manner in which violations were tabulated.

Crime itself is mediated by so many factors that it is usually far-fetched to jump from statements about its prevalence to judgments about the nature of the society at any given time. High rates of some forms of crime may even reflect improved social conditions. Take, for instance, the question of race relations. In earlier periods in the history of the United States, with a stabilized racial etiquette, there was comparatively little (though a good deal more than most persons realize) interracial disturbance. With enhanced freedom for Negroes came expanded visions, greater disappointments, and deeper frustrations. Additional violence grew out of such circumstances, but few persons would be apt to rate a social climate stressing an unrealized but emerging democratic spirit as less admirable than a social climate pre-empting freedom and emphasizing subservience and absence of opportunity for persons in certain preordained castes.

Violence in the United States is also probably as much a matter of perception as one of reality. Daniel Bell, the sociologist, for instance, has pointed out that the breakdown of class barriers has alerted many Americans to violence that was always present but rarely seen by them.[2] Residents of the suburbs may now view on television screens acts of violence formerly cushioned by their remoteness, in the manner that the slaying of former President John F. Kennedy directly involved the emotions and thoughts of so many citizens. Better forms of public and private transportation mean that today persons traverse more and different kinds of territory than they did in earlier times. Thus, it is not unusual for such persons to view people and things that their forebears never encountered.

The often artificial foundation of attitudes regarding violence is shown by a recent study conducted in Roxbury, a high-delinquency area adjacent to the city of Boston.[3] In interviews, Roxbury residents complained bitterly about the crime rate, the danger of setting forth at night, and about uncontrolled violence in the neighborhood. A group of detached workers was assigned to work with gang members. Careful records kept of their accomplishments showed that the detached workers were unable to make any impress on the amount or kind of delinquency occurring in Roxbury. Nonetheless, when interviewed later, a large number of the neighborhood residents then maintained, despite the factual evidence of which they were unaware, that they felt safer, that they were certain there was less crime and that they believed it was the new program which had brought about the improved conditions.

What is it then that may be said with certainty about crimes of violence in the United States? We can report with some assurance that, compared to frontier days, there has been a significant decrease in such activities. It also seems likely that during the past decades, and particularly since World War II, violent offenses in the United States have been increasingly committed by younger people. This situation is undoubtedly the product of an almost ubiquitous precocity that has marked youthful activities. Youngsters marry younger, learn more earlier, and are freer (in urban settings conducive to such activities) to get into and to create their own difficulties.

For particular crimes of violence, the pattern is erratic, and this erraticism highlights the difficulty of placing faith in broad generalizations. Murder, for instance, has not increased much, if at all, in recent decades. Expanded employment of competent medical examiners in place of bumbling coroners has enabled us to designate as homicide many deaths previously listed as natural. But, on the other hand, medical advances, such as the discovery of sulpha drugs and the newer techniques of surgery, save innumerable persons, who, only a few years ago, would have been added to the roster of murder victims. Such items, some tending to raise the count of murder, others tending to decrease the total, make definitive evaluations almost impossible.

Other crimes of violence are equally mercurial when we try to pinpoint their numerical character and to determine their variation over time. Criminal assault is probably much more apt to be reported to the police today than in earlier times, particularly as American women come to regard beatings less as a sign of husbandly duty and affection and more as an untoward insult. Rape too has been very responsive to changes in the moral standards of the society. Increased amounts of premarital sexual behavior, for instance, may be encouraging many more intricate near-seduction situations which (rather than the stereotyped lurking stranger) now account for the largest number of sexual assaults.

VIOLENCE AND THE MASS MEDIA

A popular assumption is that the uninhibited portrayal of violence by mass media in the United States transmits an image of aggression that is apt to be duplicated by those continuously exposed to its message. Literary violence is not, of course, a new phenomenon. Satirists are fond of dissecting the classic stories of childhood and pointing out that they are indeed a grim and gory collection. There is Captain Hook, his arm waving a spiked hook at Peter Pan, and there is Hansel and Gretel, on the verge of fiery immurement in the ugly witch's oven, after a frightening night in a dark and evil forest, having been abandoned to their fate by an indifferent father and a wicked stepmother.

Such portrayals of violence, given their extraordinary longevity and appeal, may be bereft of serious behavioral implications for children. Nobody, at least, has been able to demonstrate that children raised on such a bedtime diet are destined to reproduce similar grisly events in later life. Neither, it should be recorded, has the contrary been proven, nor is it apt to be.

There is no gainsaying, however, that the mass media in the United States often reflect patterns of violence differing in degree and intensity from those found elsewhere in the world. Viewers of television, for instance, are apt to be impressed by the ritualistic manner in which violence is portrayed. Stories in which events appear to be reasonably true to life and well within the realm of the possible will suddenly present fight sequences defying credence, with individuals inflicting punishment on each other that no one could conceivably survive for more than a few seconds. In rapid order, chairs bashed over heads will be ignored, punches that would fell elephants will be casually shrugged aside, and kicks ferocious enough to finish off any mortal will be greeted with no more than a momentary grunt on the part of the hero. The pummeling will proceed resolutely for perhaps a minute or more until (perhaps from the tedium of it all) the villain succumbs.

It is easier to caricature such proceedings, however, than to assay their importance and influence, however tempting such moralizing may be. This involves an intricate kind of research. Results to date, while far from conclusive, tend to point in the direction of culpability on the part of the media for their inordinate and disproportionate stress on violence.

THE VIOLENT MALE?

It is vital to appreciate the fact that man does not possess an inborn instinct for violence; expressions of violence represent matters learned after birth in a social context. Konrad Lorenz' *On Aggression*, a book considered to be the most important contribution on the subject in this century, points out that among the carnivores only rats and men have no innate inhibitions against killing members of their own species. It has been noted in this respect that the Latin proverb *homo homini lupus*—man is a wolf to man—represents a libel on the wolf, a quite gentle animal with other wolves.

Anthropologists have filled out the biological portrait drawn by Lorenz with ethnographic studies of preliterate tribes that find no pleasure in dominating other persons or in hunting or killing. All such groups ask is that they be left in peace, a state they can achieve in the midst of power-seeking neighbors only by retreating to inaccessible territories. To Geoffrey Gorer, a prominent anthropologist, the most common distinguishing trait of the peace-loving tribes is an enormous gusto for sensual pleasures—eating, drinking, sex and laughter. Gorer has also found that these tribes make little distinction between the social characteristics of men and women. In particular, they have no ideal of brave, aggressive masculinity. No child grows up being told that "All men do X" or that "No proper woman does Y."[4]

For Gorer and others who have studies that matter, it is here that the key to the riddle of violence lies. Violence that warps and destroys will be controlled, they believe, only when societies no longer insist that virility and similar masculine status symbols be tied to demonstrations of aggression and violence. Some observers suspect that the "hippies," those Easter celebrants noted at the outset of this piece, may in some manner sense this. Sex roles seem blurred among them, and it is sometimes difficult to distinguish the girls from the boys. The use of drugs by juveniles also represents withdrawal from combat, a disinvolvement from matters physical and forceful.

The pardox, of course, is that the United States is not an inaccessible territory, and its citizens are not likely to be able to survive without some display of traditional masculine-style truculence and aggression. Abhorrence of violence presumably will either have to become universal or the violent will prevail. The alternative, asking for violence to be expressed only toward real enemies, but to be inhibited in regard to one's fellows, is an achievement that no society has yet been able to realize.

NOTES

1. See Glen M. Duncan, Shervert H. Frazier, *et al.*, "Etiological Factors in First Degree Murder," *Journal of the American Medical Association* (November 22, 1959), pp. 1755-1758.
2. See Daniel Bell, "Crime as an American Way of Life," *The End of Ideology* (Glencoe, Ill.: Free Press, 1960).
3. See Walter B. Miller, "The Impact of 'Total-Community' Delinquency Control Project," *Social Problems* (Fall 1962), pp. 168-191.
4. See Geoffrey Gorer, "Man Has No 'Killer' Instinct," *New York Times Magazine*, November 27, 1966, pp. 47 ff.

Violence and the City

Daniel Glaser

It is difficult to know the dimensions of criminal violence in American cities because statistics on crime are collected primarily by the police, yet most violence is not reported to the police. This has been proven when the general public has been polled on their experiences as crime victims; most persons who report suffering a serious assault or a rape indicate that they consider this experience too personal or too humiliating to inform the police about it, or they simply do not tell the police as they do not expect the police to do anything about it.[1] Increases in police statistics on the frequency of violent crime in our cities could well represent only increases in the fraction of these offenses that are reported to the police and recorded by them, rather than an increase in the actual amount of violence. Periodic carefully conducted polls, asking people if they had in a recent period (e.g., the last six months) suffered an assault or other crime of violence would greatly increase our knowledge of violence trends, even though such measurement methods also are far from perfect.

Homicide statistics, however, have long been collected independently by two types of agencies, the police and the public health units of local, state, and national governments. Health department statistics on homicide come from physicians' reports on the causes of death. They are collected nationally in the Vital Statistics Reports of the U.S. Public Health Service. The fact that the F.B.I.'s homicide rates from police departments and the Vital Statistics rates from health departments have been very similar for the past 25 years suggests that both are fairly complete and accurate.

SOURCE: Daniel Glaser, ed., *Crime in the City* (New York: Harper & Row, 1970), pp. 201–6. Copyright © 1970 by Daniel Glaser. Reprinted by permission of Harper & Row, Publishers, Inc.

The most striking feature of our homicide rates is their decline. Between the 1930s and the 1950s our homicide rate was cut in half, and we have not gone back nearly to the levels of the 1930s.[2] In areas where police statistics have been compiled in a fairly consistent manner for over a century, as in Boston and New Haven, it is evident that the homicide rate of these cities was much higher in the nineteenth century than in the 1930s.[3] However, there has been some increase of homicides in the past decade, from a low of 4.5 per 100,000 in the 1950s to 6.1 per 100,000 persons in 1967.[4] There are five main causes for this recent increase.

The first is that our population now has an unusually large proportion of people in age groups highest in violence rates, especially men in their twenties. It is estimated that one-third of the increase in violence rates in the 1960s was due to the impact on our population's age distribution of the boom in babies born right after World War II.

Secondly, there has been an increase in the proportion of our population living in a "subculture of violence." This refers to the prevalence of customs and expectations in a group that make the ready use of violence to settle interpersonal differences not only expected, but considered honorable, manly, and proper. It has been vividly described in innumerable accounts of the escalation of petty arguments into deadly battles in communities where violence is most concentrated. Homicide statistics indicate where such subcultures are most intense:

a. In Latin American countries, notably Colombia and Mexico, the homicide rate is six times that of the United States. The obligation to meet rebuff by violence, and to seek violent revenge when one's honor is affronted, are part of a traditional set of values there known as "machismo" or manliness. We see portrayals on our television screen of something similar in our frontier culture. At present, in the United States as a whole, the extent and intensity of the subculture of violence seems appreciably less than in these Latin American societies. However, violence is also much greater in the United States than in the countries of Northwestern Europe, such as Britain and Scandinavia, if we can judge by differences in homicide rates.

b. Our southeastern and South Central states have long had about twice the homicide rate of the rest of the country, even though these states are lower than other regions in rates of nonviolent crime, such as theft and fraud. The tradition of settling quarrels by violence seems greater there than elsewhere, and lethal weapons are more prevalent. Another distinctive feature of homicide in the South is its higher concentration in rural areas, as opposed to large cities; in the rest of the country it is relatively more concentrated in the central cities of metropolitan areas. Yet in a national poll conducted for the President's Crime Commission there were less frequent reports from the general populace in the South of suffering aggravated assaults than there were in the North Central and western states. This difference, which contrasts with the homicide rates, was almost entirely due to assault rates being high in central cities outside the South and relatively low in southern cities.[5]

c. We have always had our highest violence rates in those sections of our major cities which have been the segregated settlements of povertous migrants from areas with intense subcultures of violence. In the 1920s it was the Sicilian and other southern Italian groups. In the 1950s and 1960s it has been the areas of settlement of poor migrants from our rural South and from Latin American countries. It is notable that in southern cities, especially the older southern large cities like Atlanta, Charleston, and New Orleans, there has not been as high a degree of spatial segregation of the Negro residents as there has been in the North, where they have been newer migrants who are more concentrated in the slums, barred by prejudice from moving out of these areas as other migrant groups did when they became more prosperous. Indeed, it has been demonstrated by Professor Thomas Pettigrew of Harvard that one can predict the Negro homicide rate of northern states by the white homicide rate of the states from which the Negro population came.[6]

Thus we have had a southern rural and Latin American subculture of violence transplanted to the slum areas of our northern and western cities. But the violence in our cities is not so much from these migrants as from their descendants. The transported subcultures of violence have been concentrated and intensified on city ghettoes by prolonged isolation of those reared there, under conditions of weak social control due to unemployment (especially of youth), poverty, poor public services, and weak social institutions.

d. On the whole, in most countries of the world, the youthful, the unskilled, and the least educated components of the population have had the highest rates of violence. The murder rate of standard metropolitan areas in the United States is very negatively correlated (−.62) with the median family incomes of the areas.[7] Opinion polls in the United States indicate that low education is especially associated with the belief that one should not allow insults to one's honor to go unpunished. More educated persons learn to settle their differences verbally or to ignore them.[8]

A third factor has been an increase in the alienation and discontent of youth, especially those already associated with subcultures of violence. Studies of rebellious behavior in youth, particularly in the high school age range, indicate that rebellion is especially associated with a failure to see a connection between conforming behavior and future status. Professor Arthur Stinchcombe of the University of California at Berkeley has demonstrated, with rather dramatic statistics, that it is the youth who are pressured to do well in school but do not, and the youth who do not expect to benefit from their schooling, who are most often hostile, sullen, malicious, and delinquent. These are disproportionately, but by no means exclusively, the youth from poorer families.[9] However, in the slum ghettoes of our urban centers, especially in the North and West, we have had a concentration of out-of-school and out-of-work youth, and their work failure plus other handicaps have demoralized those still in school. Therefore, there is much alienation from the dominant society's norms among them, and this is readily manifested as violence.

A fourth significant feature of subcultures of violence is that their traditions not only determine the readiness with which violence will be employed, but also the form in which violence will occur, augmented by such opportunity factors as the availability of traditional weapons. Thus in Texas, most killing is by shooting whereas in New York it is mostly by stabbing, cutting, and clubbing. This reflects both the emphasis on gunplay in the Texas subculture, and the ready availability of guns there, whereas a strict law against unlicensed possession of guns in New York State reduced their availability in that state. After the violent riots in Detroit, Newark, and elsewhere in the late 1960s, there was a sharp increase in the sale and the theft of small arms. Both in the ethnic ghettoes and especially in the areas around them, according to widespread reports, we approached closer than ever to a fully armed society. It is no wonder that with these conditions the proportion of homicides committed by guns increased by approximately one-sixth in 1967 over 1966.[10] The readier availability of guns would increase the proportion of assaults that are deadly even if the assault rate remained constant.

A final factor is the relative breakdown of our criminal justice system. Indeed, it might well be described as a nonsystem, with each of its three main components—the police, the courts, and corrections—operating without much concern for the consequences of their activities on the other components. The police are expected to intervene in a volume of criminal behavior so much greater than the courts could process to conviction by prescribed procedures, that police tend to evaluate their work solely by their arrest rates, and not by the consequences of the arrests. The courts cannot keep up with the volume of business given them without a combination of excessive delays and extensive failures to process to conviction on the charges indicated in the arrest report. It is well established that whenever the police are pressured to act in offenses for which there is little prospect of securing a conviction, they are inclined merely to harass, to reduce the presumed potentiality of offenses or of complaints, rather than to seek convictions. Once they are not oriented to obtaining convictions, their concern for due process decreases, and they are thus less regulated by the law of criminal procedure. This was observed years ago in the American Bar Foundation study of police handling of gambling and other vices for which convictions were unlikely.[11] I think we have good reason to infer from reports in recent years that court regulation of police behavior in dealing with violence has decreased. I also am suggesting that as a consequence of this decreased court regulation of police conduct there has been an escalation in both the ready use of violence and its provocation by counter-violence in police-community relations in many city neighborhoods with high violence subcultures.

The solutions to these problems are not easy. One can only recommend measures that should reduce violence in the long run, rather than provide instant solutions. The following are major suggestions for this purpose.

1. We should institutionalize victim survey research. An independent agency should conduct scientific inquiries with representative samples of the population to determine: (a) the extent to which the persons polled have been victims of violence in a recent period; (b) whether they contacted the police when violence occurred; (c) if they did not contact the police, why not; (d) if they did contact the police, what was the consequence; and (e) what are their attitudes and concerns regarding the use of violence. This will provide estimates of violence rates independent of the violence which comes to the attention of the police, and it will help pinpoint areas and trends of police success and failure in coping with violence.

2. One should support all measures which contribute to the transportation of subcultures of violence into customs of resolving differences by nonviolent means. This would be fostered by more educational and employment opportunity, and by increasing the extent to which youth can see prospects of a direct and somewhat immediate relationship between their educational efforts and their employment rewards. The culture of violence will be especially transformed if the ghettoes where it is concentrated can become permeable and ultimately dispersed, since it is a sociological law that social isolation promotes cultural differentiation.

3. The escalation of minor affrays into mass violence, and of temporary altercations into careers of violence, will be reduced if police, courts, and corrections officers can consistently react to violence by effective due process, rather than by counter-violence alone, which is often equally lawless.

4. The severity of personal and social damage from violence will be reduced by diminishing the ready availability of lethal weapons through effective measures of gun registration and control.

NOTES

1. Phillip H. Ennis, "Crimes, Victims and The Police," *Trans-Action*, Vol. 4, No. 7 (June, 1967), 36-44; Phillip H. Ennis, *Criminal Victimization in the United States: A Report of a National Survey* (Field Surveys II of the President's Commission on Law Enforcement and the Administration of Justice), Washington, D.C.: U.S. Government Printing Office, 1967; Daniel Glaser, "National Goals and Indicators for the Reduction of Crime and Delinquency." *Annals of the American Academy of Political and Social Science*, 371 (May, 1967), pp. 104-126.
2. Glaser, *op. cit.*
3. Theodore N. Ferdinand, "The Criminal Patterns of Boston Since 1849," *American Journal of Sociology*, Vol. 73, No. 1 (July, 1967), 84-99; Elwin H. Powell, "Crime as a Function of Anomie," *Journal of Criminal Law, Criminology and Police Science*, Vol. 57, No. 2 (June, 1966), 161-171.

4. U.S. Department of Justice, *Uniform Crime Reports for the United States, 1967*, Washington, D.C.: U.S. Government Printing Office, 1968, p. 7.

5. Ennis, *Criminal Victimization in the United States, loc. cit.*

6. Thomas F. Pettigrew and Rosalind B. Spier, "The Ecological Structure of Negro Homicide," *American Journal of Sociology*, 67 (May, 1962), pp. 621-629.

7. Richard Quinney, "Structural Characteristics, Population Areas, and Crime Rates in the United States," *Journal of Criminal Law, Criminology and Police Science*, Vol. 57, No. 1 (March, 1966), 45-52.

8. Lewis Lipsitz, "Working-Class Authoritarianism: A Re-evaluation," *American Sociological Review*, Vol. 30, No. 1 (February, 1965), 103-109.

9. Arthur L. Stinchcombe, *Rebellion in a High School*, Chicago: Quadrangle Books, 1964.

10. *Uniform, Crime Reports, 1967, loc. cit.*

11. Herman Goldstein, "Police Discretion: The Ideal Versus the Real," *Public Administration Review*, 23 (September, 1963), pp. 140-148; Wayne R. LaFave, *Arrest: The Decision to Take a Suspect into Custody*, Boston: Little Brown, 1965, chaps. 5 and 6; Herman Goldstein, "Administrative Problems in Controling the Exercise of Police Authority," *Journal of Criminal Law, Criminology and Police Science*, Vol. 58, No. 2 (June, 1967), 160-172.

Part II
The Dilemmas of
Crime Prevention

Of the seemingly endless array of social problems plaguing modern-day America, crime, especially violent crime, is undoubtedly one of the most pervasive. When the economy worsened in the recession of the midseventies and even a greater number of workers lost their jobs, and while the rate of inflation steepened, public opinion surveys accorded the problem of crime with the greatest concern by people regardless of where they lived. The articles in this Part reflect the concern of Americans with crime; violent crime, that is, crimes committed against the person by strangers are particularly feared. A substantial proportion of Americans report feeling unsafe in their own homes, and a majority of people indicate that they fear traveling the streets after dark. Painfully, the available statistics suggest that these fears are *not* ungrounded. While, statistically speaking, the *probability* that one will be murdered, assaulted, or raped (by a stranger) is slight—dramatically less than the probability that one will die or be maimed in an automobile accident—the rate of increase for these offenses is in some cases startling. Regardless of whether part of this reported increase represents improvements in data collection brought about by standardization engendered by computers, people perceive that the world is becoming an increasingly more threatening place. In addition to the perceivable and/or actual increase in the amount of crime, other aspects of criminality have changed as well. Some twenty-odd years ago, when the nation experienced its really first self-conscious move out of the cities into the suburbs, people believed that the nastier aspects of life, such as overcrowding and crime, were left behind in the city. Our recent findings have belied this utopian vision: Crime has dramatically increased in all geographic areas. Not only has it found its way into "new" areas but "new populations" of offenders are surfacing. This phenomenon will be considered in the following Part. What this implies is that both the extent and nature of criminal activity is changing; crime is becoming less specific and more diffuse. Current concern, we believe, reflects this awareness, and from this awareness and concern come strong calls for effective crime control programs and the demand for the initiation of crime prevention efforts. Citizens should once again feel safe in their homes and on their streets; yet somehow this never quite comes about. Why should this be so?

Regardless of the specific fears engendered by crime, what is needed are some general-level statements about what crime is and how it is related to both the structure and process of society. Such statements were offered by the French sociologist Émile Durkheim almost a hundred years ago. Using an organic analogy, Durkheim suggested that crime was *not* indicative of organic malfunction or breakdown but inherent in the workings of the system itself. The power to discriminate is the power to judge. Certain acts will be deemed inappropriate and the perpetrators of these adjudged as "criminals."

Yet Durkheim does not readily make the step from these to the examination of "real crimes" such as robbery and burglary. We do get the sense that men make laws, and these laws, for the most part, strike us as being just. In a very simple sense, then, people who break the law(s) are criminals. This formulation, however, is too simple because it does not really tell us where crime and criminals actually seem to be coming from.

Again, let us examine what we already know about crime. A number of things immediately strike us:

1. In a substantial porportion of cases, violent crimes such as homicide (including manslaughter) and rape are the result of acts of passion in which the victim and offender are intimately acquainted with each other.

2. To the best of our knowledge, serious crime such as robbery and burglary are primarily young men's (or increasingly *young persons'*) acts.

3. A very substantial proportion of offenders coming to the attention of control agencies are recidivists, that is, they had been processed by these (or other) agencies in the past.

4. A very substantial proportion of those who are processed by the criminal justice system are involved in so-called victimless crimes which could better be disposed of by other than criminal agencies. In a somewhat similar direction, it appears that many juvenile offenders are processed by this same system for behavior that would not be considered illegal if done by adults.

While these observations can be made about the phenomenon of crime itself, some additional comments about the nature and organization of American society are in order. Many of our most important cultural themes emphasize the acquisition and accumulation of material goods and wealth. Our place in the world can be typically defined by the amount of wealth we have been able to accumulate. The contemporary culture is also one that is noticeably "a-ascetic-ally" oriented; that is, Americans are increasingly more receptive to bodily comforts and pleasures. In this light, the interest Americans have in the use of drugs, including alcohol, and in sexual fulfillment is entirely understandable. Yet identifying these two themes points to additional problems.

As sociological researchers have been suggesting for the last two decades, while the interest and orientation toward these themes are probably universal throughout the culture, the legitimate means to their achievement are not nearly as well distributed throughout the culture. Stated somewhat differently, a society tends to order, arrange, or structure its members by given characteristics such as race, ethnicity, age, sex, wealth, and the like. And the legitimate or ac-cepted ways to achieve culturally valued goals are found to be differentially distributed on the basis of the ordered structure of the society. This then posits the assumption that while structured inequality exists along with universal com-mitment to cultural goals, we can expect to see a differential distribution of offenders, and even more basically, we can see where a significant social impetus for criminal (that is, nonlegitimate) behavior will come from. Given these ob-servations, the future of crime prevention efforts appears dim at best. It is unlikely that the culture will, in the foreseeable future, relinquish or replace these materialistic sensually oriented goals.

It is somewhat unclear, then, where the impetus for crime control will come from. As the turbulent midsixties and early seventies have amply demonstrated, behavior readily defined by the existing power structure and its supporters as "criminal" is the concomitant of social change. Mass violence, individual acts of terrorism, and robbery perpetuated in the name of revolution are not uncommon occurrences. And, for the most part, we now realize that this particular kind of criminal behavior (here, only the defined legality of the behavior is considered and *not* its morality) is associated with younger people from some of society's higher socioeconomic strata. The theoretical question that immediately comes to mind considers the relationship of such kinds of behavior and social change. Hence, given periods of rapid social change, can we invariably expect to see much criminality? Historical and anthropological evidence appears to suggest an affirmative answer. The implication is that higher class youth will be exposed to the effects of our control-specific institutions.

This exposure, of course, is nothing new to youth from other social strata who habitually find their way into the criminal justice network and tend to remain there. Our available data suggest a very high, perhaps overly high, representation of repeaters appearing in the captured criminal population. Consequently, the probability of an adult offender's having been involved with the criminal justice system as a juvenile is very high.

The implications of this lead one to speculate that if meaningful and actual access to legitimate ways of protest and legitimate means to material wealth were more readily available, the amount of crime would diminish, assumptions that much of our "crime prevention" activity has taken as being wholly valid. Although little was done in the radical-criminal area, our "war on crime" has certainly included an economic component that attempted through various social action programs to improve the socioeconomic condition of the lower class. Considering the recent increase of crime and the overall and apparently increasing fear of it, we have not been successful.

The question, then, still remains: How do we reduce crime? Focusing on the police, we must conclude that this agency is effective in only individual cases. Overall, the police achieve slightly less than a 25 percent arrest rate for reported crimes. It has been suggested that by increasing the intensity of police activity in an area, the amount of criminal activity can be drastically reduced. This was tried in Kansas City, where routine police patrols were increased in randomly selected areas of the city. Evaluative research conducted to document the experiment indicated that there was little or no real difference in the number of crimes reported between those areas with increased patrols and those without them. Perhaps with police saturation, the citizens in the target areas felt more secure and thus feared the occurrence of crime less, making the experiment politically worthwhile. Although this may be a valuable side effect of increased police activity, it still does little to solve our basic problem.

Going a step higher to the courts, it has been argued that the improvement of the adjudication of criminal justice can have a significant impact on the crime problem. By doing away with practices like plea-bargaining and shortening the lag between arrest and trial, it is suggested, we can more efficiently handle offenders and thereby better "control" the criminal population. Here too the notion seems to have had more theoretical appeal than practical value. Although intervention by various levels of government in the operations of the courts has occurred, the overall picture has become even gloomier, since it has been difficult to demonstrate the actual connection between court reform and the reduction in crime. Although we regularly operate with the notion of an integrated social system, our understanding of its operation is limited to, at best, a descriptive and *not* analytical conception.

Shifting focus somewhat to the problem of *criminalization*, our attempts at crime prevention have proceeded in a different direction. Here the main thrust of the work is aimed at keeping persons, especially juveniles and first offenders, *out* of the criminal justice system; and, if involved in the network, moving them through it and out again quickly, assuming that the social (if not the physical) person of the offender is in some way damaged through his contact with the social-control process. The criminalization process suggests that by *social labeling*, the person is in some way damaged, henceforth making his or her operation in the legitimate world problematic. In practical terms, this view finds more than a modicum of support. It is indeed true that a person with an arrest record does in fact find it more difficult to secure certain kinds of employment, or employment in general. If we extrapolate somewhat further, it is relatively easy to perceive how if one is in the enforced company of others for whom crime is literally a way of life, one might begin to assume the attitudes, argot, and skills of the more sophisticated group. Needless to say, this is one of the major arguments against the existing organization of our juvenile justice and corrections systems. But, once again, we are still at a descriptive level, perceiving a connection between a young person's involvement with the criminal justice system as he or she goes on to commit additional offenses after release from confinement. This argument is also used when one considers the status of those persons who enter the system adjudged guilty of a "victimless crime." At present, we are not quite sure what the subsequent careers of these persons will be; we believe, however, that the likelihood of future criminal behavior does increase. The basic issue is not how to keep these people from involvement with the criminal justice system, but whether their activity ought to be considered in the realm of control. This matter, like the one that defines the problem of the maldistribution of opportunity and wealth, goes to the very heart of our society. It involves a questioning of some of our basic values as well as a very critical examination of our social structure, culture, and institutions. Given the status quo, whether this examination will actually occur is, in itself, problematic. The situation is further complicated by the fact that since the solution to the problem involves major alteration of values, culture, and social structures, the question of change assumes an entirely different dimension.

More recently the problem of crime control and prevention has been approached from the perspective of the community. Attempts have been made to involve both the community's population and agencies through public education and public involvement in the parole system. Although these efforts have not been systematically evaluated, there is some reason to believe that community involvement in any ongoing crime prevention efforts can be valuable. This has been the major thrust of the federal government's efforts in crime prevention.

A major difficulty, though, is that programs have rarely been well articulated. Certainly we are impressed with concepts like "community crime control," "citizen initiative against crime," "citizen participation in the policing of their communities," but, in effect, this tells us little about what the actual outcome of such programs will be. Moreover, raised hopes regarding federal projects that are funded for a year or so and then discontinued have made communities somewhat wary of expanded federal initiative, especially when they know they will have to assume the remaining fiscal burden for crime control projects that appear to be of only minimal impact.

Finally, the last major direction in crime control has been the attempt to *change* those persons enmeshed in the criminal justice network. Until quite recently we had fully embraced the idea of "treating" criminal offenders. By providing counseling services, psychotherapy, and the like, we believed that we could in some way change them, make them turn from their criminal ways, which were, after all, indicative of some underlying conflict or inadequacy in their socialization. Quite recently this view has been under attack by those who have extensively evaluated the *results* of the treatment programs. Their findings indicate that if recidivism is considered, treatment has had little effect.

In the following essays, these issues are considered at greater length. We have chosen two selections that are quite different in both scope and approach. The first from the National Advisory Commission on Criminal Justice Standards and Goals essentially outlines the federal government's position on the issues of crime control and prevention. We believe it is valuable because it presents the statistics that are used when the issue of crime control is considered. In addition to a fairly extensive statistical discussion, the Commission presents a plan for crime prevention in the coming years. It sets definite goals whereby the incidence of crime is to be reduced by given proportions. Unfortunately, however, while the numerical goals are clearly stated, exactly how they are to be achieved is not accorded the same level of specificity. One is never quite sure what the federal government really wants to do, and exactly how it is to be accomplished. Too, since the Commission was empaneled by the Nixon Administration, the question of its autonomy must be raised. This question is particularly salient when considering problems like the decriminalization (or even legalization) of certain forms of behavior that heretofore had been accorded criminal status. Again, the major difficulty when we consider a report emanating from an official source involves separating the real policy statements from the platitudes of concerned rhetoric; in the government's war on crime this separation never quite happens.

The second selection, by LaMar T. Empey of the University of Southern California, presents a full, scholarly treatment of the issues surrounding crime control and prevention. The strength of Empey's writing lies in its comprehensiveness. He begins with a consideration of the federal government's rhetoric concerning a "war on crime" and why such a "war" quickly resolves itself into a soliloquy of saber-rattling directed at an ill-defined adversary. His analysis then shifts to an institutional and social level, helping us to see how crime (and/or deviant behavior) is generated by the very structures and processes of our society. The discussion concludes with some perspectives on how some of our essential institutional arrangements (such as the school) might be modified so that the social forces from which alienation stems might in some way be attenuated. The strength of the article also lies in its demand that we consider crime as the natural result of certain forms of organization. For only then does it become possible to consider modifying these social organizations as the only real "solution" to the problem.

Of the many perspectives regularly offered for the amelioration of social problems, it is the examination of basic values and their manifestation in social structures that seems to hold the greatest promise. It is our contention that meaningful change and planning efforts must correspond to generalized statements about social organization. Until we develop this perspective, our efforts at crime prevention will be, at best, fragmentary and futile.

A National Strategy to Reduce Crime

National Advisory Commission on Criminal Justice Standards and Goals

Crime is not a new phenomenon in American life. Scholars and commissions before this one have documented the growth and complexity of the crime problem in the United States, its causes, and its destructive effects on national life. The damage to persons, property, and spirit, and the fear of unprovoked, unpredictable violence are more than familiar.

This Commission does not offer easy solutions to those problems. But it does offer a beginning.

GOALS FOR THE DECADE AHEAD

The Commission believes that the American people can reduce the social and economic damage caused by all forms of crime. The Commission also believes that there are certain crimes that threaten the very existence of a humane and civilized society and that the rate of these crimes can be assessed and controlled. These are the violent crimes of murder and nonnegligent manslaughter, forcible rape, robbery, aggravated assault, and the property crime of burglary.

These five crimes are particularly serious when committed by a stranger on the streets and highways of the Nation. In such cases, an extra dimension is present —the dimension of fear. Thus, when these crimes are committed by strangers, the Commission labels them "high-fear" crimes and proposes a sharp reduction in their rate.[1]

SOURCE: National Advisory Commission on Criminal Justice Standards and Goals, *A National Strategy to Reduce Crime* (Washington, D.C.: U.S. Government Printing Office, 1973), pp. 7–28.

Violent crime and burglary, however, are also serious when committed by relatives and acquaintances.

Generally, the Commission proposes a two-level attack on these five crimes:

First, the rate of "high-fear" (stranger-related) crimes should be cut in half by 1983.

Second, whether the crime is committed by a relative or acquaintance, or a stranger, the crime rates should be cut by 1983 as follows:

- Homicide (murder and nonnegligent manslaughter)—at least 25 percent.
- Forcible rape—at least 25 percent.
- Aggravated assault—at least 25 percent.
- Robbery—at least 50 percent.
- Burglary—at least 50 percent.

The Commission is aware that the selection of these crimes and percentages of reduction[2] will arouse the doubts of skeptics, but the Commission submits that the proposed crime reduction goals are aspirations, not predictions. They define what could be, not what necessarily will be. To reach these goals will require a concentration of the national will and the best application of our capabilities. The Commission is confident that by improved effort, including use of the standards and recommendations presented elsewhere in its reports, the goals can be attained.

Why These Crimes?

The Commission decided to focus attention on the five target crimes because of their cost to society—economic cost to some degree but, more importantly, their cost to citizens in fear, psychic damage, and mistrust.

The economic loss resulting from the five crimes amounts to hundreds of millions of dollars.[3] According to the FBI, money and property taken from victims of robbery and burglary in 1971 totaled $87 million and $739 million respectively.[4] These figures do not show the undoubtedly large losses resulting from unreported offenses.

To add up economic costs alone would be to underestimate seriously the total cost of crime in America. No price tag can be put on the fear that, as much as any other factor, is speeding the exodus from the cities, strangling businesses, and causing people to mistrust each other.

Polls conducted by the Gallup organization indicate that fear may have become more widespread since the Violence Commission reported. In 1968, 31 percent of Gallup survey respondents said they were afraid to walk in their own neighborhoods at night. By the end of 1972, the number had risen to 42 percent.

Considerations similar to those above caused the Commission to include burglary among the target crimes. A Gallup poll late in 1972 found that one person in six does not feel safe in his own home at night.[5] While burglary is technically classified as a property crime rather than a crime of violence and might perhaps be expected to occasion less fear, widespread apprehension about personal safety in the home certainly indicates that fear of being burglarized is the subject of acute concern among many Americans.

By focusing attention on the target crimes, the Commission does not wish to suggest that other crimes are not serious problems for the Nation. Yearly arrests for shoplifting, fraud, embezzlement, forgery and counterfeiting, arson, and vandalism far exceed in number the arrests for the target crimes.

Nor do the target crimes produce the greatest direct economic loss. The President's Commission on Law Enforcement and Administration of Justice (the President's Crime Commission) estimated that in 1965 direct losses through crimes against persons, crimes against property, and the cost of illegal goods and services, amounted to about $15 billion a year. Of this loss, violent crimes and burglary were estimated to account for little more than $1 billion, or 7 percent of the total.[6]

The estimate of the President's Crime Commission did not include losses from crimes where victimization is often secondary, diffuse, and difficult to measure, such as violations of antitrust laws, building codes, pure food and drug laws, and statutes relating to the public trust (prohibiting bribery of public officials, for example). Whatever the cost of these crimes, it is certainly greater than direct economic losses from violent crimes and burglary.

The true cost of the target crimes lies in their capacity—their increasing capacity—to inspire fear. It is this fear that, in the words of the Violence Commission, "is gnawing at the vitals of urban America."

Why Set Quantitative Goals?

The use of numerical values gives a dimension to goal-setting that has been lacking in earlier proposals for reducing crime.

Previously, government reports and political leaders have spoken in broad terms, such as: crime should be controlled and reduced; administration of the criminal justice system should be improved; public expenditures on the system should be increased; Americans should redouble their efforts to eliminate the causes of crime, such as poverty, discrimination, urban blight, and disease; planning should be improved; additional research should be undertaken; citizens should become more involved; and so on.

Unfortunately, these broad statements are not easily translated into action. What, for example, does it mean to say that crime should be reduced? Which crimes? What is to be reduced—the rate, the actual number, the economic and social impact, or something else? How great a reduction is possible? How great a reduction is acceptable? How do State and local governments, criminal justice agencies, and citizens go about realizing these goals? And how is it possible to tell if a goal has been achieved?

These are not academic questions. They have practical implications in time, dollars, and lives. Goals are most useful when they are measurable, when at the end of a given period achievements can be compared with expectations and an assessment of the reasons for discrepancies made. For citizens, goals to reduce crime provide benchmarks for judging the effectiveness of criminal justice operations and other public programs. For legislators, they are guides to funding. For operating agencies, they are focal points for the allocation of men and equipment.

BASIC FACTORS IN SETTING GOALS FOR CRIME REDUCTION

In making its judgments on goals for crime reduction, the Commission considered in depth many factors. Although it is impossible to enumerate all of the factors, the Commission believes that among the most important are the following:

- Characteristics of the target crimes.
- Socioeconomic changes.
- Changes in public attitudes.
- Public support for the criminal justice system.
- New methods of measuring progress.

Characteristics of the Target Crimes

In 1971, more than 3 million violent crimes and burglaries were reported to the police in the United States (see Table 1). Since victimization surveys conducted by LEAA and the Crime Commission indicate that at least as many unreported violent crimes and burglaries occur as are reported,[7] it is highly probable that at least 6 million violent crimes and burglaries occurred in 1971.

TRENDS IN CRIME RATES. From 1960 to 1971, numbers of reported offenses and crime rates increased greatly in all five target crime categories. Except for the rate for murder and nonnegligent manslaughter, which increased 70 percent from 1960 through 1971, the rates for all of the target crimes more than doubled over the 12-year period.

Studies of reported crimes show wide fluctuations in rate from decade to decade. If the period prior to 1960 is any guide, Americans do not necessarily have to expect ever-increasing crime rates.

Although it is difficult to assess the period prior to 1933, when the FBI first began to compile national statistics, the available evidence indicates that rises and declines in crime have occurred since the beginning of the Nation. Probable peaks of violent crime in the late 19th century and the early 20th century have been identified in earlier studies.[8]

TABLE 1. Violent Crime and Burglary Reported to the Police, 1960 and 1971

	Murder and nonnegligent manslaughter	Forcible rape	Robbery	Aggravated assault	Burglary	Total
Number of Offenses:						
1960	9,030	17,030	107,340	152,580	900,400	1,186,380
1971	17,630	41,890	385,910	364,600	2,368,400	3,178,430
Percent Change 1960–1971	+95.2	+146.0	+259.5	+139.0	+163.0	+168.0
Rate per 100,000 Inhabitants:						
1960	5.0	9.5	59.9	85.1	502.1	661.6
1971	8.5	20.3	187.1	176.8	1,148.3	1,541.0
Percent Change 1960–1971	+70.0	+113.7	+212.4	+107.8	+128.7	+132.9

Source: Federal Bureau of Investigation, *Crime in the United States: Uniform Crime Reports—1971* (1972), p. 61. Publication referred to hereinafter as *UCR 1971*.

At this point it is necessary to enter a caution about the data on which the Commission based its conclusions on the extent of crime. The only source of overall information on crime on a continuing basis is the FBI's Uniform Crime Reports (UCR), which tabulate and analyze the reports of local police departments about crime in their areas. Because the FBI has succeeded in securing better local reporting over the years, it is essential, in the words of the President's Crime Commission, to "distinguish better reporting from more crime."[9]   In considering trends, it is also important to note changes in public attitudes toward reporting crime. Possibly some of the increase in the figures on forcible rape is due to the fact that women are not as reluctant as they once were to report rape.

Having said this much, the Commission points out what the UCR does show: that the number of crimes reported has risen much faster than the population. It may be assumed that the target crimes, which are widely regarded by the public as more serious, are better reported than many others. It therefore seems appropriate to make use of the UCR for basic data, with reference also to victimization surveys.

According to the UCR, the current "crime wave" did not get under way until the mid-1960's. From 1933 to 1940, the rate for one of the target crimes, forcible rape, rose 41 percent. Rates for all the others declined: criminal homicide by 14 percent, robbery by 51 percent, aggravated assault by 13 percent, burglary by 21 percent.[10] In view of the state of the early UCR figures, which have been questioned more vigorously than current statistics, no extensive conclusions can be drawn except that the crimes experiencing the greatest decreases in reported rates—robbery and burglary—probably did decrease.

From 1940 to 1963 the rates for rape, assault, and burglary rose gradually; the rate for robbery showed very little increase; and the rate for homicide declined appreciably. Beginning in the early 1960's, however, the rates for all five crimes rose steeply and continuously through 1971.

Preliminary data for 1972 released by the FBI indicate that violent crimes increased by only 1 percent over 1971. Robberies, which make up the largest number of crimes in the violent category, showed a 4 percent decrease. Murder was up 4 percent, aggravated assault 6 percent, and forcible rape 11 percent. Burglary was down 2 percent.

It thus appears that the Nation might be reaching the peak of a crime cycle, but it is quite possible that crime rates will rise again. The past does not necessarily foreshadow the future.

TYPES OF OFFENDERS AND VICTIMS. In 1969, the Violence Commission noted several chief characteristics of violent crime, which, with one or two exceptions, are linked to burglary as well:

- Violent crime in the United States is primarily a phenomenon of large cities.

- Violent crime in the city is overwhelmingly committed by males.
- Violent crime in the city is concentrated especially among youths between the ages of 15 and 24.
- Violent crime in the city is committed primarily by individuals at the lower end of the occupational scale.
- Violent crime in the city stems disproportionately from the ghetto slums where most Negroes live.
- The victims of assaultive violence in the cities generally have the same characteristics as the offenders; victimization rates are generally highest for males, youths, poor persons, and blacks. Robbery victims, however, often are older whites.
- By far the greatest proportion of all serious violence is committed by repeaters.[11]

Current statistics on arrests and offenses reported in the 1971 UCR generally support the Violence Commission's findings on violent crime. They also indicate that burglary, which is a property crime, is less confined to central cities and less likely to be committed by nonwhite offenders than is violent crime.

Almost three-fifths of the violent crimes and almost two-fifths of the burglaries reported in 1971 took place in cities with populations of more than 250,000, where just over one-fifth of the U.S. population lived.[12] Since 1968, however, violent crime and burglary rates have risen faster in the suburbs than in cities with populations greater than 250,000 (see Table 2). Serious crime is becoming less a central city phenomenon.

TABLE 2. Violent Crime and Burglary Known to the Police
(Rates per 100,000 Population)

	Urban (cities over 250,000)	Suburban	Rural
Crime Rate 1968:			
Violent Crimes	773.2	145.5	108.4
Burglary	1,665.8	761.0	387.2
Crime Rate 1971:			
Violent Crimes	1,047.5	205.7	133.4
Burglary	2,026.1	974.5	484.9
Percentage Increase:			
Violent Crimes	+35	+41	+23
Burglary	+22	+28	+25

Sources: *UCR—1968–1971*, "Crime Rate by Area."

In 1971, almost 60 percent of the arrests for violent crimes and more than 80 percent of the arrests for burglary involved young people, 24 years or younger.[13]

More than 90 percent of those arrested for violent crimes and burglaries in 1971 were males.[14] While there has been an overall increase since 1960 in the number and proportion of arrestees who are female, the percentage increase of males arrested for violent crimes has grown even faster. This has not been true of females under 18, where there was an increase of 229 percent. However, the priority crimes remain clearly the actions of males.

More than one-half of those arrested for violent crimes in 1971 were non-whites, mostly blacks. One-third of those arrested for burglary in 1971 were nonwhites, again mostly blacks.[15]

Within a group of persons arrested in 1971 on Federal charges of violent crime or burglary, from 65 percent to 77 percent had been arrested at least once before for violations of Federal or State law.[16] While FBI rearrest statistics include only those charged under Federal authority, available evidence indicates that similar high rearrest rates are the norm for States and localities as well. A reminder should be made here: arrest statistics show who has been arrested, not necessarily who committed an offense.

A national victimization survey made in 1970 by LEAA also shows that the persons most likely to be victims of violent crimes are males, youths, poor persons, and blacks.

The survey data do not indicate the sex or age characteristics of the heads of households victimized by burglary. They do show that the rate of victimization by burglary is more than one and one-half times as high for black families as for white ones. They also reveal no significant difference in the rate of victimization between households with incomes under $10,000 and those above $10,000.

This latter finding conflicts with the conclusion of the President's Crime Commission in 1967: "The risks of victimization from . . . burglary, are clearly concentrated in the lowest income groups and decrease steadily at higher income levels."[17] Because the President's Crime Commission also based its findings on a representative national survey further research will have to be undertaken to resolve the inconsistency in the two sets of data. But it is likely that a shift in the pattern of victimization has occurred since 1966.

OTHER CHARACTERISTICS OF OFFENDERS AND VICTIMS. Additional characteristics of offenders, victims, and places of occurrence of the five priority crimes suggest important contrasts in factors associated with each offense.

Murders, assaults, and rapes tend to be "crimes of passion," a label that indicates the spontaneous and noneconomic elements of these crimes. It is known, too, that victims of criminal homicide and assaults frequently precipitate attacks by using insulting language or physical force in quarrels and disagreements.[18]

Studies of homicide and aggravated assault show that a substantial percentage of offenders and victims had been drinking before the event and one study of criminal homicides revealed that either the victim or the murderer had been drinking in almost two-thirds of the cases.[19]

Alcohol appears to be only a minimal factor in robbery, according to another study. When there was evidence of alcohol, at least as many victims as offenders were drinking. The study pointed out that "this somewhat reinforces the image of the robbery offender as an individual who rationally plans his act against an unsuspecting victim, in contrast to the offender in the other major violent crimes, who often acts more passionately and impulsively."[20] No comparable information on the role of alcohol in burglaries is available.

A popular explanation of the recent rise in reported crimes has been the use of drugs, especially heroin. There is considerable evidence that heroin-dependent persons frequently engage in theft, burglary, and robbery to support their habits. There is little evidence, however, that points to heroin as a significant factor in non-income-producing violent crime.[21] From an in-depth study of the relation between drug abuse and crime, the National Commission on Marihuana and Drug Abuse reported in 1973 that heroin-dependent persons usually commit crimes against property, principally shoplifting and burglary, though occasionally when desperate they will commit an assault, mugging, or robbery.[22]

TIME AND PLACE OF CRIMINAL ACTS. The target crimes vary considerably as to where, when, and how they are committed.[23]

Victimization surveys and reported crime statistics answer many questions about where and when crimes are committed. Assaults occur about equally inside and outside buildings.[24] The home and various other inside locations are the likeliest locations for forcible rapes and homicides.[25] Sixty percent of reported burglaries occur in residences, as opposed to commercial establishments.[26] Possibly 60 percent of all burglaries and noncommercial robberies occur at night, as do two-thirds of the aggravated assaults and one-half of the rapes.[27]

Many persons are victimized more than once within relatively short time periods. About one in six robbery and assault victims during 1970 were victimized twice during the 12-month period, according to the LEAA victimization survey.

Eighteen percent of the households burglarized in 1970, according to the survey, were burglarized more than once in that year, 3 percent of them three times or more in the same year. About two in five of the burglaries reported in the survey in 1970 involved entries without force through unlocked doors, unlatched windows, or other means of access. These findings have particular relevance for crime prevention efforts by police and citizens.

RELATIONSHIP BETWEEN CRIMINAL AND VICTIM. A critical factor differentiating the five target crimes is the relationship between the criminal and his victim. It has long been assumed that a majority of murders are committed by someone known to the victim, and the same theory has been held in regard to aggravated assault and forcible rape. However, victimization surveys are indicating that the proportion of these crimes committed by strangers is increasing.

A special survey, conducted by the FBI in 1960 in cities where 38 percent of the U.S. population lived, reported that about one-third of all aggravated assaults were committed by strangers.[28] But the 1970 LEAA survey showed that nearly two-thirds of rapes and aggravated assaults were committed by strangers— i.e., the victim stated that the attacker was a stranger, or that he could not identify the attacker, or that the attacker was known by sight only (see Table 3). Almost all noncommercial robberies are committed by strangers.

TABLE 3. Offender-Victim Relationships

Offense[1]	Status of Offenders	
	Previously known to victim (percent)	Stranger[2] to victim (percent)
Forcible Rape	35	65
Aggravated Assault	34	66
Noncommercial Robberies	15	85

Source: LEAA.

[1] Attempts and actual offenses.

[2] Stranger means that the victim stated that the attacker was a stranger, or that he could not identify the attacker, or that the attacker was known by sight only.

Accurate information on relationships between burglars and their victims is not available, principally because burglars are rarely confronted by the persons they victimize. Many burglaries—probably a majority—are committed by habitual offenders—individuals who are involved in dozens, and in some cases hundreds, of offenses. For example, interviews with Dallas County inmates held by the Texas Department of Corrections in 1972 found that 48 repeat offenders admitted to an average of 65 burglaries per inmate.[29] Obviously, such persons are unlikely to confine their activities to residences and establishments of persons with whom they are acquainted.

The relationship of the offender to the victim for the five target crimes has important implications in selecting crime reduction strategies. This relationship takes on additional meaning when put in the context of possible changes in general social and economic conditions.

Socioeconomic Changes

Every serious study of crime has noted the association between fluctuations in crime rates and changes in population, social values, and economic conditions.

Among the societal conditions most frequently linked with the problem of crime are the following:

- The proportion of young people in the population.
- Metropolitan area population growth.
- Population mobility.
- Family stability.
- Income distribution.

The Commission is sure that relationships exist between crime and social justice, technological progress, and political change, although the nature of such relationships remains exceedingly ill-defined. The long-term effect of greater personal and national affluence, for example, may well depend on what type of criminal behavior is being addressed. In setting crime reduction goals, therefore, the Commission considered these two questions:

1. What significant changes will occur in society during the next decade?
2. How will societal changes affect violent crime and burglary?

The following discussion covers the factors the Commission considered most pertinent in answering these two questions.

PROPORTION OF YOUNG PEOPLE IN THE POPULATION. One important crime-related factor is the changing age structure of the population. This is especially true for young males—the group noted above as most likely both to commit crime and to be victimized by crime. Calculations made by the Commission indicated that the proportion of the population aged 15 to 24 will decrease.

Whereas young males increased as a percentage of the total population, and in absolute numbers, during the 1960's, their group will stop increasing—indeed will actually decline in both numbers and proportion of the population—by the late 1970's. The group increased by one-third—from 6.6 percent to 9.0 percent of the population—between 1960 and 1970. Its share of the population will peak around 1976 (9.5 percent) and decrease to about 8.5 percent in 1983.[30] This is about the same level as in 1968.

A similar change will take place in the youth population as a whole, including both males and females. The 15–24 age group will stop increasing relative to the total population in about 1976 and will decline in absolute numbers beginning about 1980.

Thus, the pressure recently felt by the criminal justice system due to the unusually large numbers of youths resulting from the postwar "baby boom" will be substantially lessened during the 1970's and 1980's.

METROPOLITAN AREA POPULATION GROWTH. A quite different influence on crime may be expected from other changes in American demographic patterns in the decade ahead. Projections prepared by the National Commission on Population Growth and the American Future indicate that the United States will continue to become more urbanized over the next several decades. In 1970, about 71 percent of all Americans lived in metropolitan areas. By the year 2000, the Population Commission expects 85 percent of the population to be living in metropolitan areas. The increases in most metropolitan areas will be in suburbs rather than in central cities.[31]

While estimates of the magnitude of population changes may vary as projections are updated, the direction is clear. The population density of central cities will not change drastically, and parts of surrounding suburbs will become more dense. This is significant in light of the historical association between population density and crime rates. Robbery, burglary, and other property crime rates are considerably higher in central cities than in suburbs or rural areas. As shown in Table 2, however, violent crime and burglary rates have been rising faster in the suburbs than in central cities. It is probable that the suburbs already are beginning to feel criminogenic effects of steadily increasing urbanization.

POPULATION MOBILITY. The move to urban areas will bring with it not only pressures and opportunities for antisocial behavior but also the loss of a sense of community that comes with widespread mobility.

The extent and impact of transiency in the population has been explored recently by Vance Packard, who estimates that "at least a fifth of all Americans move one or more times each year, and the pace of the movement of Americans is still increasing." He considers this widespread and constant movement to be a factor "contributing to the social fragmentation we are witnessing. ..."[32] Pervasive movement produces rootlessness which in turn leads to a sense of anonymity that is felt by segments of large urban populations.

A lack of common experience in a crowded but transient populace makes the organization of citizen crime prevention efforts more difficult. It also hinders the development of close police-community relations.

Rootlessness or mobility may also be a factor leading to criminality. A longitudinal study of delinquent males in Philadelphia, Pa., found that one of the variables significantly associated with police contacts, especially repeated contacts, was degree of school and residential mobility—the more mobility, the more police contacts.[33] Although there may be several explanations for this association, one of the most likely is that high mobility lessens ordinary community ties that restrain delinquency-prone youths from illegal acts.

In short, increasing population mobility is likely to contribute to America's crime problems during the next decade.

FAMILY STABILITY. Society has long depended on the authority of the family as a major instrument of social control and thus of crime prevention. Whether it can continue to rely so strongly on the family is open to serious question. The next 10 years will probably witness declines in traditional family stability. Steeply rising trends in illegitimate births and divorces over the last 3 decades point to weaker family ties than in the past.

INCOME DISTRIBUTION. Few developments will have greater influence on American life than changes in national income distribution. The proportion of the population in lower income brackets decreased throughout the sixties.[34] While increasing affluence is not assured, current projections are encouraging.

One analyst has estimated that by 1980 more than half of the Nation's households will have incomes of more than $10,000 a year, as against two-fifths in this category in 1970.[35] (Estimates are in 1970 dollars.) At the same time, the proportion of households with incomes of $7,000 or below will decrease to less than one-third. Thus the average will be rising and affluence will be spreading.

As these changes take place, the relationship of wealth, poverty, and crime becomes more difficult to assess. Greater affluence for the majority of the people means more valuable targets for burglary and robbery, possibly with less caution exerted by owners to protect possessions that can readily be replaced. Rising general affluence may mean that frustration and envy will in fact increase for persons in the lowest income brackets—one out of every nine families will have incomes below $3,000 a year, according to Linden's estimates—and this may lead to more attempts to supplement income by illegal acts.

On the other hand, greater affluence should mean that more citizens will have more of their basic wants satisfied than at any previous time in-our Nation's history. The basic economic pressures that lead to stickups, break-ins, and violence may well be lessened.

Changes in Public Attitudes

Changes in attitudes now widely held by the American public may well affect crime in the decade ahead. How Americans feel about their lives, their jobs, their neighbors, and their government will ultimately shape society for better or worse. Two sets of attitudes—racism and lack of confidence in government— will be specifically treated here as they have been identified in other studies as critical variables in the recent rises in crime.

FRUSTRATION OF MINORITY ASPIRATIONS. In 1969 a task force of the Violence Commission considered the paradoxical rise in crime rates in the late 1960's at the very time when inner city conditions were improving. Although substantial progress was being made toward overcoming the racial discrimination and lack of opportunity which appeared to be root causes of crime, the rates of violent crime rose faster than in the immediately preceding years. The paradox could be ascribed, the Commission concluded, mainly to minority disappointments in the "revolution of rising expectations" and the loss of public confidence in social and political institutions.[36]

Today, 4 years after the publication of that report, there is little conclusive evidence that the country will quickly solve the problems of racial injustice and minority frustration. But neither is there evidence that the races are locked in irreconcilable conflict.

A national opinion survey on perceptions of racial discrimination conducted by the Harris organization in late 1972 showed that less than half the black respondents felt they had trouble getting into hotels and motels. About half felt their group was not discriminated against in getting quality education and entrance into labor unions. But in all the other aspects of personal and community life about which they were asked—decent housing, white-collar and skilled jobs, wages, treatment by police, and general treatment "like human beings"—considerable majorities of blacks reported feeling discrimination.[37]

Significantly, however, when compared with a survey on the same subject in 1969, fewer black respondents perceived discrimination on the job and in the community in 1972. In some areas the percentage drop was substantial. In 1969, for example, 83 percent of the black respondents felt discrimination in housing; the percentage in 1972 was 66. When two-thirds of the blacks still feel discriminated against in so important an area as housing, American society has a long way to go yet toward racial justice. But, at least in the opinion of some, progress is being made.

Another interesting point about the Harris surveys is that, in some key areas, the white residents in 1972 perceived more discrimination against blacks than they had in 1969. In the earlier year, for example, 19 percent of the whites thought blacks were discriminated against by the police; 25 percent of the whites thought so by 1972. Discrimination against blacks in housing and education was also more apparent to whites in 1972 than in 1969.

Finally, it should be mentioned that in another national survey taken in mid-1972 black respondents "were significantly *more* optimistic about their personal futures" (emphasis in original) than whites.[38]

These may appear to be small gains. But if disappointment of minorities in the revolution of rising expectations is a cause of violent crime, they have some importance for the future.

Whether they have permanent significance remains to be seen. The dismal heritage of years will not pass quickly. Bold and sustained government action is essential to progress.

MISTRUST IN GOVERNMENT. In contrast to the encouraging, though small, shifts in public opinion regarding racial problems, national surveys indicate that lack of public confidence in political institutions is reaching crisis proportions.

In 1970, the University of Michigan's Survey Research Center found that between one-third and one-half of those surveyed in a national sample responded affirmatively to questions asking whether they believed (1) that their government can be trusted only some of the time; (2) that the government is run for the benefit of a few big interests; and (3) that many officials are "a little crooked."[39]   The percentages of respondents expressing these beliefs have increased significantly since the Center began periodic surveys in the late 1950's.

These findings are of great significance to the reduction of crime. In this society, citizens do not obey the law simply in response to threats by the authorities but because they acknowledge the right of the lawmaking institutions to lay down the rules and the right of the law enforcement agencies to enforce them. In other words, citizens recognize the legitimacy of the country's political institutions. As the Violence Commission put it, "what weakens the legitimacy of social and political institutions contributes to law-breaking, including violent crime."[40]

The findings are also discouraging in the light of the need for close cooperation between citizens and officials in crime-fighting efforts. Few citizens will long be willing to cooperate with officials whom they believe to have a hand in the till or to be "on the take" from illegal enterprise. Indeed, the impact of the Watergate problem and other aspects of the 1972 presidential election on the confidence of the people in this country in their government has yet to be assessed.

It cannot be said with certainty whether public cynicism about government is a deepening chronic malaise or whether it will abate along with the domestic turbulence of the 1960's and American military involvement in Southeast Asia. The Commission is hopeful, however, that public confidence will be restored by public leadership that is honest and fair.

Public Support for the Criminal Justice System

The fourth major factor that the Commission took into consideration in setting its goals for crime reduction in the decade ahead was public support for the criminal justice system.

In mid-1972 a national survey conducted by the Gallup organization showed that violence and crime were the domestic problems that most worried the respondents. And the respondents were willing to put their money where their worries were. A larger proportion of them were willing to approve government spending to combat crime than spending for any other activity, including air and water pollution, education, and mass transportation.[41]

As a matter of fact, the share of the Gross National Product (GNP) devoted to expenditures for the criminal justice system has been rising steadily for nearly 20 years. From 1955 to 1965, criminal justice expenditures rose from one-half to two-thirds of 1 percent of GNP, with an average annual increase of about one-hundredth of 1 percent. By 1971 criminal justice expenditures had risen to approximately 1 percent of GNP, with an estimated annual increase since 1966 of more than five times that shown in the 1955–65 period.[42]   Although percentage increases have undoubtedly been influenced by expanded Federal spending, all levels of government have spent more for the criminal justice system. Preliminary estimates by the Law Enforcement Assistance Administration and the Bureau of the Census indicated total spending of $10,513,358,000 in 1971.[43]

The other major evidence of public support for the criminal justice system lies in the increasing participation of citizens in the operation of the system. No hard statistics are available, but, beginning in the late 1960's, there was an upsurge of citizen activity directly aimed at reducing crime. This took the form of working for better streetlighting, setting up neighborhood security programs, and other activities. Hundreds of local projects emerged in communities across the country. Citizen participation is one of the Commission's priorities for action, and it will be discussed in detail in this chapter. The reader should also refer to the chapters on community crime prevention and on corrections, as well as to the separate reports on these subjects.

NEW METHODS IN MEASURING PROGRESS

The establishment of crime-specific goals is a meaningless exercise if the rate of progress cannot be accurately assessed. One factor in the Commission's conclusions, therefore, was the ability to measure crime.

There are now two tools for measuring national crime rates: the UCR compiled annually by the FBI, and the national victimization survey developed by LEAA.

The UCR has the inherent limitation of being based on reports from police departments. Hence it includes only those crimes known to the police.

Victimization surveys made since 1966 in various cities indicate that at least half of all crimes against persons and property are not reported to the police. Moreover, there have been findings that police departments have not recorded fully the extent of crimes that are reported by citizens, or have not accurately classified and defined reported offenses.[44] Consequently, the victimization survey is widely believed to give a more precise estimate of the volume of crime and other dimensions of criminal activity, such as cost, than the UCR.

LEAA, in conjunction with the Bureau of the Census, is now conducting an annual victimization survey of the representative national sample of households and commercial establishments.[45] Local data will be provided by supplemental sample surveys in about 35 of the Nation's largest cities. These local surveys will be updated periodically. For the five largest cities—New York, Chicago, Los Angeles, Philadelphia, and Detroit—survey information will be provided biennially.

The surveys, which are expected to continue under Federal auspices, should provide a fairly reliable estimate of the true level of rape, aggravated and simple assault, robbery, burglary, larceny, and auto theft. Attempted crimes will be counted as well as crimes actually committed.

In the case of rape, the resulting picture from victimization surveys may not be as clear as for other offenses, owing to the reluctance of victims to identify incidents. However, the interview technique may be more successful in eliciting information than the official reporting process. Discreet and indirect approaches to the incident are expected to overcome a good deal of the reporting problem. The fact that rapes are comparatively small in number will undoubtedly mean that it will take longer to establish a significantly reliable measure of change for this offense than for others which occur with far greater frequency.

The LEAA survey will ascertain the amount of property lost and recovered, attitudes toward police, fear, age and race characteristics of offenders, place of occurrence, and weapons used by assailants. Unlike UCR statistics, the LEAA survey will indicate offender-victim relationships. This will make it possible to measure progress towards reducing "high-fear" (stranger-related) crime which the Commission has set forth as a national goal.

In sum, the LEAA survey will make it possible to achieve a more precise record of the volume and rate of crime. The first complete annual picture of victimization will emerge for 1973. Preliminary tabulations of annual survey results will be available approximately 8 months after the end of each year.

It should be noted that victimization surveys also present some problems. First, victimization surveys may be interpreted as showing an increase in crime. The data should show higher numbers and rates of crime than the public is accustomed to reading and hearing. This is attributable to greater accuracy, but citizens may find it difficult to distinguish between accuracy in reporting and actual increases in crime.

Second, victimization surveys are expensive. Therefore reliance on victimization surveys to assess national progress cannot mean discarding traditional police statistics. Surveys are too costly to be run on a continuous basis by LEAA in every jurisdiction.

Most States and localities will have to continue to rely on official police statistics to determine directions of change in their crime rates. Even those cities that are surveyed yearly by LEAA will need to use information on crimes known and reported to the police. Such data are essential to effective allocation of police manpower. They are an irreplaceable indicator of the extent to which citizens are willing to bring crimes to the attention of police. Unlike the LEAA victimization survey, most police departments do not collect statistics on offender-victim relationships. The Commission, however, urges that departments expand their statistical coverage to do so.

It is unrealistic to expect any measure of crime to be 100 percent accurate. Victimization surveys should be useful in evaluating reported crime statistics and vice versa. Not only will such cross-comparisons lead to more accurate data, but they should also encourage public confidence in official estimates of the crime problem. A lessening of public debate as to whether crime has gone up or down in the Nation and communities may be a byproduct of the development of victimization surveys.

A LOOK AHEAD WITH PRIORITIES FOR ACTION

The crime reduction goals proposed in the preceding pages are not the result of using some heretofore unknown formula. Nor were they the result of abstract or wishful thinking. They were decided upon after considering the nature of the target crimes and some of the social and governmental developments—past and future—that will affect them. The Commission believes that reductions of the magnitude proposed are not unrealistic.

The Commission was led to this belief by the several signs discussed above, signs that point to the possibility of reducing the priority crimes. Among them are the probable reduction in the proportion of the population who are in the crime-prone 15-to-24 age bracket. Increasing national prosperity is an encouraging sign if it eliminates absolute poverty. Recent formation of citizen crime-prevention organizations and public willingness to approve increased government spending for the criminal justice system also augur well for progress toward the goal of reducing crime.

Among the priority crimes of murder, rape, assault, robbery, and burglary, the Commission has concluded that the greatest reduction is most likely to occur in the rates of the latter two. These differ in several key ways from the other priority offenses. Robbery and burglary are acquisitive crimes, committed for material gain, and often they are calculated and planned carefully. Usually, they are committed by persons who are strangers to the victims. They occur in environments that can be altered to reduce the opportunities open to the criminal. Large numbers of burglaries and robberies are vulnerable to relatively easily implemented deterrent strategies: police patrols, street lighting, citizen crime prevention activities, and speedy and effective court dispositions.

In addition, the Commission is convinced that society and the criminal justice system are capable of directing many delinquent youths and ex-offenders to lawful avenues of economic gain so that the attraction of the "easy money" of holdups and break-ins will be less important.

In short, there are solid grounds for optimism in deterring the acts themselves and in reducing the potential number of offenders.

The fact that the Commission has set lower percentage goals for reducing murder, assault, and rape does not mean that they are less important. Indeed, murder, rape, and assault are probably feared by the average citizen more than any other crime.

The proposed percentage of reduction is lower for these so-called crimes of passion because they are less easily controlled than the other target crimes by conventional criminal justice methods. Many of these crimes are committed by acquaintances and are impervious to ordinary deterrent strategies. Victims of assault and homicide frequently show little inclination to avoid criminal attacks. Indeed, they often incite assailants by their own speech and actions. Alcohol—a drug that has proved consistently resistant to efforts to lessen its abuse—is an important catalyst in homicides, assaults, and, to a lesser extent, rapes. To reduce these crimes, a change in values is needed—an increased respect for others and a willingness to settle disputes by means other than violence.

The Commission proposes four priorities for action for reducing all of the target crimes. These are:

- Preventing juvenile delinquency.
- Improving delivery of social services.
- Reducing delays in the criminal justice process.
- Securing more citizen participation in the criminal justice system.

The Commission submits that many of the standards set forth in subsequent chapters are easily categorized within these priorities and lead to the accomplishment of the numerical goals established earlier in this chapter.

Priority: Preventing Juvenile Delinquency

The highest attention must be given to preventing juvenile delinquency, to minimizing the involvement of young offenders in the juvenile and criminal justice system, and to reintegrating delinquents and young offenders into the community. By 1983 the rate of delinquency cases coming before courts that would be crimes if committed by adults should be cut to half the 1973 rate.

Street crime is a young man's game. More than half the persons arrested for violent crime in 1971 were under 24 years of age, with one-fifth under 18. For burglary, over half of the 1971 arrests involved youths under 18.[46]

There is strong evidence that the bulk of ordinary crime against person and property is committed by youths and adults who have had previous contact with the criminal justice or juvenile justice system. Recent evidence in support of this assumption is a study of delinquency in all males born in 1945 who lived in Philadelphia from their 10th to their 18th birthdays. Specifically the study concluded that the more involvement a juvenile had with the police and juvenile justice authorities, the more likely he would be to be further involved.[47] Of the 9,945 subjects, 3,475 (35 percent) came in contact with police at least once. Of this delinquent group, about 54 percent was responsible for 84 percent of all police contacts in the group. Eighteen percent of those having repeated contact with the police had five or more contacts and were responsible for 52 percent of all police contacts in the delinquent group.

Increased efforts must be made to break this cycle of recidivism at the earliest possible point. One approach is to minimize the involvement of the offender in the criminal justice system. Minimized involvement is not a fancy phrase for "coddling criminals." It means simply that society should use that means of controlling and supervising the young offender which will best serve to keep him out of the recidivism cycle and at the same time protect the community. It is based on an easily justified assumption: the further an offender penetrates into the criminal justice process, the more difficult it becomes to divert him from a criminal career.

People tend to learn from those closest to them. It is small wonder that prisons and jails crowded with juveniles, first offenders, and hardened criminals have been labeled "schools of crime."

People also tend to become what they are told they are. The stigma of involvement with the criminal justice system, even if only in the informal processes of juvenile justice, isolates persons from lawful society and may make further training or employment difficult. A recent survey conducted for the Department of Labor revealed that an arrest record was an absolute bar to employment in almost 20 percent of the State and local agencies surveyed and was a definite consideration for not hiring in most of the remaining agencies.[48]

For many youths, as noted above, incarceration is not an effective tool of correction. Society will be better protected if certain individuals, particularly youths and first offenders, are diverted prior to formal conviction either to the care of families or relatives or to employment, mental health, and other social service programs. Thus a formal arrest is inappropriate if the person may be referred to the charge of a responsible parent, guardian, or agency. Formal adjudication may not be necessary if an offender can be safely diverted elsewhere, as to a youth services bureau for counseling or a drug abuse program for treatment. Offenders properly selected for pretrial diversion experience less recidivism than those with similar histories and social backgrounds who are formally adjudicated.

To assure progress toward the goal of minimizing the involvement of juveniles in the juvenile justice system, the Commission proposes that the 1973 rate of delinquency cases disposed of by juvenile or family courts for offenses that would be crimes if committed by adults be cut in half by 1983.

The Department of Health, Education, and Welfare, which collects information on juvenile courts, estimates that a little less than 40 percent of cases disposed of by courts are cases of running away, truancy, and other offenses that would not be crimes if committed by an adult.[49] These are the so-called juvenile status offenses.

The remaining 60-odd percent of cases estimated to be disposed of by juvenile or family courts are nonstatus crimes, those that would be crimes if committed by adults. It is the rate of these cases which the Commission would propose to cut in half.

Meeting the goal, the Commission believes, should result in significant decreases in crime through preventing recidivism and might also prove to be far less costly than dealing with delinquents under present methods. To process a youth through the juvenile justice system and keep him in a training school for a year costs almost $6,000.[50] There is no reason to believe that the cost of a diversionary program would exceed this figure, since most such programs are not residential. Indeed, diversion might prove to provide significant savings.

One final note should be added. Minimizing a youth's involvement with the criminal justice system does not mean abandoning the use of confinement for certain individuals. Until more effective means of treatment are found, chronic and dangerous delinquents and offenders should be incarcerated to protect society. But the juvenile justice system must search for the optimum programs outside institutions for juveniles who do not need confinement.

Priority: Improving Delivery of Social Services

Public agencies should improve the delivery of all social services to citizens, particularly to those groups that contribute higher than average proportions of their numbers to crime statistics.

There is abundant evidence that crime occurs with greater frequency where there are poverty, illiteracy, and unemployment, and where medical, recreational, and mental health resources are inadequate. When unemployment rates among youths in poverty areas of central cities are almost 40 percent and crime is prevalent, it is impossible not to draw conclusions about the relationship between jobs and crime. The Commission believes that effective and responsive delivery of public services that promote individual and economic well-being will contribute to a reduction in crime. The rationale for the value of a variety of services is well expressed in the Commission's *Report on Community Crime Prevention*. Having called for citizen action on such priorities as employment, education, and recreation, the report points out:

> This is not to say that if everyone were better educated or more fully employed that crime would be eliminated or even sharply reduced. What is meant is that unemployment, substandard education, and so on, form a complex, and admittedly little understood amalgam of social conditions that cements, or at least predisposes, many individuals to criminal activity.
> Thus a job, for example, is just one wedge to break this amalgam. Increased recreational opportunities represent another. Though one wedge may not have much effect on an individual's lifestyle, two or three might.

The Commission is aware that improvement of social services to a degree necessary to have an impact on crime will take time. Building career education programs into elementary and secondary school curriculums, for example, cannot be accomplished in the next 2 or 3 years. But it must begin now if society is to realize benefits at the end of 10 years and beyond.

The Commission particularly wishes to call attention to the provision of drug and alcohol abuse treatment. Communities must recognize the diversity of drug abuse and alcohol problems and the need for a number of alternative treatment approaches. Citizens must be willing to make the investment that such treatment requires, not merely because it will reduce crime but because adequate treatment is essential to deal with an increasingly serious national health problem.

Priority: Reducing Delays in the Criminal Justice Process

Delays in the adjudication and disposition of cases must be greatly reduced and the period between arrest and trial must be reduced to the shortest possible time.

In recent years, backlogs in the courts have become a well-publicized symbol of inefficiency in the entire system. In large cities, many cases have been subject to delays of 300 to 1,000 days from arrest to trial and final disposition. Legislatures and other parts of the criminal justice system, as well as judges, defense attorneys, and prosecutors, must bear some of the responsibility for the problem. Delay in the criminal justice process frustrates law enforcement efforts and develops a sense of injustice in offender, victim, and citizen alike.

The negative byproducts of judicial delay are many. The number of defendants incarcerated and awaiting trial is reaching alarming proportions in many large cities, and detention facilities are dangerously overcrowded. The LEAA National Jail Census in 1970 revealed that 52 percent of the jail inmates were awaiting trial.[51] Pretrial incarceration is costly to the individual, for it denies him income and, in fact, may cause him to lose his job. Extended incarceration resulting from judicial delay is also costly to the public, since pretrial detainees must be fed and supervised.

Alternatives to incarceration such as bail and release on recognizance present another set of problems in cases of long delays between arrest and trial. A 1968 survey in the District of Columbia found ". . . an increased propensity to be rearrested where the release period extends more than 280 days."[52]

The pressures of heavy backlogs contribute to the notorious practice of plea bargaining. Faced with an overwhelming caseload, prosecutors seek to avoid time-consuming trials by disposing of felony indictments through negotiated guilty pleas to less serious felonies and misdemeanors. Whether viewed from a rehabilitation or deterrence perspective, workload-motivated plea bargaining is an undesirable practice that can be gradually eliminated if accompanied by less burdensome court backlogs.

Speeding up the criminal justice process may not reduce crime by itself, but when coupled with effective treatment alternatives and intelligent correctional decisions, it should have a significant impact. Additional judges will undoubtedly be needed in many jurisdictions, but much can be done to improve the adjudicatory process by streamlining court procedures.

Priority: Increasing Citizen Participation

Citizens should actively participate in activities to control crime in their community, and criminal justice agencies should actively encourage citizen participation.

The criminal justice system depends on citizen participation. Most crimes do not come directly to the attention of police; they are reported by citizens. Without active cooperation of citizen jurors and witnesses, the judicial process cannot function. Institutional education and training programs will not be useful to the offender if he cannot find employment in the community in which he is released. The best-trained and equipped police force will fare poorly in the battle against crime if the citizens it serves do not take basic precautionary measures to protect themselves and reduce criminal opportunities.

Citizens in many communities are organizing to form block crime prevention associations and court-watching groups, and to furnish volunteers to work in the criminal justice system. One striking example is a nationwide program that began with the involvement of a few citizens in Royal Oak, Mich. The Volunteers in Probation program grew from eight citizens in 1959 to an estimated quarter of a million nationwide in 1972.

The Royal Oak concept utilized volunteers and professionals together and statistics indicate that volunteers and professionals working together can provide intensive probation services that are three times more effective than those provided by a probation officer working alone.[53]

Citizen cooperation with police also has great potential, but it is largely unrealized. In 1970, 18 percent of the households in America took some form of home protection—special locks, lights, alarms, watch dogs, and/or weapons.[54] Whether the measures adopted were the most effective that could have been chosen is another matter. Certainly every police department could perform a useful service by actively disseminating its crime-prevention knowledge to citizens. It is not necessary to sell self-protection to many persons, certainly not to those who have been victimized before. Yet, in many jurisdictions, aggressive outreach programs for crime prevention are nonexistent. The Police chapter of this report identifies in greater detail what some departments have done in this area.

All criminal justice agencies can do much in their operations to encourage citizens' involvement. They first must organize their operations to increase acceptability to the citizens they serve and to encourage these citizens to support their activities. This means, for example, that police must process complaints efficiently and courteously; that courts must minimize the time lost by jurors and witnesses; that corrections must run its institutions to permit the community reasonable access to those incarcerated. These are minimums. Criminal justice agencies can do much more, if they actively seek to explain their role to citizens' groups and show how citizens themselves may participate in community crime prevention. Above all, criminal justice agencies must understand and know the communities they serve. Active personnel recruitment from all facets of the community is essential if citizens and the criminal justice system are to work together as a team.

NOTES

1. The National Commission on the Causes and Prevention of Violence pointed out in 1969 that, although violent crimes form a relatively small percentage of all crimes known to the police, their effect is out of proportion to their volume. "In violent crime man becomes a wolf to man, threatening or destroying the personal safety of his victim in a terrifying act. Violent crime (particularly street crime) engenders fear—the deep-seated fear of the hunted in the presence of the hunter." National Commission on the Causes and Prevention of Violence, *To Establish Justice, To Insure Domestic Tranquility* (1969), p. 18.

2. Crimes are defined and trends noted in Federal Bureau of Investigation, *Crime in the United States: Uniform Crime Reports–1971* (1972), pp. 6–21. Publication is referred to hereinafter as *UCR* with the appropriate date. The rate of commission of these crimes is the number of actual and attempted offenses per 100,000 inhabitants.

3. For discussion of several methods of estimating costs of crime, see Donald J. Mulvihill and Melvin M. Tumin, *Crimes of Violence*, a report of the National Commission on the Causes and Prevention of Violence (1969), pp. 394–404.

4. *UCR–1971*, pp. 15, 21. These figures do not indicate how much stolen property was recovered.

5. The Gallup Poll, "The Dimensions of Crime" (January 14, 1973), p. 3.

6. President's Commission on Law Enforcement and Administration of Justice, *Task Force Report: Crime and Its Impact—An Assessment* (1967), pp. 44, 46.

7. A preliminary national survey of several thousand households was conducted by LEAA to determine the extent and nature of victimization in 1970. The survey, a developmental step in preparation for a continuous national victimization survey, polled the population 16 years of age or older for forcible rape, robbery, aggravated and simple assault, burglary, larceny, and auto theft. Murder and nonnegligent manslaughter were not covered. The responses were for personal, not business, victimization. Hereinafter the survey will be referred to as LEAA 1970 Survey. For victimization data see also *Crime and Its Impact*, p. 17.

8. Mulvihill and Tumin, *Crimes of Violence*, p. 52.

9. President's Commission on Law Enforcement and Administration of Justice, *The Challenge of Crime in a Free Society* (1967), p. 3.

10. Crime rates from 1933 furnished by the FBI.

11. *To Establish Justice, To Insure Domestic Tranquility*, pp. 20–24, 26. (The Violence Commission defined repeaters as persons with prior contacts with police.)

12. *UCR–1971*, pp. 100–101.

13. *UCR–1971*, pp. 122–123.

14. *UCR–1971*, p. 126.

15. *UCR–1971*, p. 127.

16. *UCR–1971*, p. 38.

17. *Crime and Its Impact*, p. 80.

18. Mulvihill and Tumin, *Crimes of Violence*, pp. 224–228. Precipitation was defined as first resort to insults or force.

19. Data on the role of alcohol in violent crimes are summarized in Mulvihill and Tumin, *Crimes of Violence*, pp. 641–649. The homicide study is reported in Marvin E. Wolfgang, *Patterns in Criminal Homicide* (Wiley, 1966).

20. Mulvihill and Tumin, *Crimes of Violence*, pp. 644–646.

21. For a discussion of the relationship between drug abuse and crime, see Harwin Voss and Richard Stephens, "The Relationship between Drug Abuse and Crime," to be published in *Drug Abuse*; Richard Stephens and Stephen Levine, "Crime and Narcotic Addiction," to be published in Raymond Hardy and Cull (eds.), *Applied Psychology in Law Enforcement and Corrections* (Thomas, 1973); and James A. Inciardi, "The Poly-Drug User: A New Situational Offender," in Freda Adler (ed.), *Politics, Crime, and the International Scene: An Inter-American Focus* (San Juan, P.R.: North-South Center Press, 1972), pp. 60–69.

22. National Commission on Marihuana and Drug Abuse, *Drug Use in America: Problem in Perspective* (1973), p. 175.

23. *UCR–1971*, p. 21.

24. Mulvihill and Tumin, *Crimes of Violence*, p. 302.

25. *Ibid.*

26. *UCR–1971*, p. 21

27. Data on all burglaries, residential and commercial, are taken from *UCR–1971*, p. 21. Data on residential burglaries in LEAA 1970 Survey indicate that roughly 60 percent of these are committed at night. Data on noncommercial robbery, forcible rape, and aggravated assault are taken from LEAA 1970 Survey.

28. *UCR–1960*, p. 11.

29. Dallas Police Department, *Repeat Offender Study: Summary Report* (July 1972), p. 5.

30. Calculations derived from estimates and projections published by the Bureau of the Census. The projected percentages shown here for 1976 and 1983 are the medians of the calculated percentages of the four projections used by the Bureau of the Census. See *Current Population Reports*, Series P-25, No. 493, "Projections of the Population of the United States, by Age and Sex: 1972 to 2020" (1972); and P-24, No. 483, "Preliminary Estimates of the Population of the United States, by Age and Sex: April 1, 1960 to July 1, 1971" (1972).

31. Commission on Population Growth and the American Future, *Population and the American Future* (1972). The term "metropolitan area" refers to the Commission's definition: "Functionally integrated areas of 100,000 population or more, composed of an urbanized area or central cities of at least 50,000 people, and the surrounding counties." See also Patricia Leavey Hodge and Philip M. Hauser, *The Challenge of America's Metropolitan Population Outlook–1960-1985*, Research Report No. 3 for the National Commission on Urban Problems (1968), pp. 15–16.

32. Vance Packard, *A Nation of Strangers* (McKay, 1972), pp. 6, 8.

33. Marvin E. Wolfgang, Robert M. Figlio, and Thorsten Sellin, *Delinquency in a Birth Cohort* (University of Chicago Press, 1972), p. 246.

34. The proportion of persons in the poverty bracket declined from 22.4

percent in 1959 to 12.6 percent in 1970, and total numbers also declined. (Bureau of the Census, *Statistical Abstract of the United States, 1972*), p. 329. There was a reversal in the trend in the year 1970 as compared with 1969. But most opinion and historical experience point to a return to the trend of declining numbers of persons living in poverty and their proportion of the population.

35. Fabian Linden, "The Expanding Upper Income Brackets," *The Conference Board Record* (November 1971), p. 15.

36. *To Establish Justice, To Insure Domestic Tranquility*, pp. 38–43.

37. The Harris Survey, January 15, 1973.

38. William Watts and Lloyd A. Free (eds.), *State of the Nation* (Universe Books, 1973), p. 25.

39. "Election Time Series Analysis of Attitudes of Trust in Government" (Center for Political Studies, University of Michigan, 1971).

40. *To Establish Justice, To Insure Domestic Tranquility*, p. 42.

41. Discussed in Watts and Free (eds.), *State of the Nation*, pp. 35, 117–118. Interestingly, the means most favored to reduce crime was "to clean up the slums." Improvements in the criminal justice system received from one-third ("more police") to two-thirds ("improve jails") the number of mentions made of slum clean-up.

42. Data from *Statistical Abstract of the United States* for appropriate years.

43. "Expenditure and Employment Data for the Criminal Justice System, 1970–1971" (LEAA, unpublished).

44. The usefulness of officially reported crime statistics has been widely debated. Doubts have been expressed as to how accurately UCR data can show the extent of and changes in crime. After careful study, a task force of the Violence Commission concluded, "For individual acts of violence covered by national police statistics, limitations on the accuracy of the data are apparent." Such limitations affect understanding of the levels, trends, incidence, and severity of crime. Mulvihill and Tumin, *Crimes of Violence*, pp. 16–38.

45. The survey is described in detail in the Commission's *Report on the Criminal Justice System*, Appendix A. Information for the present brief description was also supplied by the National Criminal Justice Information and Statistics Service in LEAA.

46. *UCR–1971*, p. 121.

47. Wolfgang, Figlio, and Sellin, *Delinquency in a Birth Cohort*, chs. 6, 14.

48. Herbert S. Miller, *The Closed Door: The Effect of a Criminal Record on Employment with State and Local Public Agencies*, report prepared for the U.S. Department of Labor (February 1972), p. 100.

49. Estimates from U.S. Department of Health, Education, and Welfare.

50. Derived from "Youth Service System: Diverting Youth from the Juvenile Justice System," paper prepared by the U.S. Department of Health, Education, and Welfare.

51. Law Enforcement Assistance Administration, *1970 National Jail Census* (1971), p. 1.

52. J. W. Locke and others, *Compilation and Use of Criminal Court Data in Relation to Pre-Trial Release of Defendant: Pilot Study Report* (National Bureau of Standards, 1970), p. v.

Crime Prevention: The Fugitive Utopia
Lamar T. Empey

For most people, the idea of crime prevention is attractive. To the traditionalist, it bespeaks a kind of fugitive Utopia in which the citizenry is protected from the ravages of human predation by a vigilant and efficient system of social control. To others, the utopian society would be one in which each individual is given a stake in conformity and thereby rendered unlikely to become delinquent or criminal. But there is reason to be leery of utopian hopes because crime, like organic malfunction, seems to be a normal aspect of human life (Durkheim, 1895:chap. 3). The conceit that either can be ultimately vanquished "involves a particularly trivial kind of utopian dreaming. Out of control, malfunction and crime could possibly overcome life, but control could never succeed in more than keeping them to a level appropriate to the prevailing form of human life" (Bittner, 1970:49).

Crime is found in varying degrees in all modern nations, particularly those that are urban and highly industrialized. The particular forms that it takes in any society are related to the ways in which that society is organized (Wheeler et al., 1967:409). A society like America's, for example, that places a high premium on freedom, that fosters a tradition of wanting to get ahead, and that prizes material success is not likely to be able to contain all its members within a conventional mold. Paradoxically, the dominant values that foster a high level of aspiration and striving may also be the very ones that encourage crime as one means of achieving them (cf. Merton, 1957:chaps. 4, 5; Cloward & Ohlin, 1960: chap. 4).

SOURCE: Daniel Glaser, ed., *Handbook of Criminology* (Chicago: Rand McNally, 1974), pp. 1095-1123. Copyright © 1970 by Rand McNally College Publishing Company and reprinted by permission.

These considerations, then, should act to caution against any easy assumption that the total prevention of all crime is desirable, or even conceivable. "Its historic roots, its familiar occurrence in urban society, and its particular relation to the American value system suggest that we are dealing with a chronic problem which is unlikely to yield easily to preventive efforts" (Wheeler et al., 1967: 409-10).

THE WAR ON CRIME

During the turbulent years of the 1960s and early 1970s, concern for better methods of crime prevention and control reached a peak. Evidence from official sources indicated that crime and delinquency were on the rise. Although questions might be raised regarding the complete accuracy of this evidence, a far more important issue has to do with the ways in which it was perceived and interpreted by different groups of Americans. The contrasting ideologies that emerged may portend the future.

One significant segment of the populace responded positively to a body of rhetoric suggesting that the nation is in dire peril. As Bittner described it:

A figure of speech that has recently gained a good deal of currency is the "war on crime." The intended import of the expression is quite clear. It is supposed to indicate that the community is seriously imperiled by forces bent on its destruction and calls for the mounting of efforts that have claims on all available resources to defeat the peril. The rhetorical shift from "crime control" to "war on crime" signifies the transition from a routine concern to a state of emergency. We no longer face losses of one kind or another from the depredation of criminals; we are in imminent danger of losing everything! (1970:48)

In some cases, the immediate peril seemed to come from deviant acts that were not entirely traditional in character. Rather, these acts were often political in nature, and were perpetrated in response to the problems of a rapidly changing world. Consider Carter and Gitchoff's summary of them:

[Americans] have observed rebellion against the establishment in forms encompassing freedom riders in the South, to looters in the North. American youth in increasing numbers have withstood tear gas and mace, billy clubs and bullets, insults and assaults, jail and prison in order to lie down in front of troop trains, sit-in at a university administration building, love-in in public parks, wade-in at non-integrated beaches, and lie-in within our legislative buildings. These youths have challenged the establishment on such issues as the legal-oriented entities of the draft, the right of Negroes to use the same restrooms and drinking fountains as whites, the death penalty, and free speech. They have also challenged socially oriented norms with "mod" dress and hair styles, language, rock music, and psychedelic colors, forms and patterns. [The nation has] watched the development of the hippy, and yippy, the youthful drug culture, black, yellow, brown, and red power advocates, and organizations such as the Third World Liberation Front, The Peace and Freedom Party, and Black Studies Departments on the campus. We have been exposed to violence, vandalism, assault, destruction, looting, disruption, and chaos on our streets (1970:52).

Rhetoric favoring a "war on crime" also took strength from the FBI's annual account of traditional crime. During the decade of the 1960s, for example, crimes of violence per hundred thousand population (murder, forcible rape, robbery, and aggravated assault) went up 104 percent, while crimes against property (burglary, larceny, and auto theft) went up 123 percent. Overall, the total number of these seven offenses per hundred thousand went up 120 percent (F.B.I., 1969:4).

Ironically, available data also implied that, if a crime war were to be waged, it would have to be directed against the nation's youth. According to the President's Commission on Law Enforcement and Administration of Justice (1967b: 44), more burglaries, larcenies, and auto thefts are committed by young people, ages 15 to 17 years, than by any other group. Fifteen year olds are arrested most often, with 16 year olds a close second. For crimes of violence, those from 18 to 20 are the most responsible, with the second largest group in the 21 to 24 age range. Hence, in projecting the possibility that age-specific arrest probabilities for future years would remain the same as they were in 1965, Christensen (1967:221) estimated that the chances that a male would be arrested sometime during his life for an offense other than a traffic offense were 47 percent, and for a female, 13 percent.

Coupled with the protests and riots of a decade, the increasing incidence of traditional crimes created a climate of fear throughout the nation, especially in our large cities. Taken on a collective level, a vision was evoked that portrayed thousands, if not millions, of Americans sitting crouched behind locked doors, fearful that if they ventured forth they would become additional victims of their own, criminally disposed youth. These are among the reasons, then, why the catchwords for many Americans became, and still remain, "law and order," not "prevention and control." In place of a routine concern for crime, a state of emergency was declared.

Fearful that such a state of emergency, and all that it implied, would be destructive of basic humanitarian and democratic values, other groups of Americans expressed an opposing point of view. Some warned that a climate of fear does not abide patient study (Bittner, 1970:49). The implementation of a "war on crime," for example, projects hopes for victory that cannot possibly be realized. Worse yet, it extends the stamp of legitimacy to methods that would not be acceptable on moral and constitutional grounds. Instead, the organizational posture that is implied is a military one in which ferocity and coldly calculated expediency could or do result—a posture in which the representatives of authority, especially the police, are expected to be as unsparing of themselves as they are of the enemy. Yet, as many scholars have pointed out (Lasswell, 1950:228; Janowitz, 1968:8; Silver, 1968:12-14; Bittner, 1970:50), the trouble with such an approach is not only the danger that it poses for democratic institutions, but for the policemen who are enlisted in the crime war. Unless the police are totally brutalized, it is unlikely that they can ever be as unscrupulously ruthless against criminals as against an alien enemy, especially since the former are comprised largely of the nation's youth. The values and organizations that are needed by a democratic society to win a military victory are not the same as those needed to prevent and control crime.

Seeming to speak to this very issue, the President's Commission (1967a:41) noted that, since our system of justice holds both juveniles and adults responsible for their misconduct, and imposes sanctions upon them accordingly, it also obligates itself to provide potential criminals with educational, social, and economic means to understand and accept responsibility. A "war on crime," by contrast, and the ruthlessness it implies, not only fails to address this societal obligation but probably abides little consideration of it. Yet, the capacity of any citizenry to act in a responsible way depends, in the last analysis, on the viability of its basic socializing institutions—the home, neighborhood, school, and economy—not on the exercise of coercion or repressive military rule.

Because this notion appeals to common sense as well as scientific thinking, it has long been a popular one. In many ways, in fact, it has been the primary antidote to the ideology that favors a militaristic response. Yet, if one traces the development of social thought in recent decades, one is also struck by the emergence of additional and, in some ways, a more sophisticated rationale for concentrating upon crime prevention rather than coercion and punishment. This is the labeling approach to deviance, with its suggestion that society's customary ways for responding to delinquents and criminals may have done more to incubate the crime problem than to solve it. This approach probably is the most popular rationale today for responding to crime in other ways than making war on criminals.

THE LABELING APPROACH

In 1938, Tannenbaum argued that the final step in the making of the adult criminal occurs when youth become enmeshed in society's institutionalized patterns for dealing with them, in their experiences with police, courts, and correctional institutions. Tannenbaum felt that these experiences often tended to dramatize rather than to eliminate evil. As he put it, "the process of making the criminal is a process of tagging, defining, identifying, segregating, describing, emphasizing, making conscious and self-conscious; it becomes a way of stimulating, suggesting, emphasizing, and evolving the very traits that are complained of" (1938:30). The official process not only tends to isolate an individual from conformist influences, but makes him even more dependent upon the support and encouragement of his deviant peers.

Tannenbaum's comments mesh well with the perspective of symbolic interactionism in sociology (cf. Blumer, 1969), which emphasizes: (1) that social organization and the person are two facets of the same thing; and (2) that a person's self-conception should be seen as the product of an ongoing process of interaction, not as a static and fixed entity. Accordingly, Cressey argues that the criminal, like any other person, should be

> seen as a part of the kinds of social relationships and values in which he participates; he obtains his essence from participation in rituals, values, norms, rules, schedules, customs, and regulations of various kinds which surround him. The person (personality) is not separable from the social relationships in which he lives (1965:90).

Hence, if the person interacts primarily in conventional settings, he will likely perceive himself as a conformist and behave in a conventional way. But, if he is segregated from conventional people and forced to seek his identity among those who are deviant, he will be more likely to acquire a deviant concept of himself.

Lemert (1951:70-78), and later both Kitsuse (1962) and Erikson (1962), suggested that it is not just the deviant act alone to which attention must be directed, but the way in which others respond to it. Erikson, for example, argued that:

> Deviance is not a property *inherent in* certain forms of behavior; it is a property *conferred upon* these forms by the audiences which directly or indirectly witness them. Sociologically, then, the critical variable in the study of deviance is the social *audience* rather than individual *person,* since it is the audience which eventually decides whether or not any given action or actions will become a visible case of deviation (1962:308).

Lemert (1951:71) has also suggested that if deviant behavior is not identifed and negatively sanctioned by some audience, its impact on the individual will be minimal. In all likelihood, he will rationalize and deal with it as a function of one of his socially acceptable roles.

Lemert called this kind of unsanctioned deviance, *primary* deviance. Although it may be problematic in the sense that deviant and conformist inclinations are coincidental within the same person, it is unlikely that he will develop a deviant self-identity. Rather, as Davis (1961) suggests, he will be inclined, as most people are, to disavow the implications of his deviant acts. Since his social status has not

been changed by the reactions of others to him, he will tend to retain a conformist self-concept and avoid many of the negative consequences of being defined as
a deviant person.

If, on the other hand, the person's deviant behavior has high visibility, and if
society reacts severely to it, then the results will be markedly different. It is not
behavior per se that differentiates deviants from nondeviants, says Kitsuse, "it is
the responses of the conventional and conforming members of the society who
interpret behavior as deviant which sociologically transforms persons into
deviants" (1962:253).

In the case of the young delinquent, for example, this transformation is often
subtle and complex. Not only must he deal with the stigma associated with his
delinquent status, but he must respond to more subtle cues regarding what is
expected of him. Strong negative reactions by officials may disrupt his self-
concept and his normal roles, and the reactions of friends and associates will
also have a marked impact. Paradoxically, responses from peers, delinquent and
nondelinquent, as well as from officials, may tend to affirm his delinquent status.
Hence, to the extent that he is sensitive to the expectations and actions of
others, his behavior may easily mirror not his normal role, but a deviant one.
Even his clothes, his speech, or his mannerisms may be altered, reflecting the
appurtenances of his new role.

Lemert (1971:13) also suggests that once a person is labeled, he is expected
to adhere to an additional set of rules that apply only to him. But, rather than
helping to reduce his problems, they may only increase them. When a delinquent
is placed on probation, for example, he is often forbidden to live with an "unfit"
parent or to associate with his girl or boy friends, and he is expected to reverse
suddenly his pattern of failure at school. Any failure to adhere to these special
rules will, in itself, constitute a new act of deviance. Hence, the justice-correction
system, in attempting to "treat" the delinquent, can actually escalate the grounds
whereby his future behavior may be termed delinquent.

This increase in rules, coupled with the tendency for the delinquent to begin
behaving in accordance with the expectations of his deviant status, may result
in what Lemert calls *secondary* deviance. This kind of deviance evolves out of
the adaptations the labeled person makes to the problems created by official and
conformist reactions to his primary deviance. "When a person begins to employ
his deviant behavior as a role based upon it as a means of defense, attack or adjustment to the overt and covert problems created by the consequent societal
reactions to him, his deviation is secondary" (1951:71). Thus, even though unique historic or situational factors may have contributed to his original acts of
deviance, the reactions of society to them may actually escalate the chances that
further secondary forms of deviance will be forthcoming.

Lemert (1951:75–78) expresses doubt, however, that secondary deviance will
follow hard upon the heels of any single official, even punitive, reaction to an
individual. Rather, as Tannenbaum (1938) had suggested earlier, it is the product
of a rather long process in which the deviant will have been involved progressively

in a series of interactions with the agents of social control. The acquisition of a deviant identity and acts of secondary deviance are the product of a learning experience. Lemert failed to denote the circumstances in which interactions between the deviant and officials do not result in secondary deviance, but his analysis was extremely useful in suggesting that official processing often has the opposite of its intended effect. This occurs because deviance is escalated by official reaction, "entangling the deviant and the persons surrounding him in a web of rigidity and self-fulfilling prophecy which may become increasingly difficult to escape" (Polk & Kobrin, 1972:16).

In his definitive statement, Becker added to the labeling school themes already mentioned a stress on rule-making:

> ... *social groups create deviance by making the rules whose infractions constitute deviance,* and by applying these rules to particular people and labeling them as outsiders. From this point of view, deviance is *not* a quality of the act the person commits, but rather a consequence of the application by others of rules and sanctions to the "offender." The deviant is one to whom that label has successfully been applied; deviant behavior is behavior that people so label (1963:9).

In conclusion, the labeling perspective suggested that social groups create deviance because of the particular rules they make and enforce, and accordingly,

> acts can be identified as deviant or criminal only by reference to the character of reaction to them by the public or by the official agents of a politically organized society. Put simply, if the reaction is of a certain kind, then and only then is the act deviant (Gibbs, 1966:11).

Implications of the Labeling Perspective

The impact of the labeling perspective on social policy, as well as on social theory, has been great. Emphasis upon the negative effects of labeling helped to provide the rationale for a social movement favoring the diversion of youth and adults from the justice-corrections system, and revision of the rules and processes by which people are defined as criminal. Because this ideology stands in such marked contrast to the ideology favoring a war on crime, its moral and policy implications merit careful scrutiny. The following summary builds upon Schur's (1971:171) statement of its implications.

First, the labeling perspective reemphasizes the assertion long made by criminologists that crime is *relative* and varies according to time and place. It stresses prevention in a most fundamental sense by challenging society to examine its own rules and to determine wherein they may be harmful rather than helpful. The "injurious" quality of some criminal or delinquent acts, as Gibbs (1966:10) notes, is by no means obvious. Far from being harmful, some acts may be defined as criminal because, and only because, they are proscribed legally.

Second, by suggesting the need to scrutinize the rule-making and political processes by which crime is defined and offenders labeled, the labeling perspective highlights a growing division in sociology over two contrasting models for analyzing society, *consensus* and *conflict*.

The consensus model emphasizes the idea that all of the elements of social organization—values, norms, roles, and institutions—are a closely knit whole (cf. Dahrendorf, 1959:2). It suggests that most people share the same objectives, agree on basic definitions of right and wrong, and engage in a mutually supporting set of activities. Therefore, the various elements of social organization are presumed to reflect this consensus, and, by definition, a person who is criminal is one who rejects the basic consensus and threatens the stability of the whole.

Conflict theorists, by contrast, argue that the consensus model implies a set of values that not only favors the status quo and those in power, but also ignores reality. Modern society, they suggest, is characterized by diversity and change, and is held together, not by consensus, but by force and constraint. Although certain values predominate, they do so more by the fact that they are enforced by dominant groups and interests than by the members of society as a whole (Dahrendorf, 1958:127). The turbulence of the 1960s and early 1970s exemplifies such societal conflict over basic practices and beliefs. By stressing conflict elements and rule-making processes, labeling analysis eschews the idea that society is held together by consensus and by a static structure, emphasizing instead the importance of value and political conflict in determining how crime is defined and rules applied.

Third, because of its emphasis upon the negative effects of official processing, the labeling perspective attracts attention to deficiencies in our control and correctional structures. It helped to popularize the important notion that conformist self-concepts are forged *outside* of correctional structures, not within them, and that official processing can actually inhibit this process. Hence, there has been a rapid search for means by which to divert known and potential offenders from the stigmatizing and role-disrupting effects of the justice-correctional system.

The President's Commission (1967a:19-21) popularized the notion of youth service bureaus through which delinquents could be dealt with nonjudicially in their own communities. California instituted a probation subsidy program by which state funds are used to subsidize local counties for retaining in their communities many adults, as well as juveniles, who would otherwise have been confined in state institutions. As a result, some institutions have been closed, and new ones remain unopened (cf. Smith, 1971). In Massachusetts recently, steps were taken to eliminate entirely all of the state's juvenile training schools and to substitute community programs for them. Although cases of primary deviance would not be prevented by the closing of institutions, it was hoped that the incidence of secondary deviance would be prevented.

Such diversions contrast with the implications of the war on crime that deterrence through punishment is the best way to prevent crime. In fact, as early as 1965, the President's Commission (1967c:1) reported that two-thirds of all offenders, many of them felons, were under supervision in the community while only one-third were in institutions. Such evidence indicates that the diversionary philosophy, instigated in part by the labeling perspective, has been a powerful one.

Fourth, the flat rejection by the labeling approach of the idea that the criminal or his deviant acts are characterized by some feature that is intrinsic to them has caused scientists and professionals to question many long-held assumptions regarding the causes for crime. Most people would now agree that distinctive biological features do not characterize criminals. In fact, as Gibbs (1966:10) suggests, the possibility that such characteristics exist even for particular criminal types, such as murderers or bigamists, not only lacks scientific verification but defies logic. "Since legislators are not geneticists, it is difficult to see how they can pass laws in such a way as to create 'born' criminals." But the same kind of thinking has been applied as well to the search for unique psychological characteristics, attitudes, or values. That search for them has not been particularly successful either. As Hathaway et al. put it, personality measures "are much less powerful and apply to fewer cases among total samples than would be expected if one read the literature on the subject" (1960:439). Summaries of other studies suggest (1) that known offenders are more like than different from the general population, and (2) that measures of personality that yield deviancy variations reliably still do not distinguish criminal behavior types (cf. LaGache, 1950; Schuessler & Cressey, 1950; Short & Strodtbeck, 1965:371). It appears that legislators are unable to identify psychological aberration by passing laws any easier than they can identify born criminals.

These kinds of negative findings, as a result, lend support to labeling proponents who argue that the causes for crime cannot be found in the static structural characteristics of the offender or solely in the structural characteristics of society, but in the interaction between the two.

This concern with the dynamics rather than the structures of societal life has reinforced the need to study crime prevention on several different levels: on the societal level where rules are made, in the organizations that process offenders, and on an interpersonal level where the offender interacts with others.

Deficiencies in the Labeling Approach

Despite its contributions, the labeling perspective has some deficiencies, both as a body of theory and in its relevance for social policy. These two deficiencies are interrelated because, as Schrag suggests, the seminal capacity of any theory to produce effective social action, as well as research, depends upon its ability to meet three criteria:

First, the theory should have sound logical structure. That is, its postulates should be connected in such a manner that a number of claims or assertions can be derived from them by means of logical inference or deduction. Second, the theory should have operational significance. Some of its terms should be related by rule to observable data so that its meaning is clear and its claims can be tested by evidence and experience. Third, the theory should have high congruence with the world of experience. Its major claims should be generally consistent with the preponderance of relevant factual evidence. When these three requirements are met, the theory can be used successfully for pragmatic purposes (1962:167).

According to a number of different observers, the labeling perspective does not meet these criteria. Gibbs (1966:9), for example, argues that it does not yet contain some of the necessary elements of a substantive theory—a careful delineation and definition of concepts, and a logically developed and integrated set of propositions. These elements must be developed before the weaknesses as well as the strengths of the labeling perspective can be fully understood.

Gibbs (1966:11-12) also suggests that one major weakness lies in the failure of proponents of the labeling approach to indicate clearly whether they are seeking an explanation of deviant behavior, of reactions to it, or both. For example, the point is stressed continually that acts can be identified as deviant only by the character of reactions to them. Yet, Becker (1963:20) alludes to the existence of "secret deviance," implying that acts of deviation can be identified by reference to existing norms regardless of societal reaction. Similarly, Kitsuse and Cicourel (1963:313) assert that they do not mean to imply that forms of behavior that the sociologist might categorize as deviant have no basis in fact. And Erikson (1962:313) notes that in some societies, deviance is considered a natural pursuit of the young, while in others, license is given to large groups of persons to engage in deviant behavior in celebration of certain holidays or seasons of the year. This license, he suggests, is granted without resultant penalties or negative reactions.

What all these comments imply, of course, is that deviance can be identified, not merely in terms of reactions to it, but in terms of existing social norms. Otherwise, one could not speak of "secret deviance," or distinguish, as Lemert does, between primary (unsanctioned) and secondary (sanctioned) deviance. Moreover, the fact that norms, as well as sanctions, do have a role to play can be illustrated by drawing some fundamental distinctions between different types of deviant acts. Glaser (1971) argues that the failure of labeling proponents to do this has inhibited a clarification of the distinctive contributions they have to make.

Granted that for many acts, such as prostitution, gambling, homosexuality, drug use, drunkenness, or some juvenile-status offenses, societal rules and reactions vary greatly; "crime" in these terms is indeed relative to time and place. But what about such acts as homicide, unprovoked assault, robbery, and burglary?

Condemnation of "crime" in these forms is far more common. In all but the simplest of societies, state concern with protecting property rights, and with insuring immunity against physical attack, is virtually universal. Acts such as these, in other words, can be readily identified by allusion to existing norms, as well as by reactions to them.

Finally, the methodological thrust of the labeling approach, as Schur (1971:34) has noted, has been away from the statistical and positivistic biases of contemporary social science, and toward a greater concern with process and the social psychology of the individual. These differences in orientation are reflective, says Glaser, of two types of science—nomothetic and ideographic.

> Nomothetic disciplines seek only general laws, applicable to all phenomena of a specified class, with rules of evidence and inference modelled on those of the so-called "exact sciences." Ideographic studies, on the other hand, are concerned with understanding particular events or sequences of events, using rules of evidence and inference best exemplified in the works of historians, biographers and political commentators (1968:1).

Clearly, the labeling proponents favor a sophisticated version of the ideographic studies. They wish to discover what the processes are by which a person is labeled as deviant, or how he comes to feel and act like one. But in stressing the ideographic, they leave unanswered some basic theoretical and policy questions that nomothetic studies might answer. If, for example, there are some acts that are universally condemned, such as murder or robbery, then it may well be appropriate for social science to study these acts apart from, as well as concurrent with, the processes by which they are labeled as deviant. By the same token, since prevention programs are concerned with societal as well as individual welfare, with the victim of a crime as well as with its perpetrator, it is important to seek nomothetic generalizations about predation, to outline its differential occurrence among different subpopulations, and to seek some knowledge of its causes. Even though predatory acts occur for which no offender is apprehended or reactions applied, it is important to be aware of their incidence. Validated propositions regarding these matters surely are necessary as guides to their prevention.

It seems unlikely that members of the labeling school would be opposed to nomothetic research of this type. There are, in fact, some ways by which it could be viewed as a vital adjunct to labeling research. Studies of self-reported delinquency, for example, reveal that undiscovered illegal acts throughout all elements of the juvenile population are great (cf. Empey, 1967 for a summary). Such findings not only provide a useful means by which to compare and contrast rates of primary deviance with those of official delinquency, but raise serious questions regarding the most appropriate methods for responding to them. Clearly, if acts of primary deviance are common despite the existing control apparatus, then persons concerned with prevention must seek either to change the rules or to find remediation in other forms.

At any rate, this brief review of questions may indicate why, as Schur suggests, it has been difficult to define precisely the operational and pragmatic implications of the labeling approach. "Apart perhaps from promoting a very broad injunction 'to avoid unnecessary labeling,' the orientation does not seem to provide a clear-cut general direction for public policy toward deviating behavior" (1971:171). Hence, like the war on crime, it leaves many questions unanswered. Policy makers and practitioners have had trouble in conceptualizing and implementing successful diversionary nonlabeling programs.

Consider, for example, the major efforts since 1967 to divert juveniles and thus to prevent delinquency by creation of youth service bureaus. In 1971, a conference to exchange information on these bureaus, held at the University of Chicago, highlighted several difficulties (Seymour, 1971). Delegates were unable to agree on the basic goals and functions of youth service bureaus. Was it to change the stigmatizing effects of existing rules and practices, or to change children—to adapt children to society, or society to children? Put another way, should the bureaus be designed to provide direct services to the individual, or should they seek to alter the community so that it, rather than the bureaus, would do a better job of socializing and diverting children? These are fundamental and age-old problems and require an explicit directive from theory.

The inability of bureau delegates to agree on basic functions also meant that they could not agree on overall strategy. Some believed that the bureau should become an integral part of existing organizations in the community, while others believed that because current organizations represent the establishment, they only enhance labeling. They wanted youth bureaus entirely independent, providing whatever services are needed for whatever clientele are deemed important.

A third major problem was to decide what "diversion" means. Those who define it in restrictive terms suggest that the sole mandate of the bureaus is to divert juveniles from the justice-correctional system. This means that only those children on the threshold of entry into that system are served. Others who define diversion more broadly believe that youth bureaus should be concerned with all delinquency prevention and youth development, in preventing primary acts of deviance as well as trying to divert those juveniles whose delinquent behavior was actually discovered.

Building on his labeling perspective, Lemert (1971) provides not one but several models for diversion—a school, a welfare, a law-enforcement, and a community organization model. Yet, his analysis of existing programs probably documents more problems than workable solutions. The labeling perspective, like virtually all other conceptions in social science, is still in an embryonic state insofar as setting forth clear and testable guidelines for public policy is concerned. But, if such an elusive concept as crime prevention is to be given better substance, the strengths of the labeling perspective must be added to those of other perspectives.

DEFINITION OF CRIME PREVENTION

In the past, as Polk and Kobrin (1972) point out, the tendency has been to search out those factors that are presumed to cause crime, and then to define prevention in terms of programs that will address those causes. While such an approach has merit, it fails to specify how legitimate pursuits are cultivated. Besides indicating what one seeks to avoid, one should make explicit what is being sought. Therefore, prevention could be defined as an attempt: (1) to identify those institutional characteristics and processes most inclined to produce legitimate identities and nonpredatory behaviors in people; (2) to restructure existing institutions or build new ones so that these desirable features are enhanced; and (3) to discard those features that tend to foster criminal behaviors and identities.

A first step in operationalizing this definition is to identify the major institutional structures to which reference is being made. Ohlin (1970) has suggested that, for the purposes of prevention, they can be organized into four major categories:

1. the legitimate, normative system, which includes the legal rules, policies, and practices by which society attempts to regulate behavior;

2. the primary socializing institutions, such as the family, school, world of work, or church, all of which are expected to produce legitimate identities in young people and to prepare them for adulthood;

3. the illegitimate structures in society that support crime, all the way from organized and professional subcultures to youthful gangs and associations; and

4. the agencies of social control, such as the police, the judiciary, and corrections, whose responsibility it is to react officially to those who violate legal norms.

All of these structures are obviously central to the cultivation of either legitimate or deviant identities, but the ways in which they affect behavior, and thus the ways in which they might be involved in any crime prevention effort, are not the same. For example, one might wish to examine rules and rule-making processes, as the labeling proponents have suggested, and then make alterations in the laws that govern behavior. By contrast, changes of a much different sort might be involved where the basic socializing institutions or the illegitimate structures in society are concerned. As a method of considering the ways in which efforts at prevention might be related to these four structures, let us examine them one by one.

THE SYSTEM OF LEGAL RULES

Given the catch-all character of the legal statutes that define both crime and delinquency, and the fact that they prescribe a legal reaction to such nonpredatoy acts as truancy, neglect, gambling, drunkenness, and other kinds of "immoral" behavior that do not involve a victim, there are virtually no noncriminals. It is clear, therefore, that a tremendous amount of law-violating behavior could be "prevented" and, perhaps, the likelihood of secondary deviance reduced simply by making changes in legal statutes and policies. Many such changes are occurring, in fact.

Arguing in favor of them, Morris and Hawkins say that

we must strip off the moralistic excrescences on our criminal justice system so that it may concentrate on the essential. The prime function of the criminal law is to protect our persons and our property; these purposes are now engulfed in a mass of other distracting, inefficiently performed legislative duties. When the criminal law invades the spheres of private morality and social welfare, it exceeds its proper limits at the cost of neglecting its primary tasks. . . .

For the criminal law at least, man has an inalienable right to go to hell in his own fashion, provided he does not directly injure the person or property of another on the way . . . (1970:2).

Thus, these authors would distinguish between those acts that are predatory, and those that are not, and alter the rules to eliminate many of the latter as crimes.

The same kinds of suggestions have been made with respect to legal rules that apply only to juveniles. A number of different people and organizations (cf. Kvaraceus, 1964; Morris, 1966:643; President's Commission, 1967c:25; Rubin, 1970) all suggest that young people should not be prosecuted and receive penal sanctions for behavior that, if exhibited by adults, would not be prosecuted. Some also suggest that legal rules should not put judges and other authorities in the position of having to decide what is moral or immoral conduct for young people. Such decisions are better left to other institutions and processes.

Morris and Hawkins (1970:4-25) argue that if these kinds of changes were instituted, three major benefits would result. First, the number of people defined as criminal would be reduced by as much as three million annually, a sizeable prevention effort indeed. In numerical terms, this kind of reduction might be far greater than that achieved by more traditional and limited kinds of diversionary programs. Moreover, the pressure on police, courts, and corrections would be greatly reduced, leaving society's agents of control with much greater means for combating serious and predatory crime—violence, burglary, robbery, and professional and organized crime.

Second, prevention through the revision of legal rules would result in much less interference in the private moral conduct of the citizen, leaving the resolution of many juvenile status problems—drunkenness, drug use, sex, and gambling

—to other institutions. If the labeling proponents are correct, then many forms of secondary deviance could also be prevented.

Third, since many of the sources of income for organized crime come from the sale of such things as narcotics, gambling, and illicit sex—activities around which there is no normative consensus in the populace—these sources would be dried up. The financial power of organized crime would be seriously hurt.

While these proposed changes have considerable appeal, it is clear that, according to our definition of prevention, they would be devoted more to restructuring legal institutions and eliminating harmful practices than to indicating how legitimate identities are developed. This is not to denigrate the importance of such changes, but to indicate the many dimensions and complexities of prevention as a basic concept. Moreover, it is important to recognize that the removal of such acts as public drunkenness or drug usage as criminal offenses, while it may reduce the effects of legal stigma and the burdens on the criminal justice system, would not really solve the problems of the alcoholic or the addict. Medical detoxification clinics are being set up for the alcoholic and methadone is being administered to many addicts, but neither represents anything approaching a lasting solution for their problems. Each still continues to suffer considerable stigma and each is still costly to society. The point is that rule changes are but one of the kinds of steps needed for the prevention of even secondary deviance. And unless they are accompanied by additional forms of remediation, they may be little more than a sociological sleight-of-hand, a kind of social magic without lasting positive effect.

As a method of trying to insure that alterations in legal rules will have a desirable effect, two suggestions have been made. First, Morris and Hawkins (1970: 27) suggest that every legislature should have a Standing Law Revision Committee charged with the task of reviewing constantly the adequacy of existing rules and the impact of any changes that are made. The task of legal reform, in other words, would not be a oneshot thing; rather the committee would act as a monitor over the normative system, and be charged with the responsibility of cleaning out the debris of useless laws and policies and seeing that new ones fulfill the purposes for which they were created.

Second, Rubin (1970) suggests that any alterations, either in basic legal rules or in their administration, be tried on an experimental basis. Whenever radical alterations are made in the services rendered by the justice-correctional system, an experimental design should be set up to see if the new social alternatives are any better. Research would be conducted regularly to determine the actual effects of legal changes.

These two suggestions, while obviously debatable, approach the task of change in a reasonably systematic and rational way. Without such approaches, it will be difficult to build the knowledge necessary to test, revise, and improve existing theory and practice.

THE SOCIALIZING INSTITUTIONS

The incidence of predatory acts, highest among young people, suggests that more than alterations in the legalistic and control-oriented aspects of the criminal justice system are needed to prevent delinquency and crime. These offenses are at a very low ebb before the onset of adolescence, rise sharply after its onset, hit their peak at around 16 or 17, and decline sharply after that point (President's Commission, 1967b:44; Empey & Erickson, 1972:chap. 11). Hence, any serious effort at crime prevention would have to consider ways by which socialization per se might be made more effective.

This conclusion is based upon four assumptions, each of which is central to the definition of prevention set forth above:

1. The primary focus of prevention efforts should be upon the establishment among young people of a legitimate identity. To seek only the avoidance of a deviant identity by refraining from the use of labels or stigma is, in one sense, to approach prevention negatively. The more difficult and prior task is to insure that young people acquire a productive, satisfying, and legitimate self-concept.

2. A legitimate identity among young people is most likely to occur if they have a stake in conformity (Toby, 1957a); if, in other words, they develop a sense of competence, a sense of usefulness, a sense of belonging, and a sense that they have the power to affect their own destinies through conventional means (Polk & Kobrin, 1972:5).

3. The cultivation in young people of a legitimate identity and a stake in conformity requires that they be provided with socially acceptable, responsible, and personally gratifying roles. Such roles have the effect of creating a firm attachment to the aims, values, and norms of basic institutions and of reducing the probability of criminal involvement (Polk & Kobrin, 1972:5).

4. Since social roles are a function of institutional design and process,". . . a rational strategy of delinquency reduction and control must address the task of institutional change" (Polk & Kobrin, 1972:2-3). The changes that are sought should be capable of greatly expanding the range of legitimate roles available to young people.

In the most general of terms, these assumptions imply two things. First, if institutional change is the first order of business, a radical alteration of societal priorities is needed. Before the members of society and their elected representatives can prevent crime on any large scale, they will have to eradicate the poverty and ignorance that make life helpless for a significant minority of the American people, and break the bonds that confine many to miserable and unacceptable living conditions in our urban ghettos and rural slums. It is ludicrous to speak of fostering a legitimate identity or a stake in conformity among those for whom crime is one major way of alleviating unacceptable conditions and of realizing the American dream of getting ahead. Unless the necessary resources are forthcoming, such methods of intervention as youth service bureaus can be little more than Band-Aids on a huge and gaping wound.

It would be a mistake, however, to suggest that all crime would be eliminated were poverty removed. That is too convenient a shibboleth. Many predatory law violators are relatively affluent young people who have not acquired a stake in conformity. One reason that many of them are inclined to leave the creature comforts of their homes and to seek escape through drugs or some other means, or to justify their acts of senseless vandalism, theft, and violence, is because they feel they have no power over, or stake in, what is happening to them. The childish self-indulgence that is so common among many reflects a loss of purpose and direction. Lacking institutional constraints of a rewarding kind, some young Americans behave in an immature and destructive way.

A second implication has to do with our lack of knowledge. Even if American priorities were revised and more resources made available, it is difficult to say exactly what should be done to cultivate legitimate identities more effectively, or where and how new social roles for the young might be created. Many social action programs—whether urban renewal, the poverty program, or remedial job training—have ignored the cultural pluralism of America and the tremendous complexities associated with developing modes of intervention that are appropriate to different settings and people. No single grand strategy of prevention, invariably applied, is likely to succeed. The organizational networks in which the young are socialized vary too greatly. These problems must be confronted on both an organizational and an interactional level (cf. Empey & Lubeck, 1971: chap. 11 for a longer formulation of this analysis).

ORGANIZATIONAL LEVELS

Organizationally, there are two kinds of networks to be considered—the legitimate network consisting of home, neighborhood, school, and so on, and the illegitimate network involving the youthful gangs, the sources of drugs and vice, or career-oriented adult groups. Both are instrumental in the cultivation of deviant and legitimate idenies.

The Legitimate Network

Research has indicated that family disorganization is greater among known delinquents than among nondelinquents, but how this contributes to illegal behavior is not clear. On one hand, some studies indicate that intrafamily conflicts and tensions are differentially productive of law-violating behavior (Shulman, 1949; Monahan, 1957; Toby, 1957b; Hirschi, 1969; Chilton & Markle, 1972). On the other hand, existing evidence also suggests that intrafamily characteristics cannot be treated in isolation. Influences that may be attributed to the home may actually have their roots in ethnic, class, subcultural, and other networks of which the family is only a part. For example, in their analysis of race differentials in gang behavior, Short and Strodtbeck found that

> . . . Negro gang delinquency tends *not to be clearly differentiated from non-delinquent behavior*—that participation in the "good" aspects of lower-class Negro life (responsibility in domestic chores and organized sports activities) is closely interwoven with "bad" aspects (conflict, illicit sex, drug use and auto theft).
>
> The literature of lower-class Negro life is rich in detail which supports such a conclusion among adults as well as children and adolescents. As compared with lower-class white communities, delinquency among lower-class Negroes is more of a total life pattern in which delinquent behaviors are not likely to create disjunctures with other types of behavior (1965: 105–6).

There was much evidence throughout their study that family and community life for both adults and children was held much more in common among blacks than in other racial and neighborhood settings.

By contrast, *white* gang boys have been found to be more openly at odds with adults in their community (Short & Strodtbeck, 1965:105–12). Their activities were often seen by adults as rowdy and delinquent, and they were unwelcome in adult hangouts and groups. Much more than among black boys, their delinquent acts represented a protest against, rather than a component of, conventional family and community obligations. Thus, subcultural variations in adult-child relations and intrafamily disruptions are among a number of interdependent variables that must be taken into account. Even within families of the same social class, important differences along ethnic and other lines exist. Therefore, attempts to explain or prevent *individual* delinquent behavior without taking such differences into account are not likely to be very successful.

In all these examples, the neighborhood as a socializing institution was closely linked with that of the family. Yet, there has long been a disagreement in the literature whether those neighborhoods with the highest rates of law violations are disorganized or organized. On one hand, Thrasher concluded that illegal acts are most likely to occur in "what is often called the 'poverty belt'—a region characterized by deteriorating neighborhoods, shifting populations, and the mobility and disorganization of the slum" (1963:20–21). On the other hand, it was Whyte's (1955:viii) opinion that the slums may be highly organized, but not in the way the middle class thinks of social organization. Yet, if it is *degree* of organization that is at issue, it is difficult to see how some slum neighborhoods could be much more anonymous and unintegrated than are many white, middle- and upper-class neighborhoods. The point is that the degree and kind of neighborhood organization is likely to vary greatly from place to place, and from time to time.

Into this welter of different families and neighborhoods—white, black, brown, and mixed; lower, middle, and upper class; rural, suburban, and urban—is inserted the one institution in society that is supposed to resolve all differences, and to provide a uniform kind of socialization for all young people. This institution, of course, is the school. People expect it to provide equal opportunity for every child, and since it is the one major link between childhood and adulthood, any failure on its part has serious consequences. Yet, these expectations notwithstanding, the overall structure of the educational system, especially in our urban centers, is often ill adapted to the different localities and subcultural groups to which it must relate. Its local branches, the neighborhood schools, usually operate on centralized policies set up and administered by people whose view of the world is often vastly different from those of the children and their parents whom it is supposed to serve. Operating from a central headquarters, attempts are made to impose uniform policies and practices on widely divergent groups that have little in common. This often results in lack of communication, conflict, and deviant behavior.

The problems that have occurred in the schools illustrate those likely to occur in any other prevention or socialization effort that attempts to maintain uniform practices across different ethnic, familial, and neighborhood lines. Since these vary greatly, institutional programs designed to give the young a stake in conformity will also have to vary, if for no other reason than to foster effective communication. Before pursuing that issue further, it is important to consider the impact of illegitimate structures on socialization of the young.

Illegitimate Structures and Traditions

Often inseparable from familial, neighborhood, and educational networks are illegitimate structures in the community. Many investigators have observed that much illegal behavior results from local traditions of group-supported delinquency, some of it criminally and career-oriented, that are transmitted to juveniles (McKay, 1949; Kobrin, 1951; Thrasher, 1963; Cressey, 1964). This was indicated when Short (1963) asked the staff of a YMCA gang program in Chicago: "What are the most significant institutions for your boys?" The answer from a detached worker was revealing. "I guess," he said, "I'd have to say the gang, the hangouts, drinking, parties in the area, and the police." While these would scarcely be acknowledged as "institutions" in the conventional sense, there was agreement among other workers that the answer of the first worker was correct. One of them would have added the boys' families to the list, but the overall conclusion was that the most viable places for the boys were the street corners, the pool halls, taverns, and the "quarter parties" in which adults as well as juveniles often participated. Relating this back to the system of formal norms, it is easy to see why law violations would be high in such an area. Many of the regular activities of these juveniles, although a normal part of daily life, were officially illegal. Without any deliberate intent to be delinquent, they were law violators by definition. Therefore, both the larger society and the juvenile have problems of social organization and of defining the behaviors that shall and shall not be tolerated. The potential for conflict is high.

Information regarding the network of illegitimate "institutions" for middle- and upper-class juveniles is not so readily available, documenting a serious omission in the literature. But with their drug scene, predatory crimes, and various forms of protest—some violent and some involving vandalism—there undoubtedly are parallel conflicts in these social strata. Illegal structures, as part of the lives of diverse juveniles, undoubtedly contribute to the problems of defining effective prevention programs.

Reactions within these structures are often mixed. In their study of various adolescent groups in a long-established Italian neighborhood, for example, Kobrin and his associates (1967) found that the prestige of sophisticated delin- quents was greater than that of respectable boys, There was, they say, a touch of disdain for the respectables as "do-nothing" kids. The sources of this disdain, moreover, stemmed not only from the adolescent perspectives of the boys but from others in the neighborhood as well.

According to Kobrin et al., "there had existed for some time a firmly established integration of the legitimate and illegitimate elements of the community, mani- fested in a locally acknowledged alliance between the political leadership and that of the city's gambling, vice, and other rackets" (1967:101). Furthermore, the prestige of the respectable group may have suffered because their fathers tended to be civil servants in local government who had moved out of local social circles because they enjoyed some independence from the control of local politicians. Thus, this particular neighborhood seemed to be characterized, at the very least, by an ambivalence toward law-abiding and conventional structures, or, at the very most, by stronger ties to illegitimate than legitimate ones. Without doubt, the perceptions and behaviors of juveniles were influenced by these conflicting elements.

While this may well be an atypical community, much about it is familiar. As Daniel Bell (1959) has noted, Americans generally are characterized by an "ex- tremism" in morality, yet they also have an "extraordinary" talent for compro- mise in politics and a "brawling" economic history. American culture, as Matza and Sykes (1961) suggest, is not a simple puritanism exemplified by the middle class. It is, instead, a complex and pluralistic culture in which, among other traditions, there is a subterranean tradition of deviance. These contradictory features, as a result, form the basis for an intimate and symbiotic relation- ship between crime and politics, crime and economic growth, and crime and social change—not an oppositional relationship. The tradition of wanting to get ahead by the shortest possible route, sometimes illegal, is no less an ethic than wanting to observe the law.

Adult crime, not just delinquency, has been a major means by which a variety of people have achieved the American success ideal and obtained respectability, if not for themselves, for their children. Hence, it is likely that this deviant tradition contributes more than we realize to the behavior of younger, as well as older, people—to adolescents from all strata and communities, not only those from the lower status and deprived communities.

The task of indicating how these and the legitimate networks in any locale induce conformity or deviance will occupy scientists for a long time. Yet, research and action can be used collaboratively in the interest of promoting productive roles for the young and giving them a larger stake in conformity. One method for this would be to accompany any attempt to alter basic institutions with the analysis and construction of neighborhood typologies by which the effects of differential organization could first be cataloged, and then empirically related to efforts at change.

For example, a neighborhood typology could specify how neighborhoods are ordered along one or more dimensions, what factors determine this ordering, and how these factors are related. The typology might incorporate racial, subcultural, and institutional variables that heretofore have been analyzed separately, and relate them to legitimate or illegitimate behavior. Such a framework might indicate with greater clarity what it is about institutional operations in some settings that provides young people with a stake in conformity, but in others produces alienation and deviance.

INTERACTIONAL ANALYSIS

Few can say why, even in high delinquency areas, most young people do not become official delinquents, or why, in low delinquency areas, some juveniles violate the law. What are the institutional forces, even in ghetto neighborhoods, that encourage and foster a legitimate identity in most people, or some of the opposite even in affluent neighborhoods? Questions of this type, organizational analyses alone cannot answer. Research and innovation on the interactional, face-to-face level are needed to provide more information on the way existing institutions organize and affect interpersonal behavior: (1) what is there about the individual in a given social context that might motivate him to want to participate in either a deviant or conformist game; and (2) assuming that he is inclined to play such a game, in what position and under what circumstances would he be inclined to play it?

Using a game analogy, Cohen and Short (1971) have suggested that most human life is organized in terms of social games. Each game operates according to a set of rules, some informal, some formal. These rules specify a set of positions or roles—third baseman, teacher, pupil, minister, clerk, or con politician—and indicate what the player of each position is supposed to do in relation to the players of other positions. They also include criteria for evaluating the success of the total enterprise or the contributions of individual players. In order to "fit in," as Cohen puts it,

> you have to know the rules; you have to "have a program," so that you may know what position each man, including yourself, is playing; and you

have to know how to keep score. You cannot make sense out of what is going on, either as a participant or as an observer, unless you know the rules that define this particular sort of collective enterprise (1960:2).

The point is that each child's identity is constituted not just of characteristics peculiar to him but of the positions he plays in various games. Others are able to place him and have successful relations with him in terms of the positions he plays and the positions they play. His public reputation, his self-respect, depend upon how well he plays his position and, if he is a part of a team game, how well his team as a whole does. Too little attention has been paid, however, to game phenomena in understanding youthful behavior.

We have not been cognizant enough of the variations in rules operative among juveniles in different kinds of communities within the overall society. Thus, if one's own, or an official and conventional, definition of the situation were imposed upon them, one might not only fail to understand the games being played but would miss much that is significant. The same body of interaction occurring in different settings might have much different meaning. Behavior that might represent a disruption of ties between youth and adults in one setting might be just the opposite in another. For example, "It often shocks the unsophisticated to find that many *professional* criminals . . . are graduates of loving homes, who are successfully identifying with their fathers" (Glaser et al., 1966:20). Thus, we need to take cognizance of the way characteristics of different subcultures, neighborhoods, and communities are translated into action on the interactional level (Cohen & Short, 1971).

In the Italian neighborhood discussed above, the sophisticated delinquents were apparently tuned in to illegitimate as well as legitimate structures as a method of realizing their goals, while the "respectables," the children of civil servants, were oriented to the more conventional expectations of the larger community. There was not a serious disjunction between parents and children in either case, for both groups reflected the conflicting sets of expectations that existed side-by-side in the same neighborhood and were carried not only by juveniles but by parents.

In a black neighborhood, by contrast, Short and Strodtbeck (1965:275) suggest that reasonably common patterns between adults and children have relatively less meaning simply because neither adults nor children were tied very effectively either to legitimate or illegitimate structures.

We firmly believe that need dispositions which are required by gang membership arise in the interaction between the lack of preparation for school-type achievement in the home and in the absence of access to alternative adaptations to failure in the schools. . . . By the time boys acquire the identity associated with gang membership, a police record, or dropping out of school, the process of selectivity for failure is established (Short & Strodtbeck, 1965:275).

Thus, understanding and altering individual behavior in either case rests not only upon delineation of differences on an organizational level, but on the way differences are translated into action on the level of the child. Were policy-makers more sensitive to issues of this type, and were ongoing institutional programs better designed to account for them, socialization that was both more effective and yet more rewarding would be likely to occur.

THE INSTITUTIONAL BASE FOR PREVENTION

One problem of most prevention and control programs has been their insular character. Rather than being tied to a strong institutional base, they usually set themselves apart, even if located in the community. In terms of a medical model, they eschew a strong institutional affiliation and operate as an outpatient clinic, a recreation center, or a store-front hangout. Rather than fostering institutional change, therefore, their major targets have been single individuals. While useful functions are performed, little is done to affect the opportunity structures of the institutions themselves.

The problem is not easily solved. Polk and Kobrin (1972), however, make a strong case for using the school as the main institutional base for prevention efforts, especially when prevention is defined in terms of the means needed for young people to acquire a legitimate identity and a stake in conformity. Consider the evidence.

First, a series of studies indicates that poor academic achievement may be related more strongly to official delinquency than any other single variable (Call, 1965; Polk & Halferty, 1966; Empey & Lubeck, 1971). These studies indicate further that, while delinquency is uniformly low among boys from all social classes who are doing well in school, it is uniformly high among those who are doing poorly. Contrary to the usual assumption that it is membership in the lower class that is of crucial importance, these studies indicate that it is the child's achievement in school that is the deciding influence.

Second, in contrast to welfare, the church, or even the family, in some instances, the school is the one legitimate institution that cuts across all neighborhoods, social classes, and ethnic groups. Reflecting its capacity to have a lifelong impact on young people, the school is the one institution upon which employers and governments, as well as parents, rely for the preparation of the young for a legitimate and satisfying adulthood. As a consequence, it is the one setting where resources for the young are concentrated most heavily.

Third, the young have become superfluous in the world of work (Musgrove, 1969). The unskilled, highly routine jobs once reserved for them have disappeared, and child labor laws, designed ironically to prevent their exploitation, now exclude them from satisfying skilled work. Hence, the school has become a place of segregation for the young; if legitimate identies are not acquired there, they may never be acquired.

Finally, many cultural, recreational, and sports activities are funneled through the school. If not a part of the school, the school provides access to them. The consequence is that in many communities the school has become the major focal point for adolescent activity and a sense of belonging. Even dropouts, despite their feelings of alienation congregate at the school during lunch, recess, or other free periods. It remains a place of considerable salience to them.

These are some of the reasons why the school occupies a position of crucial importance in crime prevention. As the major avenue for legitimate achievement, a sense of belonging, and competence, the school may now be the most important youth institution and source of socialization in society, although its potential is seldom fully realized. Without it, young persons are denied access to the roles that establish them as legitimate, meaningful people, with consequences that can be disastrous both in the short and the long run. Without the school in a major role, crime prevention, as defined here, could be seriously hampered.

Despite the central position of the school, Lemert is pessimistic regarding its ability to contribute to prevention. "There is," he says, "an empty ring to all such thinking, for substantially little seems to have come of it, either in the form of organizational innovation or new philosophy to comprehend youth problems under the aegis of education" (1971:19). Judged according to past performance, one would have to agree with this conclusion. Yet, it may be unfair to suggest that the school has proven any less capable than most other societal institutions in preventing high rates of crime in recent decades. The school is particularly subject to the values and whims of the citizenry at large, and just as they have proven ineffective, so the school has proven ineffective. If, however, the school could do the following kinds of things, its capacity to give the young a greater stake in conformity might be enhanced:

1. It could do more to analyze the peculiar characteristics of any neighborhood in which it is located. Its curriculum, its organization, and its activities could then be tailored to better fit the needs of the clientele it is trying to serve. Coupled with efforts to apply some of the principles of learning theory, the academic capabilities of the school could also be improved.

2. By facilitating its linkage with other legitimate institutions in the neighborhood, other school functions could also be performed more capably. It is often true, for example, that teachers have a difficult time establishing contacts with the parents of those children who are having the greatest difficulty. Yet, only rarely have efforts been made to solicit parents or others indigenous to the neighborhood to help with this problem, either as volunteers or as employed personnel. Rather than participating in some formalistic enterprise, such as PTA, parents could be asked to join with a specific group of their own children and their children's teachers in an endeavor to improve the quality of the school experience. This would be tapping the direct vested interests of the persons involved, and would be establishing stronger ties between two major institutions.

3. Much attention could be paid to reducing the coercive methods of control upon which the school now relies so heavily, and seeking more effective normative means in their stead. As Polk and Kobrin (1972) suggest, self-study groups could be created whereby students and their families, and perhaps other adults, come together on a regular basis to analyze and deal with problems that are of concern to all. Far too often, however, there is a tendency for some teachers, administrators, and many students to think only of coercive controls. That is nonsense. No organization can exist without norms and some dedication to the collective welfare. In fact, in the Provo Experiment (Empey & Erickson, 1972), the one organizational component from which delinquents said they learned the most and gained the greatest personal benefits was that in which they helped to solve problems, make decisions, and even impose controls. Their participation in these activities seemed to reduce their sense of alienation and to promote the normative power of the organization. Added to the school, therefore, such activities might address a much larger range of childhood and adolescent difficulties than mere academic performance.

4. Traditionally, the school has failed to provide the young with the kinds of experiences that give adults a sense of usefulness and competence. Yet there are any number of constructive roles students do not now play that could be sponsored by the school: (a) in conjunction with school personnel, analyses could be made of the school's tracking, stratification, discipline, and sociometric systems to see if, in some way, these could be changed to enhance involvement rather than alienation; (b) tutorial programs could be organized so that students at all levels help others; (c) drug education programs or programs designed to reduce racial conflict or conflict with the police could be organized, and students given the chance to educate adults as well as the reverse; (d) the school could act as an advocate in behalf of its students so they contribute a youth perspective to the policy decisions made by many community groups and agencies; and (e) the school could make it possible for students to participate in constructive community programs—cleaning up the environment, registering voters, participating in crisis-intervention programs, and so on. To do these things, the school would not have to lower its academic standards; rather, the latter could be enhanced by firsthand experience and greater sense of self-worth.

It is difficult to conceive of any societal institution in which, if significant changes were made, greater results could be achieved. The school has access to virtually every young person. In many neighborhoods, it may be the only institution in which a majority of the people, young and old, have a vested interest. Hence, the opportunity it has to enlarge the number of responsible and gratifying roles for the young is probably unexcelled. Should it do that, it could have the effect of creating among young people a firmer attachment to the aims and procedures of legitimate institutions, and of reducing the probability of criminal involvement.

It must be recognized, however, that without an enlargement of its mandate, a change in educational philosophy, and greatly increased resources, the educational system could not add to its present burdens those implied here. Ordinarily, the primary institutions in society, such as the school, do not see it as their responsibility to prevent crime and delinquency. This is due probably to two things: (1) the tendency to define prevention in terms of controlling deviance rather than enhancing legitimacy; and (2) the evolution of our institutions in the twentieth century.

For a long period, responsibility for prevention, such as it was, was assigned to the agencies of control—the police, courts, and corrections—not to such agencies as the school. Not only did this free the latter from responsibility for dealing with difficult young people, but it encouraged the agencies of social control to develop a vested interest in receiving them. Their powers, budgets, and bureaucratic structures depended, in part, on maintaining that interest. In recent years, of course, the growing interest in diversion has done much to change this state of affairs. But, while diversion has emphasized a reduction in police roles, it has not really stressed the importance of an increase in the role of the educational establishment. Until that perspective is changed on the part of the citizenry as well as among educators, support for the kinds of changes proposed here may not be forthcoming.

AGENCIES OF SOCIAL CONTROL

Turning now to the agencies of social control, it should be noted that nothing said heretofore should be construed as suggesting that the control agencies should go out of the prevention business. The issue is not whether they have a role to play, but what that role should be.

In terms of preventing cases of secondary deviance or a recurrence of criminal behavior in convicted offenders, they have a central role to play. However, using the definition of prevention we have, their role is in need of clarification. Consider first a revision of legal rules and the possible consequences it might have for the criminal justice system relative to the illegitimate structures in society.

Preventing Organized and Professional Crime

Contrary to the traditional focus on processing the alcoholic, the homosexual, or the dependent juvenile, prevention efforts should address organized criminal and delinquent structures, and devise ways to deal with them. Despite continuing and growing evidence that these structures are related in a symbiotic way to prevailing business and political activities, few inroads have been made upon them. For example, greater concentration on the political and economic methods used by organized crime to purvey harmful drugs to the young could have significant consequences for prevention.

There seems little doubt that large quantities of dangerous drugs are being produced by legitimate firms, fed into illegitimate channels, and then directed to young people. The federal government regulates the amounts of dangerous drugs produced domestically, but evidently not well enough to prevent abuse. The public seems more concerned with controlling surface symptoms of drug problems—the addicted thieves and muggers who prey upon others to maintain their habit—than with finding and convicting the organized professionals who supply dangerous drugs. The most effective prevention in this case would be to shut off the sources of supply. By the same token, a greater focus upon the roots of other kinds of predatory crime—truck hijacking, auto theft rings, etc.—and upon the economic and political bodies that give them sustenance, could do much to allay public fears and to inhibit the recruitment of the young to criminal careers.

Criminal Sanctions and Deterrence

A mistaken assumption often made about those who advocate reforms of the type mentioned throughout this analysis is that they do not view crime as a serious problem. That they advocate a kind of permissiveness in which crime would only be encouraged, not deterred, is not true. But respect for the law and the use of criminal sanctions as a deterrent to the would-be predator has certain prerequisites: (1) there must be consensus on the criminal acts that are disavowed—a set of statutes concerned only with harm to persons or property might help to accomplish this; (2) the response of the criminal justice system to predatory acts must be swift and efficient; and (3) the convicted person must learn from his experience, and procure a set of alternatives to his criminal behavior.

Contrary to much public opinion, there is evidence that the fear of punishment, as well as the anticipation of reward, has a strong influence on human behavior (Bandura & Walters, 1963; Bandura, 1969:118–216; Empey & Erickson, 1972:chaps. 4, 5). Even an abstract belief that the probability of punishment is high may directly affect the likelihood of deviant behavior (Jensen, 1969). These and other studies suggest that punishment may deter, either when it is personalized or when it is believed that punishment is a probability.

On the other hand, available evidence documents a striking contrast between the belief that the criminal justice system can accomplish these ends and the way it actually operates. A clogged and overburdened system permits the most serious offenders to delay or escape prosecution, while the poor and ignorant are most likely to be prosecuted or to be treated unjustly (cf. Wittner, 1970:20–25). Thus, the system at present is not only failing to protect society from serious, criminal predators, but is also unjust and inefficient.

Because current trends and projections for the system are so preposterous, they are labeled by McEachern et al. (1970:24) as a potentially absurd system. In using the term *absurd*, these investigators indicated that if solutions are to be found vast and innovative changes will be required—less concern with nonpredatory acts now labeled as crime, a greater concentration upon the elimination of organized criminal structures, and a more efficient and progressive method for dealing with offenders. Were these steps taken, the chances would be increased that the agents of control could deter, and thus prevent, more crime.

Diversion by the Agencies of Control

With the growing emphasis upon the negative effects of official labeling, there has been an increasing tendency to divert offenders, especially juveniles, from the criminal justice system. Methods of help and control that have been utilized most effectively in middle-class communities—suspended action by the police, referral to parents, or placement in some remedial program—have been promoted in slum and lower-class settings so that diversion can be made more effective for the youth who live there. The basic goal seems to be to inhibit acquisition of a deviant identity and commission of acts of secondary deviance. To accomplish that, youth from all strata and ethnic groups require equal opportunity.

Lemert suggests that the police are in a crucial position to effect diversionary programs. "[They] encounter youth problems more frequently than other community agencies; they meet the problems at the time of their occurrence; and they wield a great deal of coercive and symbolic authority" (1971:68–69).

The available evidence regarding the willingness of police to divert juveniles, however, is mixed. In two different studies of a large number of police departments (Goldman, 1969; Klein, 1970), the proportion of juvenile arrestees who were diverted rather than referred to court varied from a low of 2 percent in one department to a high of 82 percent in another. Such striking evidence indicates that to know why some juveniles become official delinquents while others do not, one should know the determinants of such widely discrepant rates.

Several determinants have been suggested by research—the social-class level or ethnic background of the juvenile (Goldman, 1969), his demeanor at the time of his arrest (Piliavin & Briar 1964; Black & Reiss, 1970), whether the police were highly professionalized or indigenous to a neighborhood (Wilson, 1970), or whether a complainant was present to insist that the juvenile be officially charged and processed (Black & Reiss, 1970). By no means were the determinants uniform, suggesting the lack of anything approaching a universal police policy toward diversion and its utility.

Significantly, in his study of forty-six police departments in Los Angeles, Klein (1970) found that one crucial and deciding influence was whether the police had an agency, readily available, to which they could divert a juvenile— a counseling program, a capable parent, or an ongoing program of some sort.

This finding is central to the underlying assumptions of this chapter because it suggests that, even if police practices were to become more uniform, the arresting officer would still have to look for some neighborhood resource to which a juvenile could be referred. If young people are to be diverted from the justice-correction system, the primary institutions in the community—the family, school, and neighborhood—will have to take up the slack. As with primary prevention, nonjustice agencies are crucial to the success of secondary prevention.

These reasons warrant skepticism about the capacities of large and bureaucratic systems, such as probation departments or large community mental health programs, to perform this service. Instead, programs of diversion, like those of primary prevention, may have to be neighborhood-specific—related to the immediate context in which the individual lives. This is especially true for juveniles, as they often fail to see the relevance of programs that are divorced from the realities that confront them daily.

A number of neighborhood programs now use indigenous people who either work alone or in concert with the police. In some cases, these programs have used ex-felons, ex-addicts, police aides, paraprofessionals, or black and brown power advocates to serve as a resource to whom juveniles could be referred. While such programs have much in their favor, problems of continuity, funding, and lack of a strong institutional base continue to plague them, just as they plague other prevention programs. No less than others, anyone diverted from prosecution requires enduring opportunities for education, work, and even food and shelter. It is for these reasons that strategies of secondary and primary diversion require planning and resources that are immediately relevant to particular kinds of problems in specific kinds of neighborhood and community settings. Grand and bureaucratic strategies that do not take these factors into account are prone to failure.

SUMMARY AND CONCLUSIONS

This chapter has noted that, in response to high crime and delinquency rates, some segments of society are inclined to evoke a war on crime, implying that through a militaristic emphasis upon law and order, law-violating behavior can be controlled. Other segments, relying heavily upon the labeling perspective, have suggested that society's customary ways of responding to delinquents and criminals may have done more to incubate the crime problem than to solve it. Diversion from, rather than involvement in, the criminal justice system is implied as the most appropriate approach to prevention. It was pointed out, however, that both social movements failed to address a series of fundamental issues.

An emphasis upon repression or diversion fails to account for the means by which a person acquires a legitimate identity and a stake in conformity. These factors, rather than fear of punishment or avoidance of a deviant identity, consititute a primary focus on prevention.

As a method of approaching prevention in these terms, certain possibilities were suggested:

1. The system of legal rules should be changed to eliminate nonpredatory, victimless crimes from the list of criminal offenses;

2. the network of legitimate socializing institutions and the illegitimate structures in any particualr locale or neighborhood should be analyzed and prevention programs should be adapted to those explicit circumstances, for the success of these efforts depends upon the extent to which changes can be introduced into the specific institutional networks in which young people are socialized; and

3. the agents of social control should be freed to concentrate upon predatory crimes and the illegitimate structures that are at the root of the crime problem, and they should also be encouraged, in collaboration with neighborhood-specific socializing institutions, to divert many more offenders from the justice system as a means of preventing the incidence of secondary deviance.

REFERENCES

Bandura, Albert.
   1969 *Principles of Behavior Modification.* New York: Holt, Rinehart & Winston.
Bandura, Albert, and Richard H. Walters.
   1963 *Social Learning and Personality Development.* New York: Holt, Rinehart & Winston.
Becker, Howard S.
   1963 *The Outsiders.* New York: Free Press of Glencoe.
Bell, Daniel.
   1959 *The End of Ideology.* Glencoe, Ill.: Free Press.
Bittner, Egon.
   1970 *The Functions of the Police in Modern Society.* Publication No. 2059. Washington, D.C.: U.S. Government Printing Office.
Black, Donald J., and Albert J. Reiss, Jr.
   1970 "Police control of juveniles." American Sociological Review 35 (February):63–77.
Blumer, Herbert.
   1969 "Sociological implications of the thoughts of George Herbert Mead," in Herbert Blumer (ed.), *Symbolic Interactionism.* Englewood Cliffs, N.J.: Prentice-Hall.
Call, Donald J.
   1965 "Frustration and noncommitment." Ph.D. dissertation, University of Oregon.
Carter, Robert M., and G. Thomas Gitchoff.
   1970 "An alternative to youthful mass disorder." *The Police Chief* No. 37 (July):52–56.

Chilton, Ronald J., and Gerald E. Markle.
  1972 "Family disruption, delinquent conduct and the effect of subclassi-
         fication." *American Sociological Review* 37 (February): 93–99.
Christensen, Ronald.
  1967 "Projected percentage of U.S. population with criminal arrest and con-
         viction records," in *President's Commission on Law Enforcement and
         Administration of Justice, Task Force Report: Science and Tech-
         nology*. Washington, D.C.: U.S. Government Printing Office.
Cloward, Richard A., and Lloyd E. Ohlin.
  1960 *Delinquency and Opportunity: A Theory of Delinquent Gangs.* New
         York: Free Press of Glencoe.
Cohen, Albert K.
  1960 "Delinquency as culturally patterned and group supported behavior."
         Address to the 12th Annual Training Institute for Probation, Parole and
         Institutional Staff, San Francisco (mimeographed).
Cohen, Albert K., and James F. Short, Jr.
  1971 "Juvenile delinquency," in Robert K. Merton and Robert A. Nisbet
         (eds.), *Contemporary Social Problems*. New York: Harcourt, Brace &
         World.
Cressey, Donald R.
  1964 *Crime and Differential Association.* The Hague: Martinus Nijhoff.
  1965 "Theoretical foundations for using criminals in the rehabilitation of
         criminals," in Hans W. Mattick (ed.), *The Future of Imprisonment in a
         Free Society*. Chicago: St. Leonards House.
Dahrendorf, Rolf.
  1958 "Out of utopia: toward a reorientation in sociological analysis." *Amer-
         ican Journal of Sociology* 67 (September):115–127.
  1959 *Class and Class Conflict in Industrial Society*. Stanford:Stanford Univer-
         sity Press.
Davis, Fred.
  1961 "Deviance disavowal: the management of strain interaction by the visibly
         handicapped." *Social Problems* 9(Fall):120–132.
Durkheim, Emile.
  1895 *The Rules of Sociological Method.* Eighth Edition. Translated by
         Sarah A. Solovay and John H. Mueller. Edited by G.E.G. Catlin.
         Chicago: University of Chicago Press (1938 edition).
Empey, LaMar T.
  1967 "Delinquency theory and recent research." *Journal of Research in
         Crime and Delinquency* 3 (January):28–41.
Empey, LaMar T., and Maynard L. Erickson.
  1972 *The Provo Experiment: Evaluating Community Control of Delinquency.*
         Lexington, Mass.: D.C. Heath.
Empey, LaMar T., and Steven G. Lubeck.
  1971 *Explaining Delinquency: Construction, Test and Reformulation of a
         Sociological Theory.* Lexington, Mass.: D.C. Heath.
Erikson, Kai T.
  1962 "Notes on the sociology of deviance." *Social Problems* 9(Spring):307–
         314.

Federal Bureau of Investigation (F.B.I.)
    1969 *Crime in the United States: Uniform Crime Reports*– 1968. Washington,
          D.C.: U.S. Government Printing Office.
Gibbs, Jack P.
    1966 "Conceptions of deviant behavior: the old and the new." *Pacific
          Sociological Review* 9(Spring):9–14.
Glaser, Daniel.
    1968 "Research and theory on deviant behavior: nomothetic or ideographic."
          Paper presented for discussion at roundtable luncheon, American
          Sociological Association, August 28.
    1971 Social Deviance. Chicago: Markham.
Glaser, Daniel, Donald Kenefick, and Vincent O'Leary.
    1966 *The Violent Offender.* Washington, D.C.: U.S. Government Printing
          Office.
Goldman, Nathan.
    1969 "The differential selection of juvenile offenders for court appearance."
          Pp. 264–290 in William Chambliss (ed.), *Crime and the Legal Process.*
          New York:McGraw-Hill.
Hathaway, Starke R., Elio D. Monachesi, and Laurence A. Young.
    1960 "Delinquency rates and personality." *Journal of Criminal Law,
          Criminology and Police Science* 50(February):433–440.
Hirschi, Travis.
    1969 *Causes of Delinquency.* Berkeley: University of California Press.
Janowitz, Morris.
    1968 *Social Control of Escalated Riots.* Chicago: University of Chicago
          Center for Policy Studies.
Jensen, Gary F.
    1969 " 'Crime doesn't pay': correlates of shared misunderstanding." *Social
          Problems* 17(Fall):189–201.
Kitsuse, John I.
    1962 "Societal reaction to deviant behavior: problems of theory and method."
          Social Problems 9(Winter):247–256.
Kitsuse, John I., and Aaron V. Cicourel.
    1963 "A note on the uses of official statistics." *Social Problems* 11(Fall):
          131–139.
Klein, Malcolm W.
    1970 "Police processing of juvenile offenders: toward the development of
          juvenile system rates." Los Angeles County Sub-Regional Board,
          California Council on Criminal Justice, part III.
Kobrin, Solomon.
    1951 "The conflict of values in delinquency areas." *American Sociological
          Review* 16(October):653–661.
Kobrin, Solomon, Joseph Puntil, and Emil Peluso.
    1967 "Criteria of status among street corner groups." *Journal of Research in
          Crime and Delinquency* 4(January):98–118.
Kvaraceus, William C.
    1964 "World-wide story." *The Unesco Courier* 12(May).

LaGache, D.
   1950 *Psycho-Criminogenese: Tenth General Report.* Paris: 2nd International
         Congress of Criminology.
Lasswell, H.D.
   1950 *World Politics and Personal Insecurity.* Glencoe, Ill.: Free Press.
Lemert, Edwin M.
   1951 *Social Pathology.* New York: McGraw-Hill.
   1971 *Instead of Court: Diversion in Juvenile Justice.* National Institute of
         Mental Health, Center for the Study of Crime and Delinquency. Wash-
         ington, D.C.: U.S. Government Printing Office.
McEachern, A.W., R.M. Carter, H. Adelman, and J.R. Newman.
   1970 *Criminal Justice Simulation Study:* Some Preliminary Projections. Los
         Angeles: University of Southern California, Public Systems Research
         Institute.
McKay, Henry D.
   1949 "The neighborhood and child conduct." *Annals of the American
         Academy of Political and Social Science* 261 (January):32–41.
Matza, David, and Gresham M. Sykes.
   1961 "Juvenile delinquency and subterranean values." *American Sociological
         Review* 26(October):712–719.
Merton, Robert K.
   1957 *Social Theory and Social Structure.* Glencoe, Ill.: Feee Press.
Monahan, Thomas P.
   1957 "Family status and the delinquent child: a reappraisal and some new
         findings." *Social Forces* 35(March):250–258.
Morris, Norval.
   1966 "Impediments to penal reform." *University of Chicago Law Review*
         33(Summer):627– 656.
Morris, Norval, and Gordon Hawkins.
   1970 *The Honest Politician's Guide to Crime Control.* Chicago: University of
         Chicago Press.
Musgrove, Frank.
   1969 "The problems of youth and the structure of society in England."
         Youth and Society 1(September):38–58.
Ohlin, Lloyd E.
   1970 *A Situational Approach to Delinquency Prevention.* Washington, D.C.:
         U.S. Government Printing Office.
Piliavin, Irving, and Scott Briar.
   1964 "Police encounters with juveniles." *American Journal of Sociology* 70
         (September):206–214.
Polk, Kenneth, and David S. Halferty.
   1966 "Adolescence, commitment and delinquency." *Journal of Research in
         Crime and Delinquency* 4 (July):82–96.
Polk, Kenneth, and Solomon Kobrin.
   1972 *Delinquency Prevention through Youth Development.* Washington,
         D.C.: U.S. Government Printing Office.

President's Commission on Law Enforcement and Administration of Justice.
    1967a *Task Force Report: Juvenile Delinquency and Youth Crime.* Washington, D.C.: U.S. Government Printing Office.
    1967b *The Challenge of Crime in a Free Society.* Washington, D.C.: U.S. Government Printing Office.
    1967c *Task Force Report: Corrections.* Washington, D.C.: U.S. Government Printing Office.

Rubin, Ted.
    1970 "Law as an agent of delinquency prevention." Paper presented at the California Conference on Prevention Strategy. Sacramento: California Youth Authority.

Schrag, Clarence.
    1962 "Delinquency and opportunity: analysis of a theory." *Sociology and Social Research* 46(January):167–175.

Schuessler, Karl, and Donald R. Cressey.
    1950 "Personality characteristics of criminals." *American Journal of Sociology* 55(March):476–484.

Schur, Edwin M.
    1971 *Labeling Deviant Behavior: Its Sociological Implications.* New York: Harper & Row.

Seymour, John A.
    1971 "The current status of youth service bureaus." Chicago: University of Chicago Center for Studies in Criminal Justice (mimeographed).

Short, James F., Jr.
    1963 "Street corner groups and patterns of delinquency." *American Catholic Sociological Review* 24(Spring):13–32.
    1965 "Social structure and group processes in explanation of gang delinquency." Pp. 158–188 in Muzafer Sherif and Carolyn Sherif (eds.), *Problems of Youth.* Chicago: Aldine.

Short, James F., Jr., and Fred L. Strodtbeck.
    1965 *Group Process and Gang Delinquency.* Chicago: University of Chicago Press.

Shulman, Harry M.
    1949 "The family and juvenile delinquency." *Annals of the American Academy of Political and Social Science* 26(January):21–31.

Silver, Isidore.
    1968 "The president's crime commission revisited." *New York University Law Review* 43:916–966.

Smith, Robert L.
    1971 *A Quiet Revolution: Probation Subsidy.* Social and Rehabilitation Service, Youth Development and Delinquency Prevention Administration, Department of Health, Education and Welfare. Washington, D.C.: U.S. Government Printing Office.

Tannenbaum, Frank.
    1938 *Crime and the Community.* New York: Columbia University Press.

Thrasher, Frederic M.
  1963   *The Gang.* Revised Edition. Chicago: University of Chicago Press.
Toby, Jackson.
  1957a "Social disorganization and a stake in conformity." *Journal of Criminal Law, Criminology and Police Science* 48(May–June):12–17.
  1957b "The differential impact of family disorganization." *American Sociological Review* 22(October):505–515.
Wheeler, Stanton, Leonard S. Cottrell, and Anne Romasco.
  1967   "Juvenile delinquency: its prevention and control," in President's Commission on Law Enforcement and Administration of Justice, *Task Force Report: Juvenile Delinquency and Youth Crime.* Washington, D.C.: U.S. Government Printing Office.
Whyte, William F.
  1955   *Street Corner Society.* Chicago: University of Chicago Press.
Wilson, James Q.
  1970   "The police and the delinquent in two cities." Pp. 111–117 in Peter G. Garabedian (ed.), *Becoming Delinquent.* Chicago: Aldine.
Wittner, Dale.
  1970   "Log jam in our courts." *Life* 69(August 7):18:26.

Part III
New Offenders/New Crimes

Our perception of "new offenders/new crimes" comes from both a recognition of emerging patterns as well as a raised level of consciousness that allows us to view behavior in a new light. The selections in this Part relate to both of these perspectives. As we have seen, sociologists are aware of the fact that rule-violating, innovative, or criminal behavior are invariable concomitants of social change. Not only does the temporary social disorganization rendered by rapid change encourage certain forms of deviance; it also becomes possible to envision the enactment of deviant behavior as one of the engines of change. In a large way, much of the self-consciously "revolutionary" activity of the sixties and early seventies bespeaks this idea. In the following discussion, we shall consider some of these ideas within the context of the material that will be presented.

When considering social change, the only indicator we have is the observable behavior of the system's members. As the United States enters the final quarter of the twentieth century, social patterns almost unthinkable a decade or two ago are now greeted with almost total complacency. Perhaps one of the most striking changes has been the redefinition of traditional sex roles. The organized, as well as unorganized, women's movement has had much to do with raising the level of societal consciousness, thereby undoing many traditional patterns. In tandem with this form of political activity, there have been significant changes in other areas of life. For example, the revolution in sexual mores that we are experiencing rests in part, upon a technological base. For instance, it was only with the advent of the oral contraceptive and the intrauterine device (IUD) that truly effective birth control became available to women, allowing them the same sexual spontaneity that men have biologically enjoyed. Changes in patterns of work brought an even larger number of women into the social structure who could assume a more or less independent posture. The sociological ramifications of the changing status of women are rather clear: a gradual, but constant, process of desexualization is in operation, and as the future unfolds we can expect to see even fewer sex-role differences separating men and women.

All of the evidence suggests that this process has permeated the American social structure. As we posited earlier, deviant behavior and/or crime is probably one of the most sensitive indicators of change we have available to us. Following through on this assumption, we would expect to see new and different patterns and forms of criminality occurring within the female population. This hypothesis has proven itself to be entirely valid: our available data indicate both a striking increase in the incidence of crimes committed by women, as well as a dramatic shift toward patterns of criminal behavior that were traditionally believed to be entirely the province of the male.

Freda Adler's *Sisters in Crime* amply documents these assertions. Traditionally, female criminality had, for the most part, limited itself to two areas: (1) larceny, mostly in the form of shoplifting; and (2) sexual offenses, in the form of prostitution. Although women were involved in other offenses as well, their role was typically that of an accomplice to a male who both organized the crime and was the central figure in its execution. As some of Adler's case histories amply document, this role is in the process of change. In the future we can regularly expect to see more bank robberies, burglaries, and other serious offenses committed by women, either acting alone or in concert with other women; it is even likely that we will come to see males in the subordinate role of the accomplice.

Relevant here is the speculation that some of the current revolutionary activity is dominated by women. One writer went so far as to suggest that the alleged leader of the Symbionese Liberation Army, the late Donald DeFreeze, was only a figurehead and that decision-making was done primarily by the group's female cadre. Because the group wanted to encourage widespread acceptance among Third World peoples (many of whom still do not have the high level of consciousness necessary to accept female leadership), it would be necessary to symbolize the group's leadership in the hands of a black male. This, of course, is just speculation, but we do have the sense now that, in terms of violent revolutionary activity, women are *not* assuming an inferior or secondary position to men in the various movements. Even the names of the groups reflect this change. In the late sixties, Americans were concerned about the activities of a radical group known as the Weather*men*. Today a similar revolutionary group named the Weather Underground has surfaced.

It does appear that violence and females are becoming increasingly related in the revolutionary movement. But increases in women's propensity toward violence can be observed in other areas as well. Traditionally, in the relationship between prostitute and customer, or "John," it was the woman who was most in danger of being assaulted. Recently, we have more often heard the reverse—the John who has been assaulted, beaten, and even killed by a prostitute.

Exactly how widespread this is cannot be statistically documented at this time, but our impression from the increasing amount of time allocated to such incidents in the news media does suggest that it is growing. A casual scan of the media suggests, as well, that criminal activities such as gang robbery and violent assault on persons with no apparent robbery motive are also on the increase. Sociologically, such behavior indicates basic shifts in the entire organization of sex roles. At this point, it is reasonable to speculate that in the not too distant future, sex will exercise very little control over behavior.

Our second concern in the area of "new offenders/new crimes" is somewhat more difficult to define. Our impression is that when we consider offenses committed by governments in the everyday exercise of their authority, we are not talking about anything new. Certainly in other cultures, where scandal is a part of routine politics, the removal of government officials found to be using their office for private gain evokes merely a fraction of the notice that it does in the United States. For instance the resignation of both a President and Vice President of the United States in the glare of scandal was, for many people, almost unthinkable. Similarly, it is difficult to believe that those institutions ostensibly established to safeguard one's basic freedoms could be systematically eroding those freedoms with a slow but persistent stream of meaningless bureaucratic procedures. The misuse of authority in the name of expediency, the oppression engendered by the rule of order instead of the rule of law, and the widespread misuse of discretionary power held by agents and agencies of control in the enforcement of laws—all can result in offenses perpetrated by an administration against citizens.

Although it is difficult to determine whether it is the scope or severity of these assaults that have increased recently, it appears that our level of consciousness as political beings has never been higher. We are now actively questioning such shibboleths as "national security" and "law and order," asking about the extent and activities of those agencies that promulgate them.

The last two selections in this Part relate to this theme. Using a polemical approach in his "Crime in the American State," Quinney discusses the system and its agents in the context of actual law breaking. The more or less routine violation of civil liberties is set against actual crimes (such as theft) committed by the agents of social control. Then, shifting focus, he enters the controversy surrounding the issue of war crimes, cogently arguing how much of what was done in Vietnam was in flagrant violation of international law and how the issue of war crimes has never really received the attention it deserved. The fact that disciplinary action was primarily taken against a junior officer and only indirectly against his superiors is testimony to the basic disregard of human rights under which the system operates. And finally, the question of governmental involvement with organized crime at various levels is considered in the context of the Nixon Administration.

In "How the Government Breaks the Law," Lieberman describes the threads of lawlessness running throughout our culture and social structure. Administrative lawlessness is taken out of any kind of exotic, isolated context and placed in the realm of everyday operating procedure. Here one receives the feeling that it is the ponderous system itself, moving along under its own inertia, that blindly traduces the rights if not the humanity of its members.

In a broad sense, both Quinney and Lieberman give us the opportunity to speak meaningfully of crime as "the American way of life."

Sisters in Crime
Freda Adler

Characteristically, major social movements are spawned in obscurity at the periphery of public awareness, seem to burst suddenly and dramatically into public view, and eventually fade into the landscape not because they have diminished but because they have become a permanent part of our perceptions and experience. Thus it has been with the liberation of the female criminal, whose coming was foretold in song and foreshadowed in unisexual styles of dress and hair and attitude long before it appeared on police blotters. The portrait of the breathless, squeaky-voiced, empty-headed female professing awed admiration over some incredibly routine male accomplishment began to look less like a stereotype than a caricature. Even motherhood, in an era of zero-population goals and the diminishing status of homemaking, has been too closely linked with antiquated male domination to remain forever sacred. In spite of the cultural lag of white-male bias, the *Zeitgeist* of liberation has been moving irresistibly across the land. A generation militantly young, black, and female has stirred to storm and controversy previously whispered plaints whose answer, as Bob Dylan so eloquently lyricized, "is blowing in the wind." The term "social movement" is a useful abstraction to describe the distillation of innumerable events which together form a trend. But in another sense there are no social movements, only individuals reacting to the immediacy of their own felt experience. Such an individual is Marge.

SOURCE: Freda Adler, *Sisters in Crime* (New York: McGraw-Hill, 1975), pp. 5-30. Copyright © 1975 by Freda Adler and used with permission of McGraw-Hill Book Company.

Marge is forty-three years old, with brown hair headed for gray and muscular legs somewhat the worse for wear. Soft-spoken and hovering just this side of being quite plump, Marge has spent a good many years on those legs earning a living. Since her husband disappeared one day eighteen years ago, she has worked a total of fifteen years either as a waitress or a barmaid. During those years, she supported and raised two sons, one of whom eventually worked his way through a small state college and is currently a teacher. The other one, younger, died four years ago as a result of a bad bag of heroin he pumped into his arm.

Deserted, with two small children, Marge was forced to get the first job she had ever had. It was as a barmaid, in a small restaurant-lounge. Not long afterward, she gave her first serious thought to being a prostitute—like a fellow barmaid who was developing a very lucrative following among the bar's male clientele.

But soon Marge gave up the idea of prostitution—partly because of her figure which she didn't feel was suited for the trade, and partly because of her "strong Catholic upbringing." She explained, "I just never felt right in that kind of thing. Now it didn't bother me that other girls I knew were turning tricks; I just couldn't bring myself to stay with it. I guess underneath it all,.I was more strait-laced than I knew."

In place of prostitution, Marge found a more acceptable degree of reprehensibility in shoplifting. "Boosting" from department stores became a regular habit with her. At first she began by putting small items, like watches, into her pocket. Later, she progressed to more sophisticated methods. She wore large baggy coats which could conceal things like toasters and radios, then began to sew large bag-like pockets inside the coats to facilitate even larger load handling. She shoplifted for years, and was caught only once. On that occasion she was allowed to go free on her own recognizance and, although threatened with further prosecution, never heard of the incident again.

Five years ago Marge robbed her first bank. The planning took her some months. "It was something that came to me all of a sudden. . . . I had a couple of big debts and I was getting tired of working like I was. . . . I wanted a bit of easy time. I mean, the kids were getting older and I was still working and, after all those years, I needed a break. I guess maybe I got the idea from watching TV or something, I don't remember. But it surprised me; like, I first thought of it seriously and thought, 'No, I couldn't do that . . . I'm a woman,' you know? But when I thought more about it, what the hell, it didn't seem so bad. The other girls I knew were boosting or [credit] carding. They said I must be crazy when we talked about it one day. We never really thought about a woman hitting a bank before . . . but then soon after that, I heard on the radio of a lady who hit a bank and got away and I figured, what the hell, if she can do it, why can't I?"

After many months of careful planning and observation, Marge attempted to rob one particular bank. That first attempt was a failure. She walked in and approached the teller's window, but was unable to go through with the robbery. "I just asked for change for a ten-dollar bill and felt like a real smacked-ass to myself." Two months later, though, she went through with it and went on to rob two more banks before she was finally caught. After the first one it seemed easy to her. "I just walked in, walked out, and went home to count the money. I always thought it would be a lot harder . . . a lot more dangerous. I did take a gun each time, but it was never loaded and I only really had to show it to one teller. The others just put the money in the bag when I asked them to. . . . I remember that first job. It was like a cheap high afterward. I went home and turned on the radio to see what they would say about me on the news."

To her disappointment, after that first heist, police described her to the news media as a "male dressed in women's clothing." That upset Marge a bit. "Well, I mean, I know I'm no beauty queen, but I didn't think I was that bad . . . and who the hell ever saw a man with plucked eyebrows?"

During her third try, Marge was stopped on her way out of the bank by policemen responding to a silent alarm. She gave up peacefully. ("What the hell else could I do, the gun wasn't loaded or anything.") She is currently serving an indefinite prison term for robbery.

In a number of ways, Marge is typical of a new breed of women criminals making their appearance across America. She, along with thousands of others, has stepped across the imaginary boundary line which once separated crimes into "masculine" and "feminine" categories. Marge is a member of the new "liberation movement" which is spreading through the ranks of the nation's female offenders, but Marge would be the last person in the world to accredit her actions to any sort of a "liberation." She, like the majority of incarcerated women throughout the country, comes from a lower socioeconomic level and tends to identify with a value code embracing the "traditional" image of women.

"Most of the women we've gotten in the past have had what you could call a 'traditional' view of themselves as women," explained one female counselor who has worked for nearly two decades in a major East Coast correctional institution for women. "They have very strong feelings about what a woman 'should be' and that image has to do with the woman mostly as a homebody who has babies, gratifies her man's sexual wishes and otherwise keeps her mouth shut. Despite the fact that they themselves may have been quite aggressive, they hold a view that 'good' women are passive.

"I don't mean that in a derogatory way, but they tend to be from lower socioeconomic backgrounds and, among other things, they are not particularly well read or educated. Their thinking about a woman's place is even more strongly stereotyped than other women in their same age bracket who have broader, more sophisticated backgrounds.

"Prisons are just a microcosm of larger society, so like everywhere else, there is a great deal of friction between the older women and the new 'lib' type we are currently getting. Perhaps that friction is a bit more intense here than on the outside."

Marge will not tolerate the mention of women's liberation; she considers it synonymous with lesbian. She feels that "women's lib" is an organization of "kooks," and scoffs at the mention of any connection between her latest criminal actions and the beliefs of the female emancipation movement. Ironically, her feelings are similar to those expressed by countless prison administrators, police officials, and other law-enforcement authorities who believe that the women's liberation movement is in no way connected to the sharply rising crime rate of women in America. Indeed, many of them won't admit that such a female crime wave even exists. The facts, however, show not only that it exists, but also that it is growing at an alarming rate.

Part of the difficulty in understanding changes in female crime stems from the blind spots which have obstructed society's vision of women in general. Throughout centuries of male domination, even men of good will have persistently tried to unravel the mystery of women as if women were a species apart, as if women did not share the male need for status and security. If mystery there is, it is why men have been unaware that women have the same basic motivations as men; why they have exaggerated whatever natural differences may exist between the sexes; and why they have all the while pretended in their most self-righteous Henry Higgins manner that they really wanted women to be like men. The understanding of women has been unnecessarily mystified because we have reasoned backward from the observation that their techniques and approaches (wiles, if you will) are different from men's, to the unwarranted conclusion that they have basically different motivations and goals.

Once such mental sets become established, they are difficult to eradicate, for several reasons: they preserve the power structure of the male hierarchy; they form a thought pattern which tends to limit observations and speculations to preformed notions; and they are inherently satisfying as security mechanisms even to the disadvantaged group. It is little wonder that women are an enigma, if not anathema, to themselves and others.

"The fundamental fault of the female character," declared Schopenhauer, "is that it has no sense of justice." Women have been presented as being childish, devious, indirect, petty, seductive, inappropriately domineering, and incomprehensibly manipulative. It is not difficult to see that, aside from total submission, these are the only options available to the weak in dealing with the strong. To believe that these techniques are preferred by women when the more direct masculine approaches are available is to miss the point of female psychology—namely, that there is no female psychology different from the human psychology which also governs men. Isben's Nora said it simply and completely: "I believe that before all else, I am a human being." Not surprisingly, it took a woman, Karen Horney, to dispute Sigmund Freud's assumption that women labored through life under the spell of penis envy. It is not man's penis that a woman strives for but his power, and until recently the only way to achieve that has been through apparently paradoxical indirection. The phrase "she stoops to conquer," from the title of Oliver Goldsmith's play, perhaps sums up the method and the madness of women.

Interesting analogies to traditional man-woman relationships may be seen in the behavior of our closest animal relatives, the social primates. Like humans, and perhaps in response to similar biological imperatives,[1] they form structured social organizations in which emotional security and high status appear to be synonymous. Among subhuman primates where size and muscle mass usually determine dominance,[2] mature males are the dominant sex and the position of females is primarily determined by their ability to consort with and maintain relationships with high-ranking males. This is necessarily so where muscle is the arbiter of power. The parallels to human society are clear; but so are the differences, for technology has been redefining the criteria for power.

Men have historically achieved individual status through their domination of other men, labeling them in such a way that they could be perceived as not fully human and, therefore, not entitled to human rights and dignity. Men as a group have done the same to women. The primary access that women have had to status has been through men, and the price they paid was conformity to male standards for femininity—not only in how they should act, but also in how they should think and feel. For her pains, a woman was often allowed to stand close, but rarely high. Tragically, she was playing a game of submission she could not win. The more closely she approximated the mold of femininity, the less she was respected as a person in her own right. Tennyson paternalistically dubbed her "the lesser man," and LaBruyère contemptuously declared that "women have no moral sense; they rely for their behavior upon the men they love." This notion was as injurious as it was uncharitable because it led the woman as well as the man into thinking about her as an inexplicable and irrational contradiction. What other choice did she have?

All that is changing. Women are no longer behaving like subhuman primates with only one option. Medical, educational, economic, political, and technological advances have freed women from unwanted pregnancies, provided them with male occupational skills, and equalized their strength with weapons. Is it any wonder that once women were armed with male opportunities they should strive for status, criminal as well as civil, through established male hierarchial channels? The fact that women are surging so readily into male positions suggests that role playing is no more congenial to their nature than it is to men's. As with the landmark judicial decisions which broadened civil liberties for whites as well as blacks, the liberation of women has necessarily liberated men from fixed and unnatural postures.

The question we should be asking is not why women are committing male crimes, but what has taken them so long to start and why is the time now propitious. From this perspective, women are no more enigmatic than men. Like other oppressed classes they have always had the same aspirations as the dominant class but, lacking direct means, have utilized ploys, ruses, and indirection.[3]

Their resort to petty social gambits and petty crimes was a reflection more of their petty strengths than their petty drives.

"It was the radios that changed things for me: like I got a whole new look at what I was doing," said a female inmate at a California prison. Sentenced in connection with a number of drug and drug-related charges, she said that she had supported her drug addiction in part by working as a prostitute. And, according to her account, she had also moonlighted as a shoplifter . . . for a start.

"I needed more money, you know, and I was always taking these small transistor radios because there was this guy who would take all the radios I could give him for five or ten dollars each. So I needed more money for drugs, and the only thing I could think of at first was 'take more radios.' Then one day it hit me. Wow! It was weird. What the hell was I doing just taking radios all these months? I was knocking myself out for a bunch of five-buck radios. I don't know what it was at the time, but like, I couldn't see myself taking anything other than that. Like I had a block or something. Then it was like a flash. I got with a friend—she was strung out too—and we started taking color-TV sets. We got them from the loading docks of a couple of stores which left them sitting there for a while if you caught the trucks just right. We just picked one up and pushed it into the trunk and drove off. I got about a dozen of them until I got busted, you know, on the drug thing.

"I can see it now . . . how dumb I was. I mean, if I was going to rip something off, why the hell didn't I take Cadillacs for all that time instead of some goddamned radios? It took me a long while to see that. A long while."

Women are no longer indentured to the kitchens, baby carriages, or bedrooms of America. The skein of myths about women is unraveling, the chains have been pried loose, and there will be no turning back to the days when women found it necessary to justify their existence by producing babies or cleaning houses. Allowed their freedom for the first time, women—by the tens of thousands—have chosen to desert those kitchens and plunge exuberantly into the formerly all-male quarters of the working world.

There are now female admirals, longshorewomen, stevedores, and seagoing sailors (tattoos and all); there are policewomen patrolling in one-person cars, women FBI agents, and female sky marshals. Women can now be found clinging to telephone poles as installers and line workers; peering from behind acetylene welding torches and seated behind the wheels of over-the-road tractor-trailer trucks. They can be found at work as fork-lift drivers and crane operators, pipe fitters and carpenters, mail carriers and morticians, commercial airline pilots and jet-engine mechanics. Women now serve as Congressional pages. They have run for, and won, a substantial number of powerful positions throughout the American political system; and ever-increasing numbers of women continue to become judges, lawyers, and high-level executives in industry and government.

On the lighter side, many women have produced an almost carnival-like atmosphere in breaking through the discrimination barriers in such bastions of male supremacy as the Clam Broth House of Hoboken and McSorley's Old Ale House in Manhattan. They have burned their bras and staged hundreds of theater-of-the-absurd antics to dramatize their point. But these stag-bar crashers and sign-wavers are few compared with the waves of women who have quietly and effectively set up shop in a wide variety of job fields across the nation.

To be sure, the gains grow slowly, and sometimes painfully, but nevertheless women are pushing their way into—and succeeding at—innumerable jobs, occupations, and positions traditionally thought to be "for men only"! Between 1900 and 1972 the percentage of females in the total labor force has risen from 18 per cent to 37 per cent, remaining stable at about 23 per cent between 1900 and 1940, but rapidly accelerating during World War II and continuing to rise at a steady rate.[4]

But women, like men, do not live by bread alone. Almost every other aspect of their life has been similarly altered. The changing status of women as it affects family, marriage, employment, and social position has been well documented by all types of sociologists.[5] But there is a curious hiatus: the movement for full equality has a darker side which has been slighted even by the scientific community. In a recent issue of a respected sociology journal devoted entirely to the changing role of females in a changing society, not one of the twenty-one papers dealt with female criminality.[6] Therefore, it should not be surprising that this shady aspect of liberation has also escaped the scrutiny of the media, of the general public, and even of the law-enforcement agencies which have the advantage of early contact.

In the same way that women are demanding equal opportunity in fields of legitimate endeavor, a similar number of determined women are forcing their way into the world of major crimes.

• A Florida female parolee: "I don't think women are sitting down and saying, 'Oh, gee, I'll be liberated. I'll rob a bank.' Things are different today. I was living alone for years. It wasn't any real thought of 'liberation' that had to do with what I was doing. I wanted the money. If I was going to put myself out, I intended to aim as high as I could. I got caught, but a lot of others don't. Off the record I'll tell you, they'd never pinch me again because I've learned a lot now. I'd be a lot more careful."

• A Pennsylvania female inmate: "I'm not the only one. I know a lot of sisters who got tired of hanging with some dude who took all their money while they took all the heat that was coming down. I know one sister—she cut her pimp up over a five-dollar bill. It wasn't the money, see. It just got to be too much for her. I get out of here and you better believe that no man's going to do a thing on me again. I don't need them. I got it together for myself now. I can handle my own action."

• A Chicago female inmate: "It's like what they say, you know, about mountains. You climb them because they're there. Well, that's the way it is with banks and department stores; that's where the money is. It's not a question of money. That's it. Money."

It is this segment of women who are pushing into—and succeeding at—crimes which were formerly committed by males only. Females like Marge are now being found not only robbing banks singlehandedly, but also committing assorted armed robberies, muggings, loan-sharking operations, extortion, murders, and a wide variety of other aggressive, violence-oriented crimes which previously involved only men.

Like her sisters in legitimate fields, the female criminal is fighting for her niche in the hierarchy, for, curiously enough, the barriers of male chauvinism in some areas of criminal activity are no less formidable than those which confront female newcomers in the world of business. There is, perhaps, no more macho group than the traditional "family" units of organized crime. "It was just a while ago that we got our first female loan shark here in the city," said a New York assistant district attorney. "That was something new. That was strictly an organized crime thing in the past. She was a free-lancer, though. Even today, you don't get women operating on that level with the mob. They wouldn't stand for it. In a lot of ways they are a very conservative bunch of guys."

In a book which probes the inner logistics of the Mafia, Nicholas Gage points out the strict roles which are currently allowed for women with syndicate families:

> In the Mafia a woman may be a means to a profitable alliance with another Mafia "family"; a showcase for displaying her husband's wealth, status, and power; a valuable piece of property; a loyal helpmate; a good cook; a showy and ego-boosting mistress. But what she may never be is a liberated woman.[7]

Given the status of women in the Mafia, the organization clearly has a long way to go before it can be considered an equal-opportunity employer. While it is not likely that we will see the ascension of a family "Godmother" in the near future, it does appear certain that the status of women in the Mafia may well change, if only for purely pragmatic reasons. The mob, like other successful organizations, reacts to competition and accomplishment. They are not likely to ignore the increasing numbers of women who are using guns, knives, and wits to establish themselves as full human beings, as capable of violence and aggression as any man.

By every indicator available, female criminals appear to be surpassing males in the rate of increase for almost every major crime. Although males continue to commit the greater absolute number of offenses, it is the women who are committing those same crimes at yearly rates of increase now running as high as six and seven times faster than males.[8]

Like her legitimate-based sister, the female criminal knows too much to pretend, or return to her former role as a second-rate criminal confined to "feminine" crimes such as shoplifting and prostitution. She has had a taste of financial victory. In some cases, she has had a taste of blood. Her appetite, however, appears to be only whetted.

"Crime is like anything else; the people learn and explore wider areas as they go along and gain confidence," explained a Los Angeles police lieutenant, who was openly dismayed while speaking of the increasing numbers of women being brought into his station house. "You know how it is with a child . . . you can watch it grow and develop. It's like that with women we're getting. First it was a shock to be getting so many females. Now it's repeaters. You can see them grow in confidence. Like they opened a new door and realized all of a sudden that they can walk through it. The second time, they don't hesitate; they barge right in. The only way I can think to describe it is that it's like a lion cub. O.K., it gets its first taste of red meat. It doesn't wait to be fed any longer. It goes out and begins to learn how to hunt. That is what I see with a lot of these women. They've had the taste. It's not as hard as they thought to hit a drugstore or whatever. They'll go into the slammer with others and they learn to be better as criminals. It's started now and you can't break the cycle. You can only wish it hadn't started."

The extent to which women have thrown themselves into criminal endeavors can be approximated from the FBI's yearly Uniform Crime Reports, the closest thing the United States has to a comprehensive national statistical overview of its crime situation. In spite of a number of methodological problems[9]—such as a variability in number and distribution of sources, erratic reporting, and inconsistencies in adhering to a universal code of crime definitions—these statistics nevertheless suggest broad trends of criminal behavior on a national scale. During the twelve years from 1960 through 1972, the FBI monitored 2430 law-enforcement agencies across the country, recording the number and causes for all arrests. While arrests are not synonymous with crimes, they are generally a reliable indication that a crime has been committed. As one might expect, the absolute number of males arrested exceeds that of females, but what is noteworthy is that the arrest rate among females is rising nearly three times faster than males. During the twelve-year period between 1960 and 1972 the number of women arrested for robbery rose by 277 per cent, while the male figure rose 169 per cent. Dramatic differences are found in embezzlement (up 280 per cent for women, 50 per cent for men), larceny (up 303 per cent for women, 82 per cent for men), and burglary (up 168 per cent for women, 63 per cent for men).[10] Except for parity in the categories of murder and aggravated assault, the picture of female arrest rates rising several times faster than male arrest rates is a consistent one for all offenses.

Murder and aggravated assault, curiously, remain the exceptions. In these categories, the rates of men are not significantly different from those of women, although both are rising. Since these are primarily crimes of passion in which well over half of the victim-offender relationships are interpersonal,[11] as opposed to the economically motivated offenses, it would appear that the liberated female criminals, like their male counterparts, are chiefly interested in improving their financial circumstances and only secondarily in committing violence.

A thirty-eight-year-old Miami, Florida, woman currently on parole explains: "I had a gun when I went into this one place . . . it was a motel. But I never would have used it. I wanted the cash. I didn't want to hurt anyone. Most places employees understand that. They give you the cash quietly. They understand what's going on . . . you're not out to get them, you just want the money. It's a transaction between you and a large institution. There is no reason why they should get hurt. I think most of the people in the joint [jail] work the same way. It's not like they get a gun and decide to kill someone to get some money. Most are sorry that they even had a gun with them. It's harder that way when you get busted. There are some who are into the guns; who'll blast someone just for the hell of it, but they're a separate breed. Most of us are just in it for the bread. That's all. Guns, knives, and the rest are a sort of necessary window dressing . . . which at times can get out of hand."

Reports from other countries confirm the American experience that as the social and economic disparity between the sexes diminishes, there is a reciprocal increase in female crime.[12] Western Europe and New Zealand, for example, where women enjoy a high degree of equality with men, also report a rise in female criminality. The disparities between the male and female crime rate are now even narrowing in developing countries such as India, where the social distance between the sexes has traditionally been greater.

Some criminologists[13] believe that this principle applies equally well to different groups within a nation. Black males and females for instance, are more similar in their crime rates than their white counterparts, and they are also closer in their social standing to each other than are white males and females. Black women never fought for this position of parity vis-à-vis their men—economic necessity dictated the terms of the pecking order. These examples serve to verify the proposition that women are psychologically more similar to than different from men and that they are best understood as fellow humans than as a group apart.

If the adult arrest rates say anything about what is happening now, the crime rates for persons under eighteen say something perhaps even more about the woman of the future. The criminal behavior of the female juvenile closely parallels that of her adult sister,[14] portending a protracted association between females and crime. During the period between 1960 and 1972 the number of females under eighteen arrested for robbery jumped by 508 per cent, while the juvenile male figure rose 250 per cent. Likewise, other figures mounted: larceny (up 334 per cent for girls, 84 per cent for boys), burglary (up 177 per cent for girls, 70 per cent for boys), auto theft (up 110 per cent for girls, 38 per cent for boys). In this area, at least, there is no generation gap. Similar to their adult counterparts, there was no significant difference in the arrest increase for murder between males and females, suggesting that economic goals take precedence over violent ones for little sister also.

Aside from the victims, the people most directly and dangerously involved with criminals are the police. They work at the crossroads of the criminal world and society at large, and therefore give us a unique perspective, which has the advantage of being formed from direct contact with the events.

Lieutenant Peter Quinn has spent the last fifteen years with the New York City police force. Quinn's is a city notorious for having the worst happen first. What occurs criminally, as well as culturally, in New York City has an uncanny habit of being a harbinger of things to come in the rest of the country.

"Oh, it's been very obvious to me over these last years that something is happening out there," said the lieutenant, motioning toward the window in his office at the 77th Precinct Headquarters. Outside, the Bedford-Stuyvesant section was teeming in the noonday sun. "We're seeing more and more women all the time. I never really thought much about it . . . as a trend, I mean. I suppose it has to do with women's own image of themselves . . . you know, women know more about what they want, and they want more of the things that men used to have. Whatever the reasons, we see a lot more women purse snatchers, robbers, and a lot more mixed robbery teams, with men and women working as equal partners. Before, it would be only men.

"Even so," Quinn continued, "we're all still a bit less suspicious of women than we are of men. That may change, though, in the future. . . . Like I remember a few years ago, when you would have hesitated to ever put handcuffs on a woman. Not today . . . you *have* to put cuffs on them now. They'll get you just like any man will, if you don't. They've proved that to me."

A less official, perhaps, but no less authoritative view of what is happening to women can be heard from the taxi drivers who must drive in Quinn's area, as well as throughout the rest of the city. "Now I don't come here during the night," explained one driver headed out of Bedford-Stuyvesant. "I know the law says you gotta take fares anywhere, but not me. I don't get killed to collect a salary for nobody. And it ain't just men. Twice I've had women trying to pull something on me in the last year. They had guns, the whole works. And that ain't just me talking. Go see the other drivers around town . . . see if they ain't been hit by women. It's gotten awful here lately. You can't trust nobody. Men, women, they're all the same. Don't trust none of them."

In midtown New York, at the police administration building on Broome Street, Lieutenant Lucy Acerra told a similar story. The lieutenant is coordinator of the eight precincts in the city which have female police officers. In her twenty years on the force she has come in contact with innumerable women offenders.

"Now today, the majority of women you see are narcotic addicts. But even they have changed . . . their attitude about themselves, the world. Years ago, you'd have a female addict, she'd be docile, almost embarrassed. Very quiet. Today . . . they come in the door screaming and never let up. They are much more demanding than ever before."

Not far away from Acerra's office, another lieutenant in the district attorney's office shook his head while telling how the city recently apprehended its first female loan shark. It is an indication that women are getting into the nitty-gritty, big-time underworld type of operation.

During the 1971–1972 period, 3742 cities across the country reported figures similar to those which troubled New York.[15] Each had its regional peculiarities, but the basic theme was the same. In that year, arrests for index crimes (those crimes considered by the FBI to be serious and to have high reportability) of urban males under eighteen decreased by 1 per cent, while female juveniles increased by 6 per cent. For adults, the picture was similar—males dropping by 0.1 per cent and females rising by 6 per cent. Nor was this trend confined to the cities. Out past the suburbs into the traditionally conservative areas, female arrests for major crimes increased by 14 per cent, while males declined by 0.2 per cent.[16] Clearly, the same drama was playing to different crowds, city by city and section by section, across the country—and the villain in each case was the female.

In 1968, the women of America passed something of a milestone in their criminal development: while their crime rate on all fronts was quietly increasing, the first of their number made her way into the FBI's infamous "ten most wanted" list.[17] The list had been in existence since 1950 and had never included a woman before. So on December 28, 1968, it was a novelty to see Ruth Eisemann-Schier's name added for her part in a ransom-kidnaping. But the novelty soon wore off. Five months later the second woman, Marie Dean Arrington, appeared on the list. A convicted murderer, she was sought for escaping from a Florida prison farm—she had scaled two barbed-wire fences and disappeared. Since that time, the inclusion of women on the "ten most wanted" list has become normal procedure. During the past few years, women included on the list have been wanted for murder, bank robbery, kidnaping, and a variety of violent, revolutionary acts.[18]

This new national wave crested early in 1974 with the alleged kidnaping of newspaper heiress Patricia Hearst, who was later apparently converted into an enthusiastic member of the Symbionese Liberation Army. The bizarre, tumultuous, and seemingly short-lived era of the SLA may have marked a major turning point for American women. It was the peak of the movement of radically politicized females away from the historical quiescence which so characterized the preceding "silent generation" of the 1950s. In the 1960s, America became aware that increasing numbers of women were involved in the tide of social revolution that was spreading across the country, often in the form of riots, student strikes, and other types of urban guerrilla warfare. By the 1970s, it had become even more apparent that what was occurring was a revolution within a revolution. Despite their broad political pronouncements, what the new revolutionaries wanted was not simply urban social gains, but sexual equality. With a good deal of humor, the media noted that the notorious and highly violence-prone "weath-

ermen" of the late 1960s changed their name to the unisexual "Weather Underground" in the 1970s. It was no longer humorous, however, when that same
revolutionary feminism began to manifest itself in the persons of such women as
Nancy Ling Perry, Patricia Soltysik, and Camilla Hall.

These three women—all white, middle-class, and highly educated—were the
formative core of the Symbionese Liberation Army, a group of no more than a
dozen, which distinguished itself with an ongoing demolition derby of blazing
guns and falling bodies up and down the California coast. Along with their bar-
rage of volatile rhetoric, their actions included ravaging banks, robbing commercial establishments, and assassinating victims with cyanide-tipped bullets. While
the entire world watched on TV, the SLA surfaced for its criminal activities
seemingly at will, only to sink into hiding again, easily evading one of the largest
and most intense manhunts ever organized in the country's history. Curiously,
the national reaction to the SLA's maniacal escapades seemed to focus less on
the actual violence than on the group's truly unique sexual emphasis. While
"Field Marshal Cinque" was initially heralded as the "leader" of the SLA, authorities soon came to believe otherwise. Cinque was quickly identified as Donald
DeFreeze, a black man who had recently escaped from jail. As police uncovered
some of the former hiding places of the SLA, it became apparent that the women
who had organized the group had decided that it was a symbolic necessity for a
Third World revolutionary cadre to be headed by a black male. DeFreeze was the
chosen figurehead. But proof of the feminine leadership was found in much of
the voluminous written material recovered from various hideouts of the SLA—
the phrase "men and women" in various literary tracts was edited to read
"women and men."

The group's chief theorist was Patricia Soltysik, who, in background and tem-
perment, was quite typical of other SLA women. The daughter of a well-to-do
pharmacist, an honor student in high school prior to winning a scholarship to
Berkeley, she was described by former teachers as "a born leader," "a tough
competitor," and "unstoppable."[10] By traditional standards of scholastic
achievement and physical charm, she was an All-American Girl before she was
radicalized. That such women turned so drastically toward a new and highly
volatile identity caused a good portion of the nation to ask incredulously, "How
could women do this sort of thing?" Perhaps the question itself was the very
point of the episode. The fires which consumed the ramshackle Los Angeles
house where the small band staged its last shoot-out also burned away a large
part of the prevailing American illusions about women.

Women's unaccustomed involvement in crimes which require high levels of
violence or potential violence is not limited to the sensational, but can be seen
in other, less publicized areas. In the cities, for instance, young girls are now
taking to the streets just as boys have traditionally done. It has now become
quite common for adolescent girls to participate in muggings, burglaries, and
extortion rings which prey on schoolmates. Perhaps the most telling sign of
change on this level can be found in a closer inspection of the gangs which have

terrorized cities for years. Gang activity is no longer the all-male domain it once was. Girls can now be found participating in all gang activities with a greater degree of equality. Indeed, in New York City there are currently two all-girl gangs.[20] In London, where British statistics reflect a similar female crime wave, female adolescents have become a problem of major proportions.[21]

In one Piccadilly Circus incident, several young women attacked and severely beat a business executive. After taking the man's wallet and watch, the females—described later as being "in their late teens or early twenties"—attacked another man who attempted to aid the victim. That man fled. Finally, the women were approached by a lone, uniformed law officer whom they also managed to knock unconscious before they made their successful escape from the scene. Scotland Yard and public officials have recently been voicing alarm and dismay about these gangs of young girls now numbering in the dozens, who roam the city streets.[22] Armed with switchblades, razors, clubs, and fists, their members are known to delight in "granny bashing," the attack of elderly ladies, usually at night.

Throughout the United States also, it appears that older ladies of the streets are assuming a more aggressive attitude toward the world. Prostitutes—formerly considered docile body-peddlers—are now taking a much harder line toward their work and clients. In New York City and other major urban areas, hookers who have taken to mugging people on the sidewalk have become a substantial police problem. Streetwalkers from coast to coast—a large percentage of whom are now narcotic addicts—are demonstrating a new willingness to moonlight on their primary occupation and supplement their income by "rolling" their "marks" or sticking up innocent passersby.

In recent years, the prostitutes of New York have been in the headlines for a number of sensational crimes: Pasquale Bottero, an Italian glass-company executive, was stabbed to death by prostitutes outside the New York Hilton; Charles Addams, the cartoonist, rebuffed two streetwalkers' advances and received a splash of acid in his face; Franz Josef Strauss, the former defense minister of West Germany, was severely beaten and robbed near the Plaza Hotel by hookers. And these are only the headline-worthy instances.

Aside from such obvious examples of the changing way that women relate to the world, numerous other signs, somewhat more subtle but no less important, indicate where women are going. For one thing, along with killing other people more often than before, women are now taking their own lives at a steadily increasing rate. Women accounted for 35 per cent of the successful suicide attempts in Los Angeles in 1960;[23] by 1970, the figure had risen to 45 per cent, and it continues to rise.

The suicide rate is just one indicator of the inner conflicts which women are undergoing at this time, conflicts which affect their propensities toward behavior patterns which are, if not fully criminal, at least marginally deviant. In a recent study of women's role in modern society and its relation to stress, it was found that women were suffering higher rates of mental illness than men.[24] Apparently, they are having a more difficult time coping with the new status for which they strive. This is also evident in the number of women who are now dying from, or being treated for, coronary and other stress-related ailments previously thought to be "male diseases." These inner conflicts are also causing more women to involve themselves not only in divorces, but also in an unprecedented number of family desertions. Marriage counselors, psychiatrists, and detective agencies report that more women than ever before are simply walking out and leaving husband and children behind. A mother who deserted her family was unheard of a decade ago, although the practice was quite frequent among men.

Thus it is that in the middle third of the twentieth century, we are witnessing the simultaneous rise and fall of women. Rosie the Riveter of World War II vintage has become Robin the Rioter or Rhoda the Robber in the Vietnam era. Women have lost more than their chains. For better and worse, they have lost many of the restraints which kept them within the law.

The forces that have propelled females into parity with males have been as blind as justice to which side of the law they landed on. The increase in the incidence of suicide and of previously "male" psychosomatic illnesses, such as ulcers and hypertension, are some indication of the price in stress and stress-induced breakdowns that women have paid for this rite of passage. Women—criminals and legitimate workers alike—are caught up in the gears of a society which is skidding into a drastic turn, and, inevitably, some of those gears—and their cogs—are going to be broken before the turn is completed and a steady course is once again established. Increasing numbers of broken gears and bits of flying debris will be found leaping from bridges, wandering desolate city streets, and entering banks with pistols in their pockets. If our society is going to protect itself from them—as well as offer them any meaningful help once they are apprehended—it must make an effort to understand what makes females criminal. It must understand that criminal women are first human, second female, and third criminal. No one of these facets of their existence can be properly understood without the other.

An inmate at Muncy prison which has recently gone coed, integrating males into a formerly all-female population: "I felt a real change when they brought men here. I think the whole place did. After a while, I was starting to feel like a machine. Sometimes I didn't even take a shower for days. It wasn't that I wanted to be dirty, but after a while you get to feeling, like who really gives a shit what you look like in this joint. It was like I had given up on myself. Then they brought some men in. Now I got a husband outside, so it's not like I'm going to try to make one of the new guys. But just being around them made me feel alive again. I even began with the make-up and all again. I felt, well, like a human instead of a machine or something."

A counselor at Purdy prison in Washington State, where the female inmates are regularly taken to outside social affairs to mingle with males from
a nearby prison farm: "It's like a breath of life to the girls. You can see it.
That's what has to be remembered. O.K., these people are criminals, but
they are also humans and women with a very strong need to feel like
women. It can make or break their whole attitude for the rest of their life."

The women of America underwent soul-shaking changes in the 1960s. By the
end of that decade, the drive which began as sporadic protests had become a
trend—"women's liberation" emerged as a well-publicized, well-organized movement, complete with slogans, dues, and membership cards. Most of the country
came to identify the entire female emancipation effort with that organized and
highly vocal group known as "women libbers," but the actual "lib" organizations
are only the tip of the iceberg. The impetus for women's rights and equality of
the sexes began in earnest in that decade. At that time it was unheralded as a
movement, unseen as an organizational process, and unappreciated as a social
revolution. Such a trend did not gain its popularity or momentum because of a
sudden, spontaneous recognition of the oppression of women. Rather, the new,
broad-based awareness of women's place and potential developed side by side
with the civil-rights and antiwar movements, confirming Karl Marx's contention
that "social progress can be measured with precision by the social position of the
female sex."

In the early sixties, civil-rights actions swirled across the country with the
fervor of a revitalization movement, challenging Americans to reaffirm their
commitment to equality before the law, and redefining that equality to include
those previously alienated by color or age or sex. Man's characteristic tendency
to assign other people—whether they were Asians, blacks, young, poor, or
women—to a subhuman status which barred them from equal protection under
law was the real issue of the civil-rights movements, and women were now ready
to recognize their stake in it. Why this moment was propitious for recognition is
difficult to say. The theme of women as a suppressed social class had been carefully documented in 1953 by Simone de Beauvoir in her book *The Second Sex*,
but it failed to develop as a serious national concern until the mid-sixties.
America of the mid-sixties was rife with disillusionment and ripe for change. We
were fighting what Omar Bradley called "the wrong war at the wrong place at
the wrong time, and with the wrong enemy"—liberals were adding, "for the
wrong reason." In this climate of disillusionment with leadership that was white,
male, and over thirty, change was inevitable, and the seeds of liberation rooted
in fertile soil. By the decade's end, large numbers of American women in all walks
of life had begun to see themselves as Betty Friedan had portrayed them in *The
Feminine Mystique*: a systematically and subtly suppressed majority whose real
security lay in the strength of their own right arm, and whose time of delivery
had arrived.

Many of these believers gravitated to organizations such as NOW, the National Organization for Women, which has a current membership of 18,000 in 255 chapters in 48 states.[25] The women's liberation movements suffered several distortions in the press and, at the same time, added a few bruises of its own image via the actions of a few of its more outspoken members. Hence, "women's lib" came to designate—perhaps for the majority of Americans—organized groups of women who were primarily shrill-voiced witches with clenched fists and slovenly, unloosed breasts. Not so today.

There was, and is, more to women's lib. Much more. And the portrait is changing. The organization and its goals are becoming separated from its antiquated image. There is an ever-growing national awareness of women's rights which is perhaps best described as the "new feminism." The new feminism is not an organized movement, it does not hold meetings or press conferences. It is an all-pervasive consciousness which has permeated to virtually every level of womanhood in America.

The new feminism pertains to the women who may deny any sympathy for the formalized action, but who have recently secured their first job since marriage or decided to go back to school. It applies to the women who staunchly defend their "right to be feminine," and their right to define "feminine" as a variety of human rather than as a complement of masculine. They are standing up and speaking without apology at parent-teacher meetings, they are organizing demonstrations, walking picket lines, and influencing decisions at all levels of their community. It includes the nuns who are asking for rights more closely aligned with the rights which priests enjoy, and the housewives who have come to expect their husbands to share more of the duties of the home. It also means sexually honest women who expect the same orgastic satisfaction as men, and who are requiring that men do something about it. And most relevant to our subject, it describes the women who have concluded that prostitution and shoplifting are not their style: embezzlement, robbery, and assault are more congenial to their self-image.

"You wouldn't catch me doing no boosting," said one female inmate in New York who was somewhat offended by the inference that she might have been a shoplifter. The woman—in her late twenties—found the idea of shoplifting or "boosting" undignified. She did not like "small stuff." Records say she was involved in a robbery of a large movie-theater ticket office. Other inmates privately related that the same woman was nearly killed in recent underworld warfare which broke out when she was thought to have "ripped off" a local heroin dealer for a few thousand dollars' worth of his product. The others spoke of her escapades with envy and obvious admiration.

The entrance of women into the major leagues of crime underscores the point that the incidence and kinds of crime are more closely associated with social than sexual factors. This is so for at least three reasons. First, while cupidity may be universal, ability and opportunity are less evenly distributed. Housewives might pilfer from the supermarket while doing the grocery shopping, but could not embezzle from a corporation unless they work out of the executive office. Secondly, since a crime is a transgression as socially defined by the group in power, authorities are prone to overlook upper-class practices and lean a bit too heavily on the lower class. "The law," declared Anatole France, "forbids the rich as well as the poor from sleeping under bridges and stealing bread in the marketplace." Arrests for prostitution are a pertinent example. If sex on the open market is an illegal commodity, then panalties should fall on the buyer as well as the seller, particularly if it can be established that the buyer understood the nature of the transaction and was a material participant. But such is not the case. While prostitution continues to be a crime for which a significant number of women are arrested every year, the number of males arrested for consorting with prostitutes is so small that it does not even merit a special category in the Uniform Crime Reports. The third reason why kinds of crimes are more closely linked with social roles than sex has to do with mental sets. According to the group-system hypothesis,[26] behavior is directed by a largely conscious desire to please one's own significant groups, and by a predominantly unconscious tendency to conform to an early ingrained set of attitudes. So decisive is this set for the way we think and feel and act that few people breach its boundaries, even in imagination, even in deviance. We go crazy and we go criminal along the well-worn paths that our "mazeway" has constructed for us. Running amuck is not something that Bostonians do, nor do sex-kittens rob banks—they peddle their bodies as untold generations of sex-kittens before them have done. How else can we understand the female (or, for that matter, male) offender except in the context of her social role? The mother becomes the child-beater, the shopper the shoplifter, and the sex-object the prostitute. Adolescent girls have a particularly difficult task because they are attempting to negotiate puberty with nowhere near the spatial and sexual freedom of males. That they often deviate outside their narrow confines is understandable.

In the emergence of women as a socially rising group, we are witnessing an interesting phenomenon which has implications for other upwardly mobile groups. As they become more visible in positions of prestige and power, they receive more attention from the media, and are thus further bolstered in their rising achievement. Old mental sets of devaluation and self-contempt gradually yield to new ones of pride, and sometimes an overcompensating arrogance. Black shifts from denigration to beautiful. Sexually active bachelor women are no longer "ruined" but "free" or, at the very least, "the ruined Maid," as Thomas Hardy described her, exacts no small tribute of envy from her raw country sister. How quaint seem the fallen women of literature—the Charlotte Temples and Hester Prynnes and Catherine Barkleys—who earned red letters or died in childbirth to mark well for generations of women the evils of extramarital sex. They are quaint because women are increasingly imitating men's attitude toward sex rather than submitting to one he designed for her, and they are quaint because sex is no longer the best road out of the female ghetto. In her education, in her jobs, and in her crimes she has found much faster routes to travel. The journey, relatively speaking, has just begun. While the rate of increase of major crimes for women is surpassing that for males, the data[27] still provide some justification for the epithet "fair sex" in that men continue to commit the majority of crimes, and that the highest proportion of females are still arrested for larceny, primarily shoplifting.[28]

However, even here a comparison of figures for 1960 and 1972 shows an unmistakable across-the-board trend. Females are cutting themselves in for a bigger piece of the pie in every category but murder and, in a few—like the subtotal for major crimes, forgery and counterfeiting, and fraud and embezzlement—that piece is 80 to 100 per cent bigger than it had been twelve years before.

In summary, what we have described is a gradual but accelerating social revolution in which women are closing many of the gaps, social and criminal, that have separated them from men. The closer they get, the more alike they look and act. This is not to suggest that there are no inherent differences. Differences do exist ...but it seems clear that those differences are not of prime importance in understanding female criminality. The simplest and most accurate way to grasp the essence of women's changing patterns is to discard dated notions of femininity. That is a role that fewer and fewer women are willing to play. In the final analysis, women criminals are human beings who have basic needs and abilities and opportunities. Over the years these needs have not changed, nor will they. But women's abilities and opportunities have multiplied, resulting in a kaleidoscope of changing patterns whose final configuration will be fateful for all of us.

REFERENCES

1. I. Devore, "Mother-Infant Relations in Free-Ranging Baboons," in *Maternal Behavior in Mammals*, ed. H. L. Rheingold (New York: John Wiley & Sons, 1965).
2. I. Devore, "Male Dominance and Mating Behavior in Baboons," in *Sex and Behavior*, ed. F. A. Breach (New York: John Wiley & Sons, 1965).
3. For a more explicit theoretical discussion of cultural goals and institutionalized means see, Robert K. Merton, *Social Theory and Social Structure* (New York: The Free Press, 1967 [originally published in 1949]), p. 146.
4. Reproduced from "The Economic Role of Women," in *The Economic Report of the President, 1973*, United States Department of Labor (Washington, D.C.: U.S. Government Printing Office, 1973).
5. For example, see Mirra Komarovsky, "Cultural Contradictions and Sex Roles: The Masculine Case," *American Journal of Sociology*, January 1973, 78:873-84. Also, Marianne A. Ferber and Jane W. Loeb, "Performance, Awards, and Perceptions of Sex Discrimination Among Male and Female Faculty," *American Journal of Sociology*, January 1973, 78:995-1002; and Talcott Parsons and R. F. Bales, *Family, Socialization and Interaction Processes* (New York: The Free Press, 1955), p. 158.

6. *American Journal of Sociology*, January 1973, Vol. 78.
7. Nicholas Gage, *The Mafia Is Not an Equal Opportunity Employer* (New York: McGraw-Hill, 1971), p. 95.
8. Crime in the United States, Uniform Crime Reports, United States Department of Justice (Washington, D.C.: U.S. Government Printing Office, 1972), p. 124.
9. For a critique of the Uniform Crime Reports, see Marvin E. Wolfgang, "Uniform Crime Report: A Critical Appraisal," *University of Pennsylvania Law Review*, April 1963, III:708-738.
10. Uniform Crime Reports, *op. cit.*, p. 124.
11. Marvin E. Wolfgang, *Patterns in Criminal Homicide* (New York: John Wiley & Sons, 1958), Chapter 11. For a further discussion of the victim/offender relationship, see David Ward, Maurice Jackson, and Renee Ward, "Crimes of Violence by Women," in *Crimes of Violence*, eds. Donald Mulvihill, *et al.* (Washington, D.C.: U.S. Government Printing Office, 1969).
12. Edwin H. Sutherland and Donald R. Cressey, *Principles of Criminology* (Philadelphia: J. B. Lippincott Co., 1966 [originally published 1924]), p. 139.
13. *Ibid.*, p. 139. See also, H. vonHentig, "The Criminality of the Colored Woman," *University of Colorado Studies*, Series C. I. No. 3 (1942). For a discussion of the black female role in society, see, for instance, Lee Rainwater, "Crucible of Identity: the Negro Lower Class Family," *Daedalus*, Winter 1966, 95:172-216; also, Elliott Liebow, *Tally's Corner* (Boston: Little, Brown and Co., 1966).
14. Uniform Crime Reports, *op. cit.*, p. 124.
15. *Ibid.*, p. 139.
16. *Ibid.*, p. 159.
17. "Ten Most Wanted Fugitives" Program, United States Department of Justice, Federal Bureau of Investigation, Washington, D.C., December 28, 1968.
18. Among them: Bernardine Rae Dohrn, Katherine Ann Power, Susan Edith Saxe, Angela Yvonne Davis.
19. John Pascal and Francine Pascal, *The Strange Case of Patty Hearst* (New York: The New American Library, 1974), p. 92.
20. *The New York Times*, May 9, 1972.
21. *Girl Offenders Aged 17 to 20 Years*, a Home Office Research Unit Report (London: Her Majesty's Stationery Office, 1972), p. 3.
22. *Time*, October 16, 1972. In London, girl gangs are known as "bovver" (cockney for "bother," which means "fight") birds.
23. Albert Schrut, M.D., and Toni Michels, "Adolescent Girls Who Attempt Suicide—Comments on Treatment," *American Journal of Psychotherapy*, 1969, 23:243-51.
24. Walter R. Gove and Jeanette F. Tudor, "Adolescent Sex Roles and Mental Illness," *American Journal of Sociology*, January 1973, 78:812-35.
25. For a history of the National Organization for Women, see Jo Freeman, "The Origins of the Women's Liberation Movement," *American Journal of Sociology*, January 1973, 78:792-811.

26. Herbert M. Adler, M.D., and Van Buren O. Hammett, M.D., "Crisis, Conversion, and Cult Formation: An Examination of a Common Psychosocial Sequence," *American Journal of Psychiatry*, August 1973, 138:861-64; and Herbert M. Adler, M.D., and Van Buren O. Hammett, M.D., "The Doctor-Patient Relationship Revisited," *Annals of Internal Medicine*, April 1973, 78:595-98.
27. Figures calculated from data of Uniform Crime Reports, *op. cit.*, p. 124.
28. For a comprehensive discussion of shoplifting, see Mary Owen Cameron, *The Booster and the Snitch* (New York: The Free Press, 1964). See also, T. C. N. Gibbens and Joyce Prince, *Shoplifting* (London: The Institute for the Study and Treatment of Delinquency), 1962.

Crime in the American State

Richard Quinney

The major crimes that occur in the United States are bound to the political organization of our society. The state, which establishes and manages the system of social control, sometimes violates its own laws in securing this control. It may infringe the criminal code for reasons of state, and it occasionally goes further, violating laws of higher jurisdiction and even basic human rights.

These acts can be called crimes, though unlike ordinary crime, if they are uncovered, they often escape penalty. But their frequency and profound importance, and even their presence, have become marked in recent years. Any of these acts can be called criminal, whether found at the top of government or in any of its agencies.

CRIMES AGAINST HUMAN RIGHTS

Violating Civil Liberties

The state has been accused of crimes in several areas of life. The civil rights movement showed how government officials will violate the law to keep the system intact. Court decisions and legislative acts have made some of the behaviors illegal, even when committed by officials of the state. We have come to realize that many of our civil liberties are being narrowed by those who are supposed to guarantee these rights. In the name of "law and order," legal agents

SOURCE: Richard Quinney, *Criminology: Analysis and Critique of Crime in America* (Boston: Little, Brown, 1975), pp. 147-61, 321-23, Copyright © 1975, 1970 by Little, Brown and Company (Inc.). Reprinted by permission.

have slighted laws that are to protect such rights as free speech, assembly, and due process. Federal agents have violated the law in their surveillance and in their quest for evidence usable in criminal prosecution. Local police, too, have been accused of blatantly violating human rights, as well as the conventional laws of murder and assault, in running the affairs of state.[1]

The United States Constitution guarantees some rights that are not to be infringed upon. Governmental surveillance, according to Supreme Court rulings, is illegal in most situations. Such techniques as unreasonable search and seizure, interrogation, wiretapping, and various forms of electronic surveillance have been declared unconstitutional except in specified cases. Nevertheless, government agents continue to use these forms of surveillance, a fact which was dramatically brought to public attention by the disclosure that the Army was obtaining information on 18,000 civilians.[2]

It has been disclosed that several government agencies, including the FBI, also are heavily engaged in obtaining information about law-abiding citizens by these means.[3] The investigations on the Watergate crimes have uncovered the extent to which citizens are being denied their civil liberties in the name of "national security," and the many criminal techniques (including burglary) the government uses to obtain information. Agencies of the state, including the presidency, may also resort to espionage and sabotage against citizens, obtaining information illegally and even falsifying records and documents. Among the disclosures was the plan approved by President Nixon for gathering domestic intelligence. Blackmail and extortion have been used against individuals and organizations, as in the threat of income tax prosecutions if funds were not provided for campaign and other expenses. Some of these activities, such as burglary by agents of the FBI in gathering information for the presidency, have been going on for many years. These may be not only unconstitutional but may violate criminal codes. It is always problematical, however, whether these crimes will be prosecuted, because the government itself would have to do the prosecuting.

A classical strategy used by a state to promote its own security is the criminal law, which it wields against those who appear to threaten the state's existence. The state traditionally responds by establishing a legal system that defines as "criminal" any conduct that threatens it, and denying the citizen's rights of dissent. These "political crimes" form a significant part of legal history, especially in recent years.[4] This use of criminal law is usually illegal; the laws are illegal in formulation and inevitably result in criminal means of enforcement.

In the last decade the American state has gone through many political trials to promote its own interests. Those who objected to war in Southeast Asia were sometimes harassed and prosecuted. "Rioters" in the ghettoes, rebelling against the abuses they suffer, have been subjected to various laws by the state, which has used many old laws, or created new laws, to control dissent. Law enforcement agencies and the judiciary have tried to prosecute those who apparently threaten the state, but the government's strategy is not working. Trials pending for years are being thrown out of court because of the means the government used to prosecute them. Charges against such groups as the Chicago Seven, the Harrisburg Seven (the Berrigan case), the Daniel Ellsberg and Anthony J. Russo, Jr., case, and the Gainesville Eight were dropped because the police, the prosecution, or the court used criminal techniques in conducting them.[5]

CRIMES IN LAW ENFORCEMENT

Conventional Crimes by Agents of the Law

The police have traditionally been the governmental agents most exposed to opportunities for committing conventional felonies and misdemeanors while enforcing the law; crimes by the police have been documented throughout the history of law enforcement in American communities. A study of police operations in Washington, Boston, and Chicago reported that "27 percent of all the officers were either observed in misconduct situations or admitted to observers that they had engaged in misconduct."[6] The forms of crime included shaking down traffic violators, accepting payoffs to alter sworn testimony, stealing from burglarized establishments, and planting weapons on suspects. Documented elsewhere are illegal raids against innocent persons, participating in narcotics traffic, and extorting money from the prostitution business.[7] The Knapp Commission of New York City found that well over half the police force in that city are engaged in some form of crime and corruption.[8] The activities range from accepting bribes to selling stolen articles, from selling heroin to tapping telephones illegally, from blackmail to murder.

Violence is part of police work, and brutality in making an arrest is often claimed. Investigating police abuses in New York City, Paul Chevigny found that the police will make an arrest to cover up an assault committed against the suspect, concealing their own violence by arresting and charging the citizens with some offense.[9]

Crimes by the police can be understood if we look closely at police work. The police recruit, during his training, adopts a very definite outlook on his work and develops a justification for using specific procedures in the line of "duty." He learns an ideology that later affects his work:

> The policeman finds his most pressing problem in his relationships to the public. His is a service occupation but of an incongruous kind, since he must discipline those whom he serves. He is regarded as corrupt and inefficient by, and meets with hostility and criticism from, the public. He regards the public as his enemy, feels his occupation to be in conflict with the community, and regards himself to be a pariah. The experience and the feeling give rise to a collective emphasis on secrecy, an attempt to coerce

respect from the public, and a belief that almost any means are legitimate in completing an important arrest. These are for the policeman basic occupational values. They arise from his experience, take precedence over his legal responsibilities, are central to an understanding of his conduct, and form the occupational concepts within which violence gains its meaning.[10]

Many of the illegal activities of the ordinary policeman are prescribed and supported by group norms of law enforcement. Research has shown that criminal practices of police are patterned by an informal "code": "It was found that the new recruits were socialized into 'code' participation by 'old timers' and group acceptance was withheld from those who attempted to remain completely honest and not be implicated. When formal police regulations were in conflict with 'code' demands among its practitioners, the latter took precedence."[11]

In fact, the policeman may give little thought to the legality of his own actions when he is enforcing other laws. The law that is meant to protect the citizen from abuses by government authorities is more likely to be regarded by the policeman as an obstacle to law enforcement. "For him, due process of law is, therefore, not merely a set of constitutional guarantees for the defendant, but also a set of working conditions which, under increasingly liberal opinions by the courts, are likewise becoming increasingly arduous."[12] From the policeman's standpoint, the public's civil liberties impede his performance on the job. That is how the law is sometimes broken by its enforcers.

The opportunity for unlawful behavior among the police is especially acute in the black community and in political protests. Here the police already have their own group norms prescribing some illegal behavior and providing support for it. Several studies have shown that the majority of policemen are hostile and prejudiced toward blacks,[13] which can impair their ability to always keep their behavior lawful. In the ghetto riots of the late sixties, police violence was reportedly common.

Police handling of political protesters also has often been violent and illegal. The police response to the demonstrations at the 1968 Democratic National Convention in Chicago has been described as "unrestrained and indiscriminate police violence."[14] These confrontations increase the chances for violence because of the views the police share about protesters. That is, "organized protest tends to be viewed as the conspiratorial product of authoritarian agitators— usually 'Communists'—who mislead otherwise contented poeple."[15] Such ideas, combined with frustration and anger, provide ready support for harsh police actions. And because the police look on most people they find in these situations as already guilty, they think their own methods of control and apprehension are appropriate—no matter how criminal these methods may be.

Other agents of the law, such as the officials who guard and "correct" conventional offenders, violate the law in their work. These crimes correspond closely to the objectives of security and punishment. Prison guards, in particular, are to do whatever is necessary to maintain security in the prison.

These crimes are documented only when a crisis happens. Several crimes committed by correctional workers became known to the public following prison riots in New York City jails.[16] The inmates were responding to the harsh conditions in the jails, including excessive bail, overcrowding, and months of being confined without indictment or trial. After the revolt had been ended peacefully by negotiations between the inmates and the mayor's office, correctional officers systematically beat the prisoners in the courtyard of one of the jails. The beatings were recorded in photographs and eyewitness accounts. A reporter for the *Daily News* described what he saw:

> It was a gruesome scene. About 250 prisoners were sitting on the grass. Behind them, 30 Correction Department guards were lined up, all of them holding weapons—ax handles, baseball bats, and night sticks. One inmate was dragged out a doorway onto a loading platform and five guards attacked him with their clubs. They battered his head and blood flowed over his face and body. He was kicked off the platform and several other guards pounded him again with their clubs. His limp form then was lifted off the ground and thrown into a bus as another prisoner was hauled out and belted across the back with a club. Then more clubs rained down on him until he was motionless and bloodsoaked. He too was thrown into the bus. Another man was pushed out, his hands above his head. A bat caught him in the stomach and he doubled over. More clubs came down on his spine. Eight guards were slugging away at one time. A fourth prisoner emerged but the guards seemed to let go of him. He began running but the guards caught him and one put a knee into his groin. He toppled over and more guards kicked him over and over. Some more prisoners got the same treatment.[17]

As it often turns out with such incidents, three weeks after the beatings the district attorney announced the indictment of eight inmates, exonerating all the guards.

The results of crimes committed by agents of the law are usually predictable: the charges are dropped, the defendants are cleared, or, at most, an official may be dismissed. Although three students were killed and several more injured at Orangeburg State College in 1968, the South Carolina highway patrolmen who fired the shots were cleared of any wrongdoing. Similar events and results were to occur later at Jackson State College in Mississippi.

Likewise, at Kent State University in 1970, National Guardsmen killed four students, and then were exonerated of any blame. Instead, a state grand jury indicted twenty-five persons in connection with campus protests. The grand jury did not indict any guardsmen because they "fired their weapons in the honest and sincere belief and under circumstances which would have logically caused them to believe that they would suffer serious bodily injury had they not done so." (No evidence of the sniper fire that they feared could be found.) The "major responsibility" for the events at Kent State, the grand jury continued, "rests clearly with those persons who are charged with the administration of the university." The university administration, the report asserted, had fostered "an attitude of laxity, over-indulgence and permissiveness," and faculty members had placed an "over-emphasis" on "the right to dissent."[18] The idea that the government could be at fault was never entertained by the grand jury.

The killings at Attica prison in New York State demonstrate violence by the state. In September of 1971, more than forty were killed by state troopers when the prisoners demanded prison reforms. Fearing that the rebellion was a threat to law and order, Governor Rockefeller ordered in the state troopers.[19] Actions such as these are beginning to be understood by the public; crime by the state is becoming a part of the public consciousness.

Crimes of Provocation

The ideology of the American state promotes the myth that law enforcement is a neutral force that is intended to maintain the democratic process. However:

> The history of America contradicts this official image of neutrality and equal justice. The pattern is clear: when women tried to vote and Labor claimed its right to organize, at the beginning of this century, police were used as poll-watchers, as strike-breakers, and as shock troops by those who held industrial power; in the 1950's as black people began a new round in their centuries-old struggle for equal protection, police were once again used to defy the Constitution in the name of states' rights and public order; in the 1960's police again and again were sent in to disperse hundreds of thousands of citizens peacefully exercising their First Amendment rights to protest an unconstitutional war in Southeast Asia. All this time, on a day to day, face to face level the typical law enforcement slogan "to protect and to serve" meant one thing to the powerful or the passive and another to the powerless or the dissident.[20]

The practice in which a law-enforcement agency uses a policeman or an informer to encourage or plan actions that violate the law is itself a crime. Yet, we are now realizing this practice may be common. How widespread is this crime of informers becoming agents provocateurs and encouraging or committing illegal acts? The list of suspected instances includes these:

> One of the people most involved in encouraging the violence that accompanied the Chicago Democratic Party Convention was actually an undercover police officer; two members of a national peace committee who always tried to push the group into confrontations with the police were both police provocateurs; a young man who provided a bomb to blow up a Seattle U.S. Post Office was an FBI and city police informer; another FBI informer burned buildings at the University of Alabama; police agents tried to incite violence at Yale University during the demonstrations of May 1971; a Chicano activist in Los Angeles who attempted to provoke his

group into terrible acts of violence was an informer for the Treasury Department; the Weatherman group in Ohio was infiltrated by an informer who won a position for himself through advocacy of the most extreme forms of violence; the Black Panther Party "Minister of Defense" in Los Angeles, who helped bring about a shootout with the police, was actually a police informer; a New York City undercover police officer tried to convince a veterans' peace group that it should use violent tactics; another police provocateur, who had vandalized a state college campus, attempted to convert a San Diego peace march into a pitched battle with police; in upstate New York, an informer, who was on the FBI payroll, tried to set up a class to teach students at Hobart University how to make and use bombs; informers working for the FBI and local police set up a bombing attempt in Mississippi in an effort to kill two KKK members; a Chicago police informer provided the false tip which led to the killing of two Panther leaders there; a police informer led an illegal SDS sit-in at an Illinois college and later—claiming he was a Weatherman—helped to hurl the president of the college off the stage; a police informer attempted to force a militant Seattle group into taking on violent activities; two men who had led the shutting of a massive gate at Ohio State University and set off a violent confrontation with the police, were officers of the state highway patrol; and the false report claiming guns were stored in the Black Muslim Temple in Los Angeles came from a paid police informer, who claims he was instructed to make the report so that the police who employed him would have an excuse to raid the temple.[21]

Such accounts appear to be endless, making us realize that the state systematically engages in acts of provocation in attempting to protect itself. Persons and groups thought to be threats to the system have found themselves harassed by surveillance. Law enforcement agents have raided the homes of blacks, probably in response to acts of provocation by agents provocateurs among the Black Panthers.[22] Acts like these may be systematically practiced to eliminate any group that does not accept the state's legitimacy; it is, after all, supposed to be guardian of the national interest.

How far will the state go to protect its own interests? Recently revealed plans might have imposed martial law in the United States if a plot involving the 1972 Republican Convention, which was to be held in San Diego, had come off:

The plan entailed planting a number of agents-provocateurs both inside and outside the 1972 Republican Convention in San Diego. Agents were to infiltrate the groups planning demonstrations against the war and poverty. At the time of the demonstrations these agents were to provoke street battles with the police surrounding the convention hall; meanwhile, agents inside the convention hall were to have planted explosives, timed to blow up simultaneously with the "riot in the streets." The result, he [Louis E. Tackwood] claimed, would be to create a nation-wide hysteria that would then provide President Richard M. Nixon with the popular support necessary to declare a state of national emergency; the government could then arrest all "radicals," "militants," and "left-wing revolutionaries."[23]

In the Watergate crimes we recognize the full authoritarian possibilities in the modern state. The break-in at the Democratic National Convention headquarters (in the Watergate apartment complex) consisted of much more than a mere burglary and the installation of electronic listening devices. The invading team was discovered putting forged documents *into* the files. They also had incendiary and bomb manufacturing devices and implements.

> One thing was perfectly clear: this espionage mission was involved with far more than eavesdropping. As the investigation of the event unfolded during the 1972 presidential campaign, it became clear that Watergate was but the tip of the iceberg. Hundreds of thousands of dollars and scores of men were revealed as part of a national network for political espionage, sabotage and provocation. The contacts for the provocateurs who were recruited turned out to be men from the White House, some of the President's closest advisors.[24]

Crimes of provocation now come from the highest sources; this could be a design for our country's future.

Crimes of War

Criminologists, content to study criminal acts by individuals against society or the government, have neglected international incidents that could also be called criminal, in which the government itself or its agents are implicated. One of these is war, today entirely a governmental function. War is, obviously, violence. Many violent acts that are forbidden without question in peacetime are accepted as necessary in wartime and as a natural part of that unnatural business. Some acts of this kind, though, go beyond even the laws that nations have accepted as governing their behavior at war. These are war crimes.

Sociologists, confronted with these acts, conveniently ignore them, suggesting that they are not "crimes" as they define them, that these acts are not a system of behavior, or that only history can determine which acts are crimes. They fail to realize that these acts (1) are covered by the criminal laws, (2) can be systematic, integral parts of a political and economic system, and (3) are crucial in a nation's history. If we do not consider such crimes, we abdicate both our integrity as scholars and our responsibilities as human beings.

An elaborate body of international laws covers the crimes of war. The laws of war are of ancient origin, and up to the eighteenth century were mostly preserved by unwritten tradition.[25] Gradually the laws were codified and courts were established to try violations of the laws. In the last hundred years international laws and treaties have firmly codified an international law of war. The United

States is party to twelve conventions pertinent to land warfare, including the detailed Geneva Conventions of 1949. The most authoritative and encompassing statement of war crimes is found in the Chapter of the International Military Tribunal at Nuremberg, where war crimes are defined as

> Violations of the laws or customs of war which include, but are not limited to, murder, ill-treatment or deportation to slave-labour or for any other purpose of civilian population of or in occupied territory, murder, or ill-treatment of prisoners of war or persons on the high seas, killing of hostages, plunder of public or private property, wanton destruction of cities, towns or villages, or devastation not justified by military necessity.[26]

"The laws of warfare are part of American law, enforceable in American courts, not only because the United States is party to most of the major multilateral conventions on the conduct of military hostilities but also because the laws of warfare are incorporated in international customary law, which under the Constitution is part of American law."[27] The United States also recognizes that the laws of war apply to us in the *Field Manual* of the Department of the Army. The Manual makes it clear that the international laws are also "the supreme law of the land," and that "the law of war is binding not only upon States as such but also upon individuals and, in particular, the members of their armed forces."[28] The international laws of war are part of American law, and may be enforced against both civilians and soldiers, by national or intenational courts.

Now, let us see how international law can be applied to a country accused of monstrous acts in a long war: the United States in Vietnam. We assume that the government and its representatives discussed here are guilty of these crimes. How are they guilty, and how can the international courts prove their guilt and bring the guilty to trial?

At the Nuremberg war crimes trials, Chief Prosecutor Justice Jackson of the United States Supreme Court declared: "If certain acts and violations of treaties are crimes, they are crimes whether the United States does them or whether Germany does them. We are not prepared to lay down a rule of criminal conduct against others which we would not be willing to have invoked against us." Years later many believed the United States had put itself in the respondent's position. But those who level the charge of war crimes against the United States are not the obvious victors. The countries in Southeast Asia, though continually advancing their own condition, are not yet in a position to conduct a war crimes trial. And other nations have not been inclined to convene an international trial. Nevertheless, the words of Justice Jackson are coming back to haunt many Americans.

Our century has been dominated by a single view of reality: the liberal view, which may have been the source of both our problems as a nation and our inability to understand these problems. So it is that the war in Southeast Asia and the crimes associated with it may be made understandable by another theory of reality, a socialist theory. What did liberals predict about our involvement in Southeast Asia?

> Did they predict that the American government, continuously advised by university professors, would persist for several years in methods of warfare and of pacification that are criminal in international law and custom, and that are modeled on communist methods? Did they predict that the American government, in pursuit of its presumed strategic interests, would prop up, by fire-power and money, any puppet, however repressive, provided only that he would not have dealings with Russia and China? Did they anticipate that the principles of the Nuremberg trials and pledges to international order would be brought into contempt so soon and by a democracy?[29]

The liberal theory always held that the Vietnam war was, at most, a mistake. The socialist theory, scoffed at by most intellectuals in the late fifties and early sixties, suggested another meaning. Rather than viewing the war as an accident or miscalculation, an event that would cease with immediate American withdrawal, that theory predicted the United States would extend the war.

What the United States did, and continues to do in various ways, in Southeast Asia is a logical outcome of policies that have long existed. That the United States has intervened in the affairs of other nations has been taken for granted. Its right to interfere in the development of these countries, including the right to suppress national revolts, has been patently accepted. To overthrow revolutionary governments and to replace them with military dictatorships has been recognized as good foreign policy. Instead of questioning a foreign policy that is guided by corporate capitalism, in which national interests are defined as business interests, liberals have proclaimed this arrangement. And these arrangements and ideas helped bring about the Vietnam war.

The dramatic disclosure of a massacre involving more than 500 civilians in the My Lai #4 hamlet of Son My village raised the first serious consideration of war crimes by the United States in the Vietnam war. That disclosure, not made until several months after the March 16, 1968 massacre, suggested a series of war crimes over a long time:

> The official policies developed for the pursuit of belligerent objectives in Vietnam appear to violate the same basic and minimum constraints on the conduct of war as were violated at Songmy. B-52 pattern raids against undefended villages and populated areas, "free bomb zones," forcible removal of civilian populations, defoliation and crop destruction and "search and destroy" missions have been sanctioned as official tactical policies of the United States government. Each of these tactical policies appears to violate the international laws of war binding upon the United States by international treaties ratified by the U.S. Government with the advice and consent of the Senate. The overall conduct of the war in Vietnam by the U.S. armed forces involves a refusal to differentiate between combatants and noncombatants and between military and nonmilitary targets.[30]

The implications of Son My are far-reaching. The United States government seems to have pursued official policies of warfare that constitute war crimes: "It would, therefore, be misleading to isolate the awful happening at Songmy from the overall conduct of the war. It is certainly true that the perpetrators of the massacre at Songmy are, if the allegations prove correct, guilty of the commission of war crimes, but it is also true that their responsibility is mitigated to the extent that they were executing superior orders or were even carrying out the general line of official policy that established a moral climate in which the welfare of Vietnamese civilians is totally disregarded."[31]

Let us, then, examine some of the specific acts by the United States government in Southeast Asia that are defined as criminal in the international laws of war.

Murder and Ill-treatment of Civilians

The Son My massacre of civilian men, women, and children took place in a standard American military operation. Trying to trap a Vietcong unit, an American brigade (C Company of Task Force Barker) appear to have killed almost every villager they could lay hands on, although no opposition or hostile behavior was encountered.

The tragedy of Son My cannot obscure the fact that the killing of civilians by American forces became an everyday occurrence in Vietnam. Estimates have suggested that American or South Vietnamese forces killed or wounded ten civilians for every Vietcong.[32] Civilian casualties in South Vietnam ran into the hundreds of thousands. The Kennedy Subcommittee on Refugees estimated that there were about 300,000 casualties in 1968. According to a conservative estimate for the years 1965 to 1969, 1,116,000 South Vietnamese civilians were killed and 2,232,000 were wounded: between a fifth and a quarter of the population was killed or wounded by military operations in the war. Not included in these figures are the unknown number of casualties from disease and malnutrition brought on by the war. Likewise, these figures do not include the casualties suffered by the civilians of North Vietnam, many as a result of massive bombing. Thousands of other civilians were killed as the war was "wound down."

Destruction of Nonmilitary Targets

The United States engaged in heavy aerial bombardment in Vietnam. The bomb tonnage exceeded that delivered in all the allied bombing in Europe and Asia during World War II. By February of 1969, 3,200,000 tons of bombs had been dropped on an agricultural country slightly larger than New York State: 180 pounds of bombs for every man, woman, and child in Vietnam, or 25 tons of bombs for every square mile of North and South Vietnam.[33]

The strictly legal question is whether or not these bombs fell on military objectives:

> Under the traditional approach to the war-crimes concept, no legal issue is presented with respect to the bombing of genuinely strategic military targets such as factories, ammunition depots, oil refineries, airports, and—particularly in the Vietnam context—roads, bridges, viaducts, railroad tracks, trucks, trains, tunnels, and any other transportation facilities. Furthermore, we assume that accidental and incidental damage to non-military and non-strategic targets is not a war crime. [34]

But the kind of bombing carried out by the United States government appears to have been quite different; it is accused of carrying out a deliberate, nonaccidental bombardment of nonmilitary targets. In North Vietnam, B-52 bombers were said to have continuously attacked schools, churches, hospitals, private homes, dikes, and dams.[35]

In South Vietnam, bombing of rural villages was a standard military policy. Any area could be more or less indiscriminately bombed. "While such strategy violates all international law regarding warfare and is inherently genocidal, it also adjusts to the political reality in South Vietnam that the N.L.F. is and can be anywhere and that virtually the entire people is America's enemy."[36] Military policy, the accusation says, turned an entire nation into a target.

Murder and Ill-treatment of Prisoners of War

The laws of war concerning the treatment of prisoners of war are precise: it is a war crime to murder or torture prisoners. "According to the Nuremberg precedents, captors may not shoot prisoners even though they are in a combat zone, require a guard, consume supplies, slow up troop movements, and appear certain to be set free by their own forces in an imminent invasion. The Hague conventions of 1907 require that prisoners be humanely treated, and the Geneva Convention of 1949 prohibits 'causing death or seriously endangering the health of a prisoner of war.' In particular it stipulates that 'no physical or mental torture, nor any other form of coercion, may be inflicted on prisoners of war to secure from them information of any kind whatever.' "[37]

Yet there are numerous reports of the murder and ill-treatment of prisoners by American military forces as well as by the American trained and supported South Vietnamese Army.[38] Detailed accounts have been given of the beheading and shooting of wounded prisoners and of torture. Instead of incarcerating prisoners, execution is often carried out at the time of capture. Some combat soldiers characterized these actions as "everyday things," "expected" combat behavior, and "standard operating policy." Violations of the international laws of war became an issue of American military policy in Southeast Asia.

Other Crimes

American armed forces, working with the Army of South Vietnam, sprayed more than 100 million pounds of herbicidal chemicals on about half (5 million acres) of the arable land in South Vietnam. The object was "to defoliate trees affording cover for enemy forces and to kill certain plants, including rice, which furnish food for Vietcong forces and their civilian supporters.[39] In addition, 14 million pounds of CS gas, which incapacitates combatants and civilians, was used. In other words, the United States relied extensively on chemical warfare in Vietnam and later in Cambodia.

The Geneva Gas Protocol of 1925 states that the "use in war of asphyxiating, poisonous or other gases, and of all analogous liquids, materials, or devices, has been justly condemned by the general opinion of the civilized world," and prohibits the use of such weapons. Even with the most limited interpretation of the protocol, as lethal devices, the liquids and sprays used by the United States in Southeast Asia were in violation of international law.[40] Napalm too was widely used in Vietnam and surrounding countries.

In officially conducting a war against the population of Vietnam, the United States and some of its leaders could be charged with genocide, a crime against humanity, a crime covered by international treaties and for which all but two of the defendants at Nuremberg were convicted.

"The case for these stark accusations is based on the conclusions that both South Vietnam and the United States violated the Geneva Declaration of 1954 by hostile acts against the North, unlawful rearmament, and refusal to carry out the 1965 national elections provided for in the Declaration, and that the United States likewise violated the United Nations Charter by bombing North Vietnam."[41] The United States attempted to legitimize its war by claiming that self-defense measures were required in response to documented armed attacks.

But whether or not the sweeping accusations of genocide and aggression are invoked, the United States position before the traditional laws of war is open to one question: how can these violations be understood and what legal or moral recourse is there for the people of Southeast Asia and for the world community?

World Justice

Only a few war crime violations have been prosecuted—and these by military courts. Lieutenant William Calley stood a court-martial trial for his part in killing civilians at Son My. It became clear at the trial that Calley was being used as a scapegoat for decisions made by others at higher levels of command. But crucial questions about individual responsibility were raised during the trial.[42] According to the Nuremberg principles and the Army's *Field Manual,* members of the armed forces are bound to obey only *lawful* orders; orders violating international law are not to be obeyed. Moreover, questions were raised about war crimes by the United States, and according to international law, those who make and administer these policies must be held responsible. In the Tokyo War Crimes Trial, the defendant, General Yamashita, was convicted and executed for failing to restrain his troops from committing crimes against civilians in the Philippines during the closing months of World War II. That trial established for international law that "A leader must take affirmative acts to prevent war crimes or dissociate himself from the Government. If he fails to do one or the other, then by the very act of remaining in a government of a state guilty of war crimes, he becomes a war criminal."[43]

There are considerable grounds, therefore, for regarding policy-makers and those who administer policy as war criminals. One noted legal scholar, Telford Taylor, who was chief counsel for the prosecution at Nuremberg, has suggested that with the precedents in international law, several civilian leaders and military officers be held criminally responsible for their acts.[44] The Rusks, McNamaras, Bundys, and Rostows, as well as the military leaders, such as the Joint Chiefs of Staff (especially General Westmoreland), should have borne responsibility for the war crimes in Southeast Asia.

To invoke the law, if it could be done beyond the manipulations of the regime themselves, is probably to expect too much of legal institutions. The war crimes of the United States cannot be probed adequately in a court-martial proceeding when the responsibility lies higher. It seems more critical to develop a moral judgment on our recent history.

A national or international board of inquiry may be the most appropriate way to deal with war crimes. The main objective of this approach, as Richard Falk argues, is to achieve a measure of rectitude as a result of *moral clarification*. Moreover:

> Such a focus is not punitive, the idea is not to catch, convict and punish individuals, but to expose, clarify, and repudiate their conduct. Such an enterprise can only be effective if it represents as authoritative a collective judgment of mankind as a whole reached in a proceeding that was fair, but honest. Americans concerned at once with avoiding any deepening polarization at home, and with renouncing crimes committed on their behalf, should join together in calling for an *external* process of inquiry and jugdment, perhaps in the form of a specially constituted U.N. Commission of Inquiry. For Americans of conscience that is the time for neither insurgency, nor silence.[45]

In the end, everyone is responsible for the acts of government. It is the responsibility of all peoples of the world to remove the oppression of national empires and to achieve world justice and human liberation.

CRIME, BUSINESS, AND AMERICAN POLITICS

Crime as an economic enterprise depends on the symbiotic alliance between politics and business, which in turn enhances all three realms. In fact, in many areas of the American political economy the distinctions between criminal and legitimate activity are becoming obsolete. Criminal politics and criminal business, corrupt politicians and political officials serving business, threaten to become an institutional arrangement. Crime is reaching into the highest levels of politics and business; it is becoming nationalized.

Roughly since Prohibition, an unseen alliance has gradually developed in the United States, entangling organized crime, politicians, public officials, and agencies of law enforcement and administration of justice. Organized crime has become a part of politics, and politics has infiltrated organized crime. Organized criminals have found it necessary to get into politics to protect their operations from governmental interference. Their liaison with public officials is a passport to immunity from the law, preventing interruption to their business, which is amassing large economic gains. People in politics discover that involvement in organized crime furnishes lucrative financial rewards. Collaboration with organized crime also gives the political system a way of controlling the country's social and economic organization. The political, economic, and criminal realms are increasingly becoming rolled into one.

The known examples illustrating how deeply business and politics are involved in crime are overwhelming. Small cities as well as large ones have their own cases of systematic crime. A few documented cases will show this tainted, self-sustaining relationship. In Reading, Pennsylvania, we can see how a syndicate controlled an entire community:

> Operating in conjunction with a local underworld figure, most of the municipal administration from the mayor on down was corrupted. As a result, the biggest illegal still since Prohibition was tied into the city water supply, the biggest red-light district on the East Coast was set up, and the biggest dice game east of the Mississippi, within an easy drive of either Philadelphia or New York, was launched. Nothing was done for the city. Industry started leaving; downtown Reading became an eyesore. When murmurs of public discontent grew too loud, mob-controlled "reformers" were promptly whisked on the scene. As the city steadily began to wither, a Justice Department task force noticed that the only sign of civic improvement was new parking meters. The company involved in the installation of these meters had a history of kicking back to municipal governments to get the business. It was this thread that eventually unraveled the whole mess, but until outside aid arrived, the local citizenry was truly helpless.[46]

The case in which New York City official James L. Marcus was involved shows how organized crime can infiltrate city politics and economics:

The manner in which organized crime may effectively sink its claws into public officials can be seen in the case of James L. Marcus, former Commissioner of Water Supply, Gas and Electricity, in New York City and a close advisor and member of Mayor Lindsay's inner circle. Deeply in debt from business investments and Wall Street plunges, Marcus was referred by a business associate to Anthony Corallo, a reputed lieutenant in the Thomas Lucchese Cosa Nostra "family" with a reputation as a labor racketeer and loan shark. Paying interest to Corallo on cash loans said to be at an annual rate of 104 percent, Marcus sank further in debt, and was finally pressured into doing business "favors" to the Cosa Nostra loan shark and his associates. The result was a tangled web of rigged municipal contracts, bribes, and illegal real-estate deals. In 1968, Marcus pleaded guilty to taking a $16,000 kickback in return for awarding a $835,000 city contract to clean a Bronx reservoir and received a fifteen-month sentence for his part in this and several other conspiracies.[47]

Collusion is further illustrated in Newark, New Jersey:

Illustrative of this wide scope of political corruption is perhaps the city of Newark, New Jersey, which in 1969 was rocked by a major scandal involving public officials, law-enforcement agents, and organized crime. In the first of two mass indictments, a federal grand jury charged the mayor, Hugh Addonizio, with income-tax evasion and sixty-six counts of extortion involving a share in payoffs totaling $253,000 from a business firm that had contracts with the city. Also included in the indictments were eleven current or former city officials and a reputed prominent member of the Cosa Nostra. Barely a day before this action by the grand jury, a series of gambling raids by some 100 FBI agents (apparently sparked by information derived from wiretaps) in Newark and surrounding suburbs resulted in scores of arrests and led to another mass indictment of fifty-five persons. Almost a dozen of those indicted were reported to be Cosa Nostra members, including Simone Rizzo Decavalcante, alleged boss of one of the six Cosa Nostra "families" in the New York metropolitan area. (This huge interstate operation, extending as far as Troy, New York, reportedly brought the syndicate $20 million a year.) The indictments of these gambling figures also charged that some of them had "solicited and obtained" tipoffs from Newark city police on any impending gambling raids.[48]

Lasting control over an American city by organized crime, involving a relationship between local politicians and business, is documented in a study of "Wincanton," pseudonym for an Eastern industrial city controlled by a crime syndicate for the last fifty years. The Stern syndicate, operating gambling enterprises in the city, was able "to put cooperative politicians in office, to buy off those who occupied strategic enforcement positions, and to implicate most city officials in various forms of corruption so completely that they would be unable to turn upon him."[49] City officials have added to their syndicate payoffs by demanding bribes from individuals and companies doing business with the city.

Many city, state, and federal laws were violated, and the law enforcement apparatus was under illegal control. Only those not involved in the established politics and business of the community, namely, the majority of the citizens, were excluded from this arrangement. The city had a local ruling class, deeply involved in and dependent on crime.

Similar associations between city officials, members of organized crime, and business leaders were found in a western city. Investigating corruption there, William Chambliss observed that the arrangement has become institutionalized in the city.

> I have argued, and I think the data demonstrate quite convincingly, that the people who run the organizations which supply the vices in American cities are members of the business, political, and law enforcement communities—not simply members of a criminal society. Furthermore, it is also clear from this study that corruption of political-legal organizations is a critical part of the life-blood of the crime cabal. The study of organized crime is thus a misnomer; the study should consider corruption, bureaucracy, and power. By relying on governmental agencies for their information on vice and the rackets, social scientists and lawyers have inadvertently contributed to the miscasting of the issue in terms that are descriptively biased and theoretically sterile. Further, they have been diverted from sociologically interesting and important issues raised by the persistence of crime cabals. As a consequence, the real significance of the existence of syndicates has been overlooked; for instead of seeing these social entities as intimately tied to, and in symbiosis with, the legal and political bureaucracies of the state, they have emphasized the criminality of only a portion of those involved. Such a view contributes little to our knowledge of crime and even less to attempts at crime control.[50]

That the intimacy binding crime, economics, and politics has reached the national level is dramatically shown in events of recent years. Resignation by a vice president of the United States is startling evidence of how high the infection has climbed. Vice President Spiro T. Agnew resigned from that office after pleading no contest—the equivalent in law of a guilty plea—to a charge of income tax evasion, and permitted the court to publish evidence that he had extorted bribes for a decade.[51] From the time he was county executive in suburban Baltimore until he reached the second highest national office, Agnew received cash in kickbacks and payments from engineers who wanted government business.

In return for his bargained plea, Mr. Agnew was assured that the government would drop all other prosecution against him.[52] He was free to proclaim his innocence of any wrongdoing, and the court settled for a sentence of three years of unsupervised probation and a fine of $10,000. Now a convicted felon, he was also (unlike most felons) free to pursue his private life, which undoubtedly would include business as well as pleasure. The state once again remained relatively exempt from a searching examination. The public, however, had one more indication—this time from the top—about the close relationship among crime, economics, and American politics.

Investigations have uncovered other instances of collusion: organized crime's part in policies toward revolutionary Cuba.[53] Distressed that Fidel Castro tossed organized crime operations out of Cuba, closing down gambling casinos and brothels, syndicate figures and Cuban rightwing exiles cooperated with the CIA in planning and executing the attempted Bay of Pigs invasion and the subsequent attempts to assassinate Castro. Some of these same people and forces were later to surface in the crimes related to Watergate.

The connection between organized crime and government has been covered up by the federal government's law enforcement agencies. The FBI has long tried to perpetuate the idea that organized crime is limited to a few persons of Italian descent and that there is no such thing as a national crime syndicate.[54] To disclose a nationwide criminal conspiracy would have required the FBI, then under J. Edgar Hoover's direction, to investigate and expose gangster friends and supporters who were deeply involved in business and politics. We now have better evidence, however, on how far organized crime reaches in the United States: "The gray area between crime and business and politics deepened and widened until in the 1970's it is impossible to say where one ends and the other begins."[55] We need realistic understanding of this kind to start looking for thoughts and actions that will provide an alternative to a future built on the association of crime, business, and politics.

WATERGATE—BENEATH AND BEYOND

From the time the offices of the Democratic National Committee in the Watergate buildings in Washington, D.C., were broken into in June of 1972, Americans gradually became aware of crimes committed by the state, its leaders and officials, and those hired to commit criminal acts. Acts of spying and sabotage were directed from the White House, whose purpose (as former President Nixon said) was to "stop security leaks and to investigate other sensitive matters."[56] As the disclosures multiplied, crimes far beyond Watergate were exposed.

Still more crimes were committed as the investigations went forward, to cover up the criminal world that made Watergate possible or necessary. The name "Watergate" came to include not only a plot within the president's reelection committee and the coverup activities, but all the schemes the state and its leaders resorted to.

Watergate uncovered a "second government" in the United States, or perhaps better, a previously unsuspected form of influence and control spreading through the government. Watergate was but the tip of a coolly rational bureaucratic iceberg; the real forces lay in the political depths below.

Beneath Watergate is a government with "a combination of vast and complicated interlocking forces, pulling in the CIA here and organized crime there, using politicians one time and émigré thugs the next, which seems to regard government as a tool for financial enrichment."[57] These operations are usually beyond the reach of citizens. "Other scandals—whether called by that name in the press or not, as with the Watergate 'caper'—are also sure to follow, for it seems obvious that the kind of milieu in which the President has chosen to immerse himself will continue to produce policies self-serving at best, shady at average, and downright illegal at worst, and that at least some of this will break through to public attention."[58] This power will not be washed away by investigations, prosecutions, or the new administration; the underside of the United States is likely to reign for some time, until politics and economics can be changed.

The secret government's clandestine operations tell us of some forces involved in established politics and economics. These operations are connected with government and business agencies; when discovered they are covered by lies. A pattern visible in these spy and sabotage operations consists of the agents who reappear in many of the same assignments. This listing of the men indicted in the Watergate break-in reveals some of the complex criminal operations in the American state, and the key roles played by the CIA and the FBI.

Bernard L. Barker (alias Frank or Fran Carter). Half-Cuban American who lived in Cuba for a number of years and left after Castro's revolution. Former employee of the Central Intelligence Agency and reported to have had a role in the abortive Bay of Pigs invasion of Cuba. Founded Barker Associates, a Miami real estate firm, in 1971.

Virgilio R. Gonzalez (alias Raul or Raoul Godoy or Goboy). Cuban who emigrated to United States at time of Castro's rise. Employed as locksmith.

Eugenio R. Martinez (alias Gene or Jene Valdes). Former pre-Castro Cuban legislator. Exile reportedly active in anti-Castro movement. Said to have been associated with CIA. Member of Barker's real estate firm.

James W. McCord Jr. (alias Edward J. Warren and Edward J. Martin). Former FBI agent. CIA employee for 19 years until retirement in 1970. Salaried security coordinator for the Republican National Committee and Nixon's re-election committee until day after his arrest.

Frank A. Sturgis (alias Frank Angelo Fiorini, Edward J. Hamilton and Joseph DiAlberto or D'Alberto). Reportedly former American gun-smuggler for Castro, later active in anti-Castro Cuban exile activities, including Bay of Pigs invasion. Said to have had extensive links with CIA. Described as an associate of Barker.

E. Howard Hunt Jr. CIA employee, 1949–70. Reportedly had key role in 1961 Bay of Pigs invasion. Writer of spy novels. Part-time consultant to White House counsel Charles W. Colson from 1970 until March 29, 1972. Consultant projects included declassification of the Pentagon Papers and intelligence work in narcotics enforcement.

G. Gordon Liddy. Former FBI agent. Special assistant to assistant Treasury secretary, 1969–71, when he was reportedly fired for unauthorized activities. Joined White House staff in July 1971 and said to have suggested bugging *The New York Times* during Pentagon Papers controversy. Joined Nixon reelection committee in late 1971, where he was finance counsel at time of Watergate break-in. Dismissed by Mitchell for refusing to answer FBI's questions.[59]

As the Watergate investigation proceeded, it seemed clear that these men were agents for criminals much higher in the American business and political establishment. This and other events of recent years suggest not a series of isolated incidents, but a conspiracy led by powers within the United States. An observer with close ties to the intelligence establishment said: "A look at the power and history of the 15 years lying behind Watergate—at the CIA and the espionage establishment tied to Gordon Liddy's bungling burglars and the bright young men who proposed Gestapo-like plans for the White House—suggests that there was indeed a conspiracy—possibly one whose reach extended beyond CREEP [Committee to Re-elect the President] and even the White House itself."[60] Other events, involving United States foreign as well as domestic operations, may be similarly connected.

Inquiries into Watergate and the subsequent coverup disclosed many other alliances and related criminal operations, connecting the United States government, organized crime, and clandestine intelligence networks. Not the least of these discoveries is the possible connection of some of the Watergate figures, agencies, and operations to past political assassinations: John Kennedy, Martin Luther King, Robert Kennedy, and the attempted assassination of George Wallace were conspiratorial plots to maintain control over the established political and economic system in the United States by those groups, persons and forces which arranged Watergate.[61] From the assassination of John Kennedy in Dallas to the Watergate burglary in Washington, a single path appeared to be traceable.

The path of crime, it seemed, led finally to the highest level of the United States government, the presidency itself. Politics, business, and organized crime appeared tightly intertwined in the circle of people and events around the career of Richard Nixon. In an extensive investigation, a researcher uncovered hints about Nixon's business and organized crime dealings in Florida and the Caribbean since the late forties:

Nixon visited Miami numerous times in the late Forties, contrary to all of his official biographies. While there, he yachted with Richard Danner, Bebe Rebozo, and Tatum "Chubby" Wofford of the syndicate-controlled Wofford Hotel. Danner also had mob connections at that time.

Nixon has invested in two southern Florida land deals; others involved in both projects have had links with organized crime. Two men in particular—Leonard Bursten and Nathan Ratner—have had business connections with organized crime.

Nixon concealed his ownership of a Key Biscayne lot for four years until a mortgage held by another Lansky associate, Arthur Desser, was paid off.

Nixon's closest friend, Bebe Rebozo, was a war profiteer in the early Forties in the tire recapping business. Three of his associates served on the Dade County tire allocation board, in clear violation of OPA regulation No. 3C-118. At the same time Nixon was working in the legal interpretations unit of the OPA in Washington, D.C.

Nixon technically concealed his employment with the OPA until he was President.

Nixon is linked to the "Havana Connection"—a funnel for organized crime and reactionary Cuban politics. Indictees in the Watergate case also figure in this connection.

Nixon has received campaign contributions from two men who have had direct connections to organized crime.

Nixon has appointed a number of men, including John Connally, William Rogers, and Will Wilson, who have indirect ties to organized crime.

The mob-favored Miami National Bank was the chief creditor in a bankruptcy case which led to a $300,000,000 suit, still pending, against Nixon and other members of his New York law firm for their alleged part in skimming over $5,000,000 off the bankrupt firm's accounts.

Nixon's rise to wealth and power has required the silent loyalty of a wide range of personalities whose names only occasionally surface in the glare of scandal—with good reason. Richard Nixon would not be where he is today were it not for his uncanny ability to thrive on political crisis. As much as anything else it is his self-proclaimed poker-playing instincts—the cautious, calculating, close-mouthed style and the ability to keep a stone face in rough as well as smooth times—that has carried Nixon to the Presidency.[62]

The full extent of crime in the American state is just beginning to surface; some of the criminal associations and dealings were revealed by Watergate. The Nixon administration's operations this time overstepped the bounds of trickery and deceit acceptable in American politics, and the administration was called to account for *some* of its criminal acts.

NOTES

1. For documentation on crimes by the government, see Jethro K. Lieberman, *How the Government Breaks the Law* (New York: Stein and Day, 1972); Theodore L. Becker and Vernon G. Murry, eds., *Government Lawlessness in America* (New York: Oxford University Press, 1971).
2. Richard Halloran, "Army Spied on 18,000 Civilians in Two-Year Operation," *The New York Times,* January 18, 1971, pp. 1 and 22.
3. The documentation is extensive. See, for example, the reports of the various congressional committees, such as the hearings conducted by the Senate Subcommittee on Constitutional Rights and the hearings of the Senate Watergate Committee. Also see the daily coverage by *The New York Times.*

4. See Marshall B. Clinard and Richard Quinney, *Criminal Behavior Systems: A Typology*, 2nd ed. (New York: Holt, Rinehart and Winston, 1973), pp. 154-186.

5. Homer Bigart, "Berrigan Case: A Strategy that Failed,"*The New York Times*, April 9, 1972, p. E2; John Kifner, "Court in Chicago Frees 5 in 1968 Convention Case," *The New York Times*, November 23, 1972; "Ellsberg Case: Defendants Freed, Government Convicted," *The New York Times*, May 13, 1973, p. E1; John Kifner, "Eight Acquitted in Gainesville of G.O.P. Convention Plot," *The New York Times*, September 1, 1973, p. 1.

6. David Burnham, "Misconduct Laid to 27% of Police in Three Cities' Slums," *The New York Times*, July 5, 1968, p. 1.

7. Fred J. Cook, "How Deep Are the Police in Heroin Traffic?" *The New York Times*, April 25, 1971, p. E3; Andrew H. Malcolm, "Violent Drug Raids Against the Innocent Found Widespread,"*The New York Times*, June 25, 1973, p. 1; Ralph Blumenthal, "Officer in Albany Says Fellow Police Joined in Thievery," *The New York Times*, September 21, 1973, p. 1; Ralph Blumenthal, "Brothel Boss Tells of Albany Bribes," *The New York Times*, September 25, 1973, p. 39.

8. *The Knapp Commission Report on Police Corruption* (New York: George Braziller, 1972).

9. Paul Chevigny, *Police Power: Police Abuses in New York City* (New York: Random House, 1969), pp. 136–146.

10. William A. Westley, "Violence and the Police," *American Journal of Sociology*, 59 (July 1953), p. 35.

11. Ellwyn R. Stoddard, "The Informal 'Code' of Police Deviancy: A Group Approach to 'Blue-Coat Crime,' " *Journal of Criminal Law, Criminology and Police Science*, 59 (June 1968), p. 212. Also see Barbara Raffel Price, "Police Corruption: Analysis," *Criminology*, 10 (August 1972), pp. 161–176.

12. Jerome H. Skolnick, *Justice Without Trial: Law Enforcement in Democratic Society* (New York: John Wiley, 1966), p. 202.

13. See Donald J. Black and Albert J. Reiss, Jr., "Patterns of Behavior in Police and Citizen Transactions," in the President's Commission on Law Enforcement and Administration of Justice, *Studies in Crime and Law Enforcement in Major Metropolitan Areas*, vol. 2, Field Surveys III (Washington, D.C.: U.S. Government Printing Office, 1967), pp. 132–139.

14. The Walker Report to the National Commission on the Causes and Prevention of Violence, *Rights in Conflict* (New York: Bantam Books, 1968), p. 1.

15. Jerome H. Skolnick, *The Politics of Protest* (New York: Ballantine Books, 1969). Also see Rodney Stark, *Police Riots* (Belmont, Calif.: Wadsworth, 1972).

16. Paul L. Montgomery, "Crisis in Prisons Termed Worst Mayor Has Faced," *The New York Times*, October 15, 1970, p. 1.

17. Quoted in Jack Newfield, "The Law Is an Outlaw," *The Village Voice*, December 17, 1970, p. 1.

18. John Kifner, "Jury Indicts 25 in Kent Disorder; Guard Is Cleared," *The New York Times*, October 17, 1970, p. 1.

19. *Attica,* The Official Report of the New York State Special Commission on Attica (New York: Bantam Books, 1972).

20. Citizens Research and Investigation Committee and Louis E. Tackwood, *The Glass House Tapes* (New York: Avon Books, 1973), p. 259.

21. Paul Jacobs, "Informers, the Enemy Within," *Ramparts,* 12 (August-September, 1973), pp. 53–54.

22. Other cases of provocation against the Black Panthers are presented in Paul Chevigny, *Cops and Rebels: A Study of Provocation* (New York: Random House, 1972). On the sociological implications of provocation, see Gary T. Marx, "Thoughts on a Neglected Category of Social Movement Participant: The Agent Provocateur and Informant," *American Journal of Sociology,* forthcoming.

23. Citizens Research and Investigation Committee and Louis E Tackwood, *The Glass House Tapes,* p. 42.

24. Ibid., p. 173.

25. Telford Taylor, *Nuremberg and Vietnam: An American Tragedy* (Chicago: Quadrangle Books, 1970), pp. 19–41.

26. Nuremberg Principle VI, clause b. The full text can be found in *The Nation,* January 26, 1970, p. 78.

27. Anthony A. D'Amato, Harvey L. Gould, and Larry D. Woods, "War Crimes and Vietnam: The 'Nuremberg Defence' and the Military Service Resister," *California Law Review,* 57 (November 1969), p. 1058.

28. U.S. Department of the Army, *The Law of Land Warfare,* Field Manual No. 27–10, 1956. On the applicability of the international law of warfare to an undeclared war in Vietnam, the Manual clearly states: "As the customary law of war applies to cases of international armed conflict and to the forcible occupation of enemy territory generally as well as to declared war in its strict sense, a declaration of war is not an essential condition of the application of this body of law. Similarly, treaties relating to 'war' may become operative notwithstanding the absence of a formal declaration of war."

29. Stuart Hampshire, "Russell, Radicalism, and Reason," *New York Review of Books,* 15 (October 8, 1970), p. 3 Also see Noam Chomsky, *American Power and the New Mandarins* (New York: Vintage Books, 1969).

30. Richard A. Falk, "War Crimes and Individual Responsibility: A Legal Memorandum," *Transaction,* 7 (January 1970), pp. 33–34.

31. Ibid., p. 34.

32. Quoted in Edward S. Herman, *Atrocities in Vietnam: Myths and Realities* (Philadelphia: Pilgrim Press, 1970), pp. 43–45.

33. Herman, *Atrocities in Vietnam,* pp. 54–60.

34. D'Amato, Gould, and Woods, "War Crimes and Vietnam," pp. 1081–1082.

35. John Gerassi, *North Vietnam: A Documentary* (Indianapolis: Bobbs-Merrill, 1968).

36. Gabriel Kolko in Erwin Knoll and Judith Nies McFadden, eds., *War Crimes and the American Conscience* (New York: Holt, Rinehart and Winston, 1970), p. 57.

37. D'Amato, Gould, and Woods, "War Crimes and Vietnam," p. 1075.

38. For some of the sources of documentation, see ibid., pp. 1077–1081.

39. Arthur W. Galston in Knoll and McFadden, eds., *War Crimes and the American Conscience,* p. 69.
40. D'Amato, Gould, and Woods, "War Crimes and Vietnam," pp. 1091–1093.
41. Taylor, *Nuremberg and Vietnam,* pp. 96–97.
42. See *The New York Times,* December 20, 1970, p. 8.
43. Falk, "War Crimes and Individual Responsibility," p. 39.
44. Taylor, *Nuremberg and Vietnam,* pp. 154–207. Also *The New York Times,* January 9, 1971, p. 3.
45. Richard A. Falk, in *The New York Times Book Review,* December 27, 1970, p. 14.
46. Peter Maas, *The Valachi Papers* (New York: G. P. Putnam's Sons, 1968), p. 274. Quoted in Stuart L. Hills, *Crime, Power, and Morality: The Criminal-Law Process in the United States* (Scranton, Pa.: Chandler, 1971), p. 121.
47. Hills, *Crime, Power, and Morality,* pp. 121–122.
48. Ibid., p. 123.
49. John A. Gardiner, *The Politics of Corruption: Organized Crime in an American City* (New York: Russell Sage Foundation, 1970), pp. 22–23.
50. William J. Chambliss, "Vice, Corruption, Bureaucracy, and Power," *Wisconsin Law Review,* 1971 (No. 4, 1971), pp. 1172–1173.
51. See Anthony Ripley, "After the Defiance, Guilt and Resignation," *The New York Times,* October 14, 1973, p. E2.
52. "How Agnew Bartered His Office to Keep from Going to Prison," *The New York Times,* October 23, 1973, p. 1.
53. Hank Messick, *John Edgar Hoover* (New York: David McKay, 1972), pp. 172–176.
54. Ibid., pp. 190–191.
55. Ibid., p. 254.
56. On the Watergate events, see J. Anthony Lukas, "The Story So Far," *The New York Times Magazine,* July 22, 1973, pp. 1–41. Also *Watergate: Chronology of a Crisis* (Washington, D.C.: Congressional Quarterly, 1973).
57. Kirkpatrick Sale, "The World Behind Watergate," *The New York Review of Books,* 20 (May 3, 1973), p. 14.
58. Ibid., p. 15.
59. *Congressional Quarterly Almanac,* 1972, vol, 28 (Washington, D.C.: Congressional Quarterly Inc., 1972), p. 91.
60. L. Fletcher Prouty, "Watergate and the World of the CIA," *Ramparts,* 12 (October 1973), p. 50.
61. Much of the evidence is summarized in Mae Brussell, "Why Was Martha Mitchell Kidnapped?" *The Realist,* No. 93 (August 1972), pp. 1, 27–47.
62. Jeff Gerth, "Nixon and the Mafia," *SunDance,* 1 (November-December, 1972), p. 32. Also see Hank Messick, *Lansky* (New York: Berkley Medallion Books, 1973); Lucian K. Truscott IV, "The Rebozo Connection," *The Village Voice,* 18 (August 30, 1973), pp. 1, 24–34; "Nixon and Organized Crime," *NACLA's Latin America & Empire Report,* 6 (October 1972), pp. 3–17.

How the Government Breaks the Law

Jethro K. Lieberman

A HEALTHY CONTEMPT FOR THE LAW

Let's put crime in perspective and openly admit that we couldn't get along in America unless we were all willing to break the law. Despite gloomy ruminations over the sorry state of things in this most apocalyptic of centuries, we Americans do remain steadfastly cheerful about at least one thing—the life of crime. That unremitting moralist, Senator Strom Thurmond, spoke for every American when he tongue-lashed a policeman who was dimwitted enough to attempt to arrest him for running a red light. Senator Thurmond did not deny the crime; he merely reminded the officer that a Senator cannot constitutionally be arrested for committing traffic violations when the Senate is in session. "He didn't understand the system," the Senator later complained of the hapless cop.

In pursuing our way of life, Americans generally share Senator Thurmond's healthy contempt for the law (if not always his immunity). When we have wanted to do something that disturbs our moral sense, we have seen to it that a law is put on the books and have then gone right ahead anyway, secure in the knowledge that we have discharged our moral duty. And we all break laws, those of us who decry the breakdown of law and order no less than others.

When morality is on the books, it is accounted for. Fornication and adultery are crimes, but Americans—even law-abiding Americans—are guilty of them nonetheless. There were tens of thousands—maybe millions—of drinkers during

SOURCE: Jethro K. Lieberman, *How the Government Breaks the Law* (Briarcliff Manor, N.Y.: Stein and Day, 1972), pp. 17-27, 233-55. Copyright © 1972 by Jethro K. Lieberman. Reprinted with permission of Stein and Day/Publishers.

Prohibition, but Congress refused to authorize adequate funds to permit the alcoholic ban to be enforced. Drug laws and children aren't what they used to be: if some unlucky individuals are convicted of smoking marijuana, most are not—by mutual consent of the police and the governed. Congressmen don't like other people to accept bribes; but they are more equivocal when it comes to judging their own behavior, and eager officials in the Justice Department would rather not indict until the candidate has lost. You're a sucker if you think the Internal Revenue Service will spot every bit of padding, and you are not supposed to jaywalk or speed, but everyone does. A free nation of activists need hardly be deterred by restrictions everyone knows were never intended to be enforced. It is the pact we Americans have made with ourselves: condemnation without injunction. So many laws and so little reason to abide by any of them. Even more than baseball or professing self-righteousness, law-breaking is the national pastime.

To be sure, some among us profess disgust with crime. Some even deplore the "crime rate" and its inevitable, drum-rolling increase. Candidates of most persuasions, suburbanites, depraved city dwellers, and even some honest folks have expressed alarm at the rape and robbery index. The Governments of the United States pour out torrents of statistics to show us how worried we should be. But surely many of our esteemed citizens are joking, for they own guns and glorify bad men by paying high prices at movies to be nourished by violent deeds. Surely these protestations of innocence are merely the subtle jokes of a people more sophisticated than most suspect. But perhaps not. For the crime statistics measure only "hard" crime, and the lawbreaking in which most Americans indulge is "soft" or "petty" crime, not usually measured because it is rarely detected. So the irate citizen who takes a few office supplies home for his personal use or pads an expense account is not necessarily inconsistent—and may be innocent in outlook, if not in deed—when he decries the steady increase in larceny.

This "soft" lawbreaking would be inconsequential and scarcely worth noting, except that it establishes a moral climate conducive to a grander form of lawbreaking. Petty thievery is obviously a business expense; speeding, of itself, hurts no one; "nickel-and-dime" cheating on a tax return hardly affects the size or operations of the federal Government. So none of these incidents of lawbreaking causes any general crisis in confidence about America itself. They do, however, provide the foundation for our tolerance of the most serious threat to law and order: "official" lawbreaking by the Government itself.

Nowadays when Presidents of the United States and other officials of high rank—like Kings and Premiers—exhort their citizenry to obey the law, the implication is obvious that the governments they head are virtuous upholders of the law of the land. It is, in fact, more than an implication: every President likes to say that his administration will enforce to the limit all the laws, without fear or favor, equally and without discrimination.

Thus, President Eisenhower at a news conference in 1954 shortly after the Supreme Court ruled public school segregation unconstitutional, said: "The Supreme Court has spoken and I am sworn to uphold the constitutional processes in this country; and I will obey."* And President Nixon, similarly asked of his policy with regard to the Supreme Court's decision in 1969 ordering immediate school desegregation, said: "To carry out what the Supreme Court has laid down. I believe in carrying out the law even though [I disagree with the Supreme Court decision] . . . . But we will carry out the law."

It was not always so. Years ago kings were not wont to disguise their conceits: "L'état, c'est moi," said Louis XIV, and no one supposed a public would react to the belief with an overbearing display of moral indignation. Kings were above the law, not of it. Since they made it, they scarcely were required to abide by it. In our time, even Mao Tse-tung has proclaimed his empire a "People's Democracy." Though the conceit may be the same, "democracy" has made its claim so strong that few would seriously support another name. It means, no matter how dazzling the rationalization may sometimes be, that governments are creatures of the law.

We should not be fooled by the claim. Unhappily, not all governments today abide by the proposition that the state is subservient to law. In the Soviet Union, for example, it is a commonplace that Russian citizens are subject to a rule of men. Suspects of suspect crimes are locked up on bureaucratic whim, sentenced to long prison terms for abusing the freedoms of speech and press which the Soviet Constitution purports to grant. Secret police monitor the activities of the citizenry. Thirty-five years ago, millions were murdered during bloody purges. Torture was countenanced. Nations were illegally invaded on trumped up charges in the name of threats to security. Some would contend these things happen still in Russia.

Nor is the greatest ideological foe of the United States the only nation to which an accusing finger can be pointed. Brazilians and Greeks and Pakistanis know torture. In Italy, people can be detained in prison without charges for months, on the flimsiest of grounds; Italian law makes American "preventive detention" seem a polite interlude in a civilized proceeding. In China, there is massive slaughter in the name of revolution. In South Africa, people are detained without cause, placed under a house arrest that continues for years without charges ever being preferred, and political prisoners are tortured and some are killed. Throughout the world repressive juntas, cabals, dictatorships, and elites are commonplace.

The orthodox view is that it doesn't happen here. This is not merely the official line; it is the unblushing opinion of sincere citizens throughout the nation that

---

*When asked three months later whether he had given any thought ot seeking legislation from Congress to back up the Supreme Court decrees mandating integration, President Eisenhower said: "The subject has not even been mentioned to me."

the Government is a doer of good and that our good will should be accorded it.

There are dissenters. Professor Joseph LaPalombara, a political scientist at Yale University, has charged that the foundations of modern America are sunk deeply into crime and corruption. This, he asserts, is not merely true, it is inevitable: corruption is a necessary mechanism in the development of backward societies, our own not excluded, and our AID officials ought to stop feeding pap to local missions about how to organize and manage pure and sincere development programs. He urges our administrators not merely to tolerate but to appreciate the existence of a little hanky-panky. Professor LaPalombara thinks that in twentieth-century America there is still need to blink at a few honest examples of corruption and official crime.

Just as the private citizen must commit crime to get along in this modern world, the argument runs, so the Government can hardly be expected to sit back and obey the laws which some Puritans among us forced into enactment. The double standard is un-American, and therefore the Government must break the law in a thousand ways; it must break the law in as many ways, in fact, as there are reasons to do so.

When a man is fired from his job for telling the truth to Congress about the scandal in his federal office, his boss has broken the law (but other employees have learned a lesson).

When young children are forced into slavery by the wardens of reformatories, no one can doubt the law has been at least politely overlooked (but someone gets free labor).

When a judge increases the sentence of a convicted felon because the criminal wants to appeal his conviction, the Government has broken the law (but it has forestalled troublesome proceedings).

When the police raid your house because they don't like the discussion that is taking place, the Government has broken the law (but it has warned others against quarrelsome conversations).

When the Defense Department forges documents to be given to a Congressional committee, the Government has committed a crime for which ordinary mortals, unloved by Congress, have been sent to jail (but luckily the federal officers cannot be imprisoned, since they were clearly politically motivated).

When the Government decides that some polluters, but not all polluters, ought to be prosecuted, the Government as well as the polluters have violated the law (but the laudable ends are obvious).

When the President of the United States appoints a man constitutionally ineligible to hold a seat on the Supreme Court, and the Senate confirms the nomination, and the man takes that seat, the Government has merely flouted a silly rule in the Constitution.

When a major general is permitted to hold a job that he may not legally hold, and a lieutenant is told he has forfeited his commission under similar circumstances, the Government has breached the law (but the general is protected).

When a high Government officer changes official policy to suit the needs of a prized campaign contributor, bribery has occurred (but the official gets re-elected).

When a prosecutor puts into a case evidence he knows to be false, the Government has committed an illegal act (but it has upheld the "rights" of the public).

The President breaks the law when he commits the United States Government to policies not submitted to the Senate for ratification as required by the Constitution (but he thereby gets policies he might not otherwise have got).

When judges declaim from the bench, as they occasionally do, that they know the law is other than they say, they have broken the law in the name of the state (but the conviction is secured, at least temporarily).

When state legislators, knowing that their constitutions require them to apportion their seats in accordance with a scheme that would not suit them politically, do suit themselves by failing to reapportion for more than seventy years, the legislature has engaged in a willful and continuing flouting of law (that unfortunately has led to federal control we all naturally detest).

When the governmental agencies choose to disregard their own regulations, on the theory that if you make them you can break them, they have violated law (but they do not undermine confidence in the administrative process—if no one finds out).

When clusters of governments, agencies, boards, and bureaus choose to weasel around clear policies against discrimination, they have degraded themselves and disgraced principles for which American constitutional law stands (but they do keep the blacks out a few years more).

And when the Government requires soldiers to obey orders that it may well be unlawful to obey, and condemns these soldiers for obeying the same orders when it becomes clear that they were illegal, some think the Government's lawbreaking skirts visible national disaster, whereas it is perfectly clear that the Government is simply trying to uphold freedom in a time of turbulence, if only the people would let it alone, shut up, and forget about it.

Of course, the Government is merely an odd assortment of people paid by the public treasurer. The "Government" in the abstract does not break the law. Men and women do. When ordinary private citizens break the law against murder or robbery or extortion, we call them "common criminals" or "thugs," depending on their body weight and resemblance to a Nordic ideal of physical beauty. When extraordinary private citizens (those with higher salaries or better connections) break the laws against bribery or price-fixing, we tend to call them "corrupt" or "misguided," depending on the number of times they have been divorced and whether we believe in their product.

So with politicians and officials on the take: he who accepts a bribe or a favor or a suspiciously large campaign contribution has been corrupted, and that is too bad, and a little depressing, to be regretted and condemned; but the fault is peculiar to the criminal and should not reflect on you or me (so long as it is not too widespread a phenomenon; so long, that is, as we don't know about it).

Because nothing much hinges on it, the petty corruption of elected and appointed criminals is not new and is rather boring, except around election time when a man can suddenly be simultaneously a despicable hound and a martyr the likes of whom has not been seen since Giordano Bruno was burned at the stake.

Certain people would have us believe, however, that when public officials break the law for and on behalf of the Government, and not on their own account, crimes of a different order and consequence have been committed. It is said that a democratic society can tolerate random lawbreaking by robbers, rapists, murderers, and even self-styled revolutionaries, but that it cannot avoid serious damage, or even survive, in the face of sustained "official" criminal activity. Historically, the argument is nonsense, since the Government has been breaking the law consistently during the past two centuries and we have not collapsed yet. Rhetorically, however, the argument has a certain surface plausibility: Government lawbreaking, our theorists conclude, is fundamental to the ills of society, for nothing can be more conducive to the breakdown of law than the Government's own willful disinclination to obey it.

The full argument runs something like this: when citizens become criminals on their own account the community has a way of rallying around the agents of "justice." There is little resistance to the notion that those who violate most classes of prohibitory laws are to be condemned, and even among those who advocate "civil disobedience" there is a strong undercurrent of belief that those who break the law for higher ends must be prepared to accept the consequences. Socrates's willingness to accept capital punishment is still generally regarded as a moral act of the first magnitude.

When the Government breaks the law, however, the psychological reactions are far more complex. The community is split. No one need defend a criminal, but "our Government" (as opposed to "the bureaucracy") must be sustained and defended; illegal activity, when committed by the Government, quickly becomes fuzzy and political, thus salving the conscience of some, since staunch and "sincere" political beliefs are highly prized. And when the political activity is illegal, it can put even the most fair-minded citizen in a terrible dilemma, for he is part of the citizenry that nurtures the Government. Thus, whenever the Government takes some action, part of the populace—whether a larger or smaller part depends on the issue—will automatically support it simply because it is action taken in the name of the Government. The resulting ambivalence of individuals and antagonisms among citizens of different political opinions can tear society apart.

At first blush, the foregoing argument may seem to have intrinsic appeal. Indeed, the logic is inescapable but for one glaring assumption—namely, that the laws are all perfect expressions of social policies to be enforced or carried out. And obviously, this assumption is fallacious. Laws are often wrong, or sloppily worded, unclear, troublesome, or even dangerous.

A Government cannot be expected to obey laws that are inconvenient or unsuited to the needs of the times, for what good is governmental power if it cannot be used? If social illness from Government crimes is the price we must pay for law and order, we ought to be willing to bear it. No less than the common man, the Government must have a healthy contempt for the law if it is to govern at all.

That is the composite answer to the argument against government criminality. More ingenious and narrow answers are made whenever

The President of the United States,

The Army,

The Navy,

Other military services,

The Attorney General,

Other Executive officials,

Prosecutors,

Judges,

Congress, and

The police

break the law. They all have their lawyers. This healthy contempt for the laws, without which society would probably collapse from the strain of trying to remember, much less abide by, the entire rulebook, is a subject that scholars and popularizers sorely neglect, except in bits and pieces, now and then. To illuminate this heretofore dark byway of social science and American mores, the following discussion will chart the ways by which the Government comes to grips with the law—and defeats it.

It is not ordinary to think of the Government as a lawbreaker, though it is quite usual to berate it for stupidity, cowardice, and folly. Yet in modern times, charges against the Government have taken on a new dimension—not mere hardship born of unwisdom, but rank oppression sired by blatant violations of the law. Hear the rollcall: Mylai, the Panthers, Kent and Jackson State, Attica. Scandal that came to light once in a while and merely titillated or mildly shocked is now a torrent rushing forth, and it horrifies.

But back off. The Government is no citizen, though it is run by citizens—and even the citizen is conceded to have the right to disobey certain laws whose complete depravity convince the Supreme Court of their unconstitutionality. The Government is an instrument designed to bring order out of social chaos. Should it be bound by formalistic legalisms? That is the counterargument, but it will not wash.

Proponents of civil disobedience often point to the moral necessity of disobeying particular laws, while adhering to a belief that "the law" or "law" must continue to be respected, even revered. "The rule of law," they say, has a value intrinsically superior to that of any particular law, moral or immoral, wise or unwise. Though they may break a law to protest it, they will suffer the consequences.

Less conservative advocates of civil disobedience contend that it is a prime fallacy to say "that the rule of law has an intrinsic value apart from moral ends." A law student, in a book review lauding a series of radical essays on law, summed up one extreme view when he recommended that the book "top the reading list of all lawyers who think humanity might be more important than the law."

At the other extreme, of course, some people deny there is ever a cause to disobey any law.

The debate is a fundamental one because it concerns the nature of human freedom—if people are free only as they obey their own laws, what must they do about laws that deprive them of freedom or are otherwise unjust? Can we be free without law? Can we be free with unjust laws? The debate continues to rage wherever it is conceded that people are ends in themselves, and not means to other ends.

The argument is altogether different, however, when the question is whether the government must submit to "the rule of law." For the government is surely a means to an end, not an end in itself. Moreover, it is a means created by law and endowed with great power, which untempered by the charter of its existence, becomes irrational and unreasoning armed might. The government's disavowal of the rule of law—exemplified by its violation of particular laws—is far stronger than the citizen's protest against a particular law: the citizen will be forced to stand the consequences of his act, whether or not he should morally be required to do so; the government will rarely be rebuked in ways that count.

This book is devoted to the government's violation of the rule of law. Some examples are of how the government breaks particular laws; others are instances of the government's failure to enforce particular laws. But this is not a book about particular policies; it is not a book about raw injustices; it is not about unwise acts; it is not even about bad or harmful laws, except insofar as they may be unconstitutional. It is not a book about the injustice of racial conditions in the United States (except insofar as they are the reflection of government criminality), nor about the injustice of poverty, war, or inequality; again, except insofar as these conditions spring from the disobedience of government to the rule of law.

Of course, the most clearly seen goal can be thwarted by the awkward fuzziness of reality. "The law" is rarely clear, and therefore, what is unlawful is not always easy to discern. The legal profession has thrived in Western culture for more than five centuries because of that plain fact.

The lack of clarity and certainty in law not only creates confusion for the citizen; it spawns political institutions of vast and ill-defined powers. A government of many and diverse powers and its attendant bureaucracy, created to control the infinite variety of private crimes, undesirable practices, and acts of moral turpitude high and low, carries with it an amazing degree of discretion. Statutes creating administrative agencies are always vague. The laws allow to the administrators, and even their clerks and assistants, a wide latitude of possible moves. If this is an evil to be deplored, it inheres in the nature of things. Regulatory authority cannot be clear-cut. If the aim is to put an end to discriminatory and shady business practices, a clear definition of what is prohibited would permit any moderately intelligent lawyer to show his client a dozen ways to avoid the law. So it is said.

Bureaucracies are not the only governmental agencies with the power of discretion. All law confers some degree of discretion. Judges who apply the laws of ordinary crimes, of contracts, and of fiduciary responsibility must be guided by their sense of equity and by their own judgment, for these laws talk in terms of "reasonableness" and "substantiality," terms that give those who must judge room in which to wander. Thus, much of what a trial judge decides will not be upset on appeal even though the higher judge thinks it wrong, because the law permits the trial judge the leeway of discretion, and often only clear abuses are reversible.

On final analysis, this is as it has to be. Decisions must be made in life, and people have to know they can rely on what has been decided. A course of conduct that calls for a decision to move this way or that cannot forever be held in abeyance because it is subject to being second- and third-guessed. This is true of personal life as well as public life and mistakes should be tolerated because there is no realistic alternative. The code of law that dispenses with all discretion is and always will be an impossibility.

Unfortunately, this fact stands obstinately in the way of controlling—even judging—both undesirable and unlawful government behavior. If it is imperative to grant the Government discretionary powers, it is correspondingly difficult to block their usage. The result is that the Government takes actions that are immediately denounced by partisans as being unwarranted, unwise, or unlawful.

Legality is a slippery concept. Like most complex abstractions, it is subject to daily abuse. The temptation is often overwhelming to denounce what we despise as not merely wrong, misguided, or evil, but as actually unlawful or even unconstitutional. "They can't do that," we say. The capacity to distrust Government and to be discontented by what it does is nearly infinite; the United States, we like to remind ourselves somewhat mistakenly, was founded on just that distrust and skepticism.

Lack of agreement does not convert otherwise lawful action into crime, however. Though there can be nearly unanimous agreement that some laws are unwise or unjust, it will not wash to describe actions taken pursuant to such laws as illegal. The oil depletion allowance is condemned by many people, conceivably even by a public majority. You can say the allowance is unwise and unjust. Yet deductions taken pursuant to it cannot therefore be regarded as unlawful. Neither can the Government's refusal to grant deferments to those young men who conscientiously object to certain wars be branded as unlawful, though you may deplore the spirit and the reach of the Selective Service Act, which allows draft boards to deny such requests. Even obvious Government oppression is not necessarily illegal, though the dividing line between lawful oppression and un-lawful acts is often extremely difficult to discern.

For the most part, governmental actions explored in this book can be tested against the standards of the laws. One agency will give us trouble: the Supreme Court of the United States. For just as a king might be perplexed to know how he could be bound by the law that he fashioned and could unfashion, so it is difficult to contend that the Court can act unlawfully when it interprets the Constitution or other laws. As Justice Robert Jackson once said: "We are not final because we are infallible, but we are infallible only because we are final." This is not to say that the Court has not made some outrageous decisions; every-one agrees it has. It is only to say that we will have to proceed with some caution in alleging errors in measurement against the holder of the yardstick.

Because the Court is likely to change the meaning of the Constitution at un-predictable times, it is sometimes unfair to charge that an official agency has acted unconstitutionally before the Court has so characterized the agency's activities. While the supremacy of the Court's constitutional decisions is unques-tioned here, they will for the most part be used to test the legality of govern-mental action prospectively. To take an obvious case, racial segregation of public educational institutions, while regrettable and oppressive in 1953 and before, was not unlawful in states that had laws permitting it, because the Supreme Court itself had sanctioned the practice in 1896. In 1954, however, after the Supreme Court ruled such practices unconstitutional, further adherence to the policy became blatantly illegal. (There are, however, occasions when it is clear that a Supreme Court decision should be used to test the legality of Goverment activity retroactively, for the Government frequently acts in ways never judicially sanctioned.)

The test for illegality is not easy to apply, though the extent of governmental illegality is widespread enough to make for easy pickings. Often a law will be clear enough on its face that anyone who denies the violation is saying merely that "no" is "yes," a definitional process that happens more often than it should. More regularly still, owing to the fact that courts must interpret the muddy sentences of legislatures, judicial decisions make it unmistakably clear that the law means that the Government may not do what it commonly does. In response, the Government will sometimes simply remain silent. Occasionally, Government will attempt to shift the focus by accusing its accuser of crimes. Most often the Government, caught with its pants down, will attempt to create a haze of justification and block from view those delicate sights sure to cause it and its admirers embarrassment. That the technique of law-avoidance requires the government to assert that what is a crime is not, that it is really just some routine, discretionary, managerial, executive function, ought to fool no one. Painting a leaky ship will not prevent it from sinking, even if those who believe the defect has been remedied stay aboard.

CAUSES AND EFFECTS

Causes

It ought to be obvious that there are many different causes of Governmental lawbreaking. Just as we may ascribe to the private crimes of individual citizens many different motives, so too the reasons for the Government to disregard the law are complex. Though different strands of explanation can be described, they do not individually explain Government lawlessness, any more than individual strands explain the strength of braided rope. To varying degrees, the causes fit together.

LAWLESSNESS GENERALLY. The primary, underlying cause for the lawlessness of the Government in modern times is that in a very direct sense it is without law. Its power is delegated from legislative bodies, and such delegation in the Twentieth Century has been almost entirely standardless. That is, Congress has transferred power to the Executive Branch without prescribing how that power is to be used. Regulators and administrators are free to carry out "public policy" on their own.

In the absence of strict legal controls, the classic American response to the potentiality of dictatorial power is to co-opt it. As has often been observed, administrators tend to be captured by those they oversee. Tough policy at the enactment stage cries out for soft policy at the enforcement stage.

But actions undisciplined by explicit standards can become lazy and slovenly habits; and when the administrator sees he has nothing to fear by cooperating with his wards, he becomes by degrees bolder when his actions and their interests hurt others. So powerful does the habit become that he can close his eyes when he or his minions cross the line into illegality; so automatic is the reflex that his response unvaryingly tells us he has rationalized again. Without standards, rationalizing is easy, and the administrator may actually believe he has done right or at least not done wrong. The sincere lawbreaker—especially when he is cloaked with the governmental imperium—is hard to beat.

Kenneth Culp Davis, a scholarly observer of the bureaucracy, has concluded that "perhaps 80 or 90 percent of the administrative process involves discretionary action in the absence of [the safeguards of hearings or judicial] review." The armed forces process hundreds of thousands (and sometimes millions) of soldiers, sailors, and airmen every year. Senior officers make millions of decisions affecting their lives under sweeping regulations that provide little scope of review.

Regulatory agencies of all types are likewise required to pass upon enormous numbers of applications, cases, and other matters and to dispose of them under the vaguest of guidelines. As Davis has noted:

For the fiscal year 1969 the SEC passed upon 4,706 registration statements, but it had only 103 formal cases. It probably issued about 5,000 no-action letters. For the same year the FCC disposed of more than half a million transmitter applications, but it had only 197 formal cases. The Immigration and Naturalization Service handled the huge number of 20,109 formal cases, but it disposed informally of 993,324 applications. The Social Security Administration passed upon 4,600,000 claims for benefits, but it had only 24,048 formal cases; the number of persons covered by insurance increased to 101,000,000. The Internal Revenue Service received 110,000,000 tax returns and examined 2,544,000; it recommended 1,049 prosecutions (in each instance making a very important determination), but it decided only 37 formal cases.

As the discretionary powers of Government increase in number, the burden of regulation and enforcement increases correspondingly. As bureaucracies grow larger, increasing amounts of time are required to be devoted to internal housekeeping, management, and liaison. The substantive, underlying regulatory goal is often lost. Also, the increase in the number of bureaucrats diffuses the responsibility for decision-making (and multiplies instances of lawbreaking).

Administrative errors are rarely one person's fault. The seizure of the U.S.S. *Pueblo* by the North Koreans showed just how diffuse accountability had become in the United States Navy, where theoretically each higher rung of the chain of command is responsible for mistakes of the lower rungs. But precisely because responsibility ran up a chain of command, the Navy was reluctant to assign blame to any one person or any particular level. The top man, Admiral Thomas H. Moorer, Chief of Naval Operations, was later rewarded with a promotion to the chairmanship of the Joint Chiefs of Staff.

In the common-sense view of things, we usually blame the man who pulled the trigger, not the many people in the deviant's past who one way or another helped fashion the criminal personality. But in the case of Government, where each level of bureaucracy is merely "following orders," the lack of an accountable boss and the possibility of pleading that any action taken was within the lawful discretion of the administrator very often means that anything goes. Thus, practices deriving from lawful bureaucratic activity may become agency policy even though they are unlawful.

Administrative discretion does not mean that the Government always violates the law out of malice or vindictiveness; far more often it means that sloppy staff work, laziness, and lack of the necessary follow-up—all conducive to unlawful acts—flourish in the discretionary wilderness. The need and prerogative of discretion become so thoroughly ingrained in Government that when there are signs of trouble administrative agencies usually permit an investigation by their own investigators only, which is something like the Attorney General's asking the Mafia to engage in a little "self-regulation."

Discretion can, of course, breed contempt for the law directly. Someone long accustomed to having his own way is not often inclined to permit others to test his actions, and malice works best under cover.

Administrative discretion poses the same difficulty for the investigator that an impenetrable jungle provides for the explorer. Justice Brandeis's statement to the effect that sunlight is the best disinfectant is often quoted; but in a modern state with tens of thousands of ordinances, regulations, statutes, and judicial decisions, the difficulty of uncovering lawbreaking, much less of making it public, is immense. As one essayist has put it:

> Like so much else in the bureaucracy, its illegality is strikingly devoid of flair, of passion, and of individuality. If it is hidden from the public, it hides not behind a well-constructed shield of secrecy, but behind a camouflage of boredom. Federal lawlessness is the result of a systematic series of decisions that become impersonal and eventually uninteresting, except to the victims. It is no thrill; it is a sure thing, accomplished from nine to five, with regular coffee breaks.

When occasional examples of corruption or lawbreaking are revealed, they are more often than not passed over with nonchalance or perhaps "deplored," with no further action being taken.

Moreover, standardless legislation means that social policies can be defeated as easily, and sometimes far more easily, at the enforcement stage than at the enactment stage. The prelude to legislation is highly visible: the arguments pro and con are discussed volubly, and the news media focus popular attention on legislative deliberations. Most new laws will be effective over a very broad spectrum of society because legislation by nature is general; the statute (usually) establishes broad precepts or commandments. And once a law is enacted, it is recorded for all who know where to find it to read.

Enforcement of the laws, to the contrary, is not universal; it is particular. It is not a one-time declaration; it is a never-ending process. Legislation is centralized; enforcement, decentralized. Enforcement is not open, visible, and voluble; at least, it need not be. It is often hidden, difficult to find, and lacking in pattern. Reporters find it more difficult to write about the lack of law enforcement—because it is difficult and dangerous to prove that criminal activities are taking place in the enforcement area—than to write about the passage of laws, news of which is usually handed to them in a press release by a proud President or legislator.

Furthermore, the effort to promote general legislation or to defeat it is very expensive because so much is being bought; the cost of corrupting an administrator to deter him from enforcing a law in a particular instance is far cheaper, because protection for everyone is not necessary. The promise of a $30,000-a-year industry job is obviously cheaper than a million-dollar advertising campaign. Finally, vague policies may slip by and become law; application against a particular offender is invariably objected to. That is why policies in the public interest occasionally become law and are then rarely enforced: witness campaign laws, pollution laws (at least until lately), and other laws regulating health, safety, and welfare.

Special interest groups have economic and other motives for attempting to influence bureaucrats. But the public's interest is too diffuse even to demand effective implementation and administration of the many regulations to warrant the time and money it costs to monitor the Government.

Read through Title 32, Chapter XVI, of the Code of Federal Regulations—the rules dealing with the Selective Service System—and you will be struck immediately by the gap between the promises on paper and the personal experiences of husbands, sons, and brothers before their draft boards. The names of board members, for instance, are supposed to be posted. Yet there are dozens of examples in the burgeoning legal literature of selective service law of board members unaware or contemptuous of the regulations, who refuse to give out their names, especially after having made an unlawful, unwise, or impolitic comment at a hearing. Their reactions are perfectly understandable even if they are often unlawful. But who can monitor all these examples of petty illegality by petty officials and hold them to account?

The American political system tolerates bad laws passed openly (no matter how difficult the legal language in which they are couched). It does not, however, formally tolerate the cheaper alternative of private control over law enforcement. When the Government is implicated, the unlawful activity must be justified as within the bounds of administrative discretion. Doing this is usually an easy matter because of the inflexible operation of Lieberman's Law.

LIEBERMAN'S LAW   The Law explains the paradoxical fact that the lack of law in the administrative process is due largely to the superabundance of law. The Law runs as follows:

Legal rules proliferate to support their loopholes. The Law perceives the increase in legal rules as a dynamic tendency: the lack of law produces more law, and when there is too much law there is no law at all.

Description of the Law. The rule can best be described as a wall of lattice-work: the thin strips of wood represent all of our legal rules, but the pervasive holes are very prominent; indeed, but for the holes there would be no design at all.

Quantitative Formulation. The rate of expansion in laws is at least geometrical. That is, let us say a rule is created and four loopholes in it are discovered. So another rule is promulgated, with four parts, one to plug each hole. But in order to pass the new rule, other rules have to be announced to prevent misuse of the four-part rule. Each of these new rules and each part of the four-part rule are then discovered to have their own loopholes. So the process begins again, with ever-increasing rapidity.

Personnel. The system of creating rules, applying them, and attempting to plug the loopholes (usually called regulation or law enforcement) requires personnel—

called bureaucrats—for its operation. Laws are not self-executing. The human agencies required to implement every regulatory scheme may abuse their power, so an ever-lengthening set of rules is concocted to control the power. But these controls are not self-executing either so more agencies and divisions and subdivisions are necessarily created to act as counterweights (appeal boards, advice boards, offices of general counsel, public relations and information offices, liaison offices) to insure that each office talks to the others. More rules, internal rules, are promulgated to ensure that these offices all get along.

The ratio of bureaucrats to rules (B/R) has never been systematically explored. So hazy is our understanding, in fact, that we have two common contradictory versions: the first has it that the country is crawling with bureaucrats whose number far outstrips the demand created by legal rules and who, consequently, wind up shuffling papers. The second version has it that there are an overwhelming number of rules whose enforcement is greatly impeded by the paucity of monitoring officials. These versions can be reconciled by the simple corollary to the Law that *creating rules is far more important than enforcing them.* This corollary follows because enforcement is conceived of as a method of plugging loopholes and, by the Law, Americans plug loopholes by creating more rules.

One example of the Law in operation should suffice. The coal mining industry in the United States has neglected the welfare of its workers for years. The Federal Coal Mine Health and Safety Act of 1969 was supposed to change all that. The measure permitted stiff fines of up to $10,000 to be assessed against violators. Because previous laws had rarely been enforced, the Bureau of Mines in early 1971 published a "fee schedule" listing the range of fines (between $5,000 and $10,000) it said would be imposed on operators whose mines are ordered closed because their violations pose an "imminent danger." But the Bureau also established two loopholes for the one rule:

> If it is determined (A) that the operator did not or could not, with the exercise of reasonable diligence, know of the violation, or (B) did not or could not have available to him at the time of inspection the equipment, material, personnel or technology to avoid the violation

the penalties would not be assessed. Translated, the rule means this: the operator is immune from penalty for subtle safety violations; he is also immune, by the second part of the rule, from penalties for gross violations. Whether anything falls in between is up to the benevolence of the Bureau of Mines, which had failed to enforce the law before and had established these new regulations ostensibly to overcome the bureaucratic difficulty of making a choice. Lieberman's Law leads ineluctably to the conclusion that the only way to get respect for law is to wipe out most of our laws.

Administrative discretion does not explain all of governmental lawlessness. Human activity springs from a variety of motivations, and institutional arrangements are subject to deterioration and decay from a variety of causes. Some of these are briefly discussed below.

INABILITY TO ADMIT MISTAKES. The typical politician has a congenital indisposition to heed Cromwell's injunction to think that he may be mistaken. When President Nixon pronounced guilt on Charles Manson, then being tried in California for the sensational slaying of movie actress Sharon Tate and others, the headlines were quick to point out the error. The President was equally quick in backtracking. The President and his aides "explained" what he earlier "meant" or "intended."

The President's original statement follows:

> I think the main concern I have is the attitudes that are created among many of our younger people and also perhaps older people as well, in which they tend to glorify and make heroes out of those who engage in criminal activities. This is not done intentionally by the press. It is not done intentionally by radio and television, I know. It is done perhaps because people want to read or see that kind of story. I noted, for example, the coverage of the Charles Manson case when I was in Los Angeles, front page every day in the papers. It usually got a couple of minutes in the evening news. Here is a man who is guilty, directly or indirectly, of eight murders without reason.

Shortly after these remarks were delivered to journalists at a Law Enforcement Assistance Administration (LEAA) conference in Denver, Ronald Ziegler, the press secretary, personally "clarified" the "intent of the President's remarks":

> The President, in his remarks to you in this room earlier, was, of course, referring to the focus of attention and the dramatics that are oftentimes put on various criminal acts, alleged criminal acts. Quite obviously, the President in his remarks regarding the trial now underway was referring to allegations that had been raised and are now in a court of law. If you take the President's remarks in the context of what he was saying, there is no attempt to impute liability to any accused. The gist of his statement was just the contrary. I think when he concluded his statement in reference to the system, including his remarks to you, he made it very clear that it is important in our system, as it does exist, that individuals have the right of fair trial, although, apparently, many of you understood it to mean something other than the President intended it in his total remarks, to suggest that he was referring to something other than the obvious, and that is the fact that he was referring to the allegation against Mr. Manson and the others on trial in Los Angeles.

That clarification, inarticulate because of haste in making it, was further refined by the President as he returned to Washington; a statement was prepared aboard the Presidential plane and distributed to reporters as the passengers disembarked at Andrews Air Force Base:

I've been informed that my comment in Denver regarding the Tate murder trial in Los Angeles continues to be misunderstood despite the unequivocal statement made at the time by my press secretary. My remarks were in the context of my expression of a tendency on the part of some to glamorize those identified with a crime. The last thing I would do is prejudice the legal rights of any person, in any circumstances. To set the record straight, I do not know and did not intend to speculate as to whether the Tate defendants are guilty, in fact, or not. All the facts in the case have not yet been presented. The defendants should be presumed to be innocent at this stage of their trial. To repeat what I said at the LEAA conference in Denver, our American system of justice requires the constant support of every citizen, to insure a fair trial for the guilty and innocent alike.

The "mistake" was thus explained away as a semantic misinterpretation.

Four months later the President finally owned up to the mistake. At a news conference the following colloquy took place:

Q: Mr. President, at a previous news conference you said that what happened at Mylai was a massacre. On another occasion, you said that Charles Manson is guilty. On another occasion, you mentioned Angela Davis by name and then said that those responsible for such acts of terror will be brought to justice.

My question concerns the problem of pretrial publicity and the fact that it could jeopardize a defendant's rights at a trial. How do you reconcile your comments with your status as a lawyer?

THE PRESIDENT: I think that's a legitimate criticism. I think sometimes we lawyers, even like doctors who try to prescribe for themselves, may make mistakes. And I think that kind of comment is probably unjustified.

This humble confession of error has not signalled any willingness on the President's part to subscribe to the cognate necessity of keeping an open mind. He has said, for instance, that he would pay no heed to any recommendation of his National Commission on Marijuana and Drug Abuse that marijuana be legalized, even though the Commission was only beginning to undertake a study of the problem when the statement was made.

The statement about Manson's guilt is a relatively trivial, though prominent, example of the failure of our political and legal institutions to be able gracefully to admit errors and mistakes. A component of the prosecutor's decision to suppress evidence in the case against Lloyd Eldon Miller was his fear that an acquittal would show a mistake had been made. Jim Garrison, the notorious district attorney of New Orleans charged Clay Shaw with perjury after his acquittal in a Kennedy conspiracy trial in order to cover up Garrison's shenanigans. The cover-ups by high-ranking Army officials in connection with the massacre at Mylai stemmed in part from the same impulse.

After the May Day demonstrations in Washington, Police Chief Jerry V. Wilson denied that false arrests had been made: "The fact that we cannot in every case prove the case in court does not make it a false arrest," he said; "I don't think I would agree that we violated [the demonstrators'] civil rights." It would not have been difficult or even very damaging in terms of his public posture to admit that in the heat of the moment some arrests may have been made without cause. Chief Wilson might have pledged an "investigation" and later exonerated his men; but somehow he and the Attorney General knew almost before the demonstrations had ended that police abided by the law one hundred percent of the time. Babe Ruth himself never hit above .400. Wilson said after the arrests that the only alternative would have been "martial law, which is much worse, because the individual doesn't even get released." Whatever the merits of that legal argument, declaration of martial law would at least have told innocent bystanders and gawking spectators to stay off the streets.

The deeply ingrained and all-too-human reluctance to confess error permits minor mistakes and infractions of the rules to develop into full-blown unlawful policies.

CORRUPTION. Ward politicians brought up on a diet of corruption and conditioned to blink at the law are not readily convinced, once they are elected to high office, that they should always abide by the law. Moreover, the example of officials who blink at or ignore the law is not wasted on their subordinates. Much police corruption stems in part from the tacit understanding that superior officers at the station house will pretend not to see what is going on about them.

The temptation to corruption is understandable, as one policeman explained to an investigator for the President's Commission on Law Enforcement and Administration of Justice:

> These people really work on you. They make it seem so logical—like you are the one that is out of step. This bookie gave me this kind of line: "It's legal at the tracks, isn't it? So why isn't it legal here? It's because of those crooks at the Capitol. They're gettin' plenty—all drivin' Cads. Look at my customers, some of the biggest guys in town—they don't want you to close me down. If you do they'll just transfer you. Like that last jerk. And even the Judge, what did he do? Fined me a hundred and suspended fifty. Hell, he knows Joe citizen wants me here so get smart, be one of the boys, be part of the system. It's a way of life in this town and you're not gonna change it. Tell you what I'll do. I won't give you a nickel; just call in a free bet in the first race every day and you can win or lose, how about it?"

Sometimes the laws directly incite corruption in the administrative agencies created to implement policy. The Texas Youth Council, for example, administers a program whose budget depends directly on the number of children condemned to its reformatories. The budget was established at approximately ten thousand dollars per child in 1969 and 1970; when newspaper revelations of the "agreed judgment" technique for sending children to schools operated by the TYC caused an outcry in El Paso, the TYC revoked the paroles of a much higher number of children than usual to make up for the decrease in the number of those sent directly to the schools for the first time. Thus the budget level was roughly maintained.

POLITICAL PRESSURE. Closely related to rank corruption is the distortion of the legal process caused by political pressures. Even obvious violations of the law are covered up by the apparent governmental policy of firing employees who reveal violations. Thus Ernest Fitzgerald.

Thus, also, the difficulties of the New York State Division of Human Rights (SDHR), which has been almost totally lethargic in enforcing that state's tough antidiscrimination law in the construction trades. An official of the Division said: "I won't say if we're really meeting the problem because if I answer that I'd lose my job." Moreover:

> It was no black militant, but still another official of the SDHR, who said that only the political power of the construction trade union, or fear of it, prevented action. It was a young attorney in the office of the attorney general who told us nothing is being done because of the "political climate," that his superior is a "politician" and that action against discrimination would be unpopular because the electorate is composed of what he called "Procaccino's people." It was an official of the State Department of Labor who stated that the department did not "tangle" with the labor unions, because if it did "its appropriations would be cut off."

The dismal record of the United States Bureau of Mines in policing mines and insuring their safety can be traced in part to the appointment of officials who lack any qualifications whatsoever. The Federal Coal Mine Health and Safety Act of 1969 required that the Interior Department Advisory Committee on Coal Mine Safety Research consist of persons "who are knowledgeable in the field of coal mine safety research." In February, 1971, Acting Secretary of the Interior Fred J. Russell unlawfully appointed to the thirteen-member Committee seven persons without any mining experience. Mrs. Jo Anne Gray, Republican National Committeewoman from Colorado, was put on the committee because "Mrs. Gray's mother's folks were coal miners." Mrs. Sara Abernathy, the widow of a doctor and an employee of Republican Senator Henry L. Bellmon of Oklahoma, was named to the post, according to an Interior Department spokesman, "because a doctor's wife knows a lot about medicine." Two of the new appointees were officials of the two mining companies whose safety policies were so poor that they had the highest death rates due to safety-related defects in the 1960's.

Mr. Russell appointed these people from a list prepared for him by an aide to the Assistant Secretary for Mineral Affairs. The aide had worked for the Colorado Mining Association, a trade association, before his appointment to the Interior Department. The annals of American politics are filled with similar examples of bypassing professional qualifications in choosing personnel.*

STUPIDITY, INSENSITIVITY, AND OVERSIGHT. Stupidity, insensitivity, and oversight are sometimes the causes for lawbreaking, but the surface appearance may be a mask for cunning. In 1971, for example, the Attorney General justified "national security" wiretaps without first applying for court authorization by claiming "by the time enough evidence is obtained to show probable cause, it may well be too late." He added, however, that "when the national security is threatened, prevention is the first consideration. We first need intelligence on the movements of suspected conspirators, not formal evidence on which to convict them." The shift between "probable cause" and "formal evidence" may be a matter of stupidity, insensitivity, or oversight; in all events, it heightens the dramatic tension.

The Attorney General went on to claim that if "enough evidence to show probable cause for a court order to wire tap" existed "we could probably prevent the threat in question without needing a wiretap." That statement, in turn, leaves dangling the question why wiretaps are ever needed when there are legal grounds to get them; but his audience was not enlightened.

In 1970, the new Chief of Naval Operations, Admiral Elmo R. Zumwalt, had issued sixty-seven of his famous "Z-grams," which laid down broad guidelines for modernizing the naval service. A few days before Christmas, the Admiral's military lawyer called over to his counterparts in the Office of the Judge Advocate General, asking them to read over each of the sixty-seven Z-grams in one afternoon to determine whether they were in every respect consistent with Navy Regulations. If they were not consistent, he said, a new Z-gram would be promulgated stating that all the other Z-grams would take precedence over the Navy Regulations. Of course, the Regulations were issued by higher authority even than Admiral Zumwalt, and his Z-grams could have no such legal effect. But it is this kind of oversight and failure to think things through at the proper time that is capable of producing many acts against the law.

---

*Many other advisory committees, operating partly with Government funds, have only industrial representation; for instance, the short-lived Civil Aeronautics Board Finance Advisory Committee and the National Industrial Pollution Control Council. When an occasional advisory group is required by law to contain certain kinds of members, the President has been loath to appoint them. The Advisory Council on Environmental Education, established by the Environmental Educational Act of 1970, required among its members ecologists, students, academicians, and medical, legal and scientific representatives. A year after the Act was signed into law by President Nixon, he had appointed no one to its membership.

MISTAKES AND IGNORANCE. There are so many laws that it is impossible for any Government official to guarantee that his department or agency will not violate one. Sometimes the laws make sense and other times they are hopelessly muddled. It has been said that the Interior Department's Indian Affairs Manual "fills 33 volumes that stack some six feet high and contains more than 2,000 regulations, 389 treaties, 5,000 statutes, 2,000 federal court decisions and 500 opinions of the Attorney General." It is inevitable that the Government will often react to situations out of ignorance or by mistake.

Sometimes the mistake is that of a junior official who understands neither his own function nor the political subtleties that surround him. When Yehudi Menuhin, the world-famous American violinist, accepted honorary Swiss citizenship, he was informed by letter from the American consulate in Berne that a "preliminary decision" of the State Department had been made that his acceptance revoked his birthright.

A stinging letter from Menuhin to Secretary of State William R. Rogers brought forth the reply that "a preliminary finding" had not been reached. Nevertheless, Winifred T. Hall, chief of the consular section of the American Embassy in Switzerland, had written Menuhin that "the Department of State requested us to inform you that your obtention of naturalization as a Swiss citizen is regarded as highly persuasive evidence of your intention to relinquish United States citizenship. The surrounding circumstances and purposes are not considered to negate such intent. Consequently, the Department of State holds that you expatriated yourself. . . . This decision by the Department of State that you have lost your United States citizenship is a preliminary one. The final decision will be made by the Department of State in the next several months."

Switzerland does not award medals or other honors to those it holds in high esteem; its only "form of public honor," according to Menuhin, is the granting of honorary citizenship. In that spirit, Menuhin said, he had been honored to accept the grant. Upon learning of the "preliminary decision," Secretary Rogers ordered that the incident be "investigated promptly" and said he was "distressed" to hear of the Department's letter. Officials noted the next day that the "routine" procedure would be altered to avoid future misunderstandings.

Under the law, the Government must prove that a citizen has voluntarily relinquished his citizenship before it can deny him a passport; there is no legal procedure by which the Government can strip a person of his citizenship. Shortly thereafter, Rogers wrote Menuhin that "your acceptance of an honorary citizenship did not place your United States citizenship in jeopardy."

Mistakes can also result from insufficient or sloppy methods of administrative organization. Examples of loose auditing procedures presented elsewhere in these pages illustrate the problem.

LACK OF PROFESSIONALISM. Many times Government officials break the law and are permitted to break the law by their superiors because they are insufficiently professional. American policemen are consistently underpaid and under-trained; the temptations leading to corruption are abundant. Frequently law enforcement officials perceive their roles along narrow institutional lines and do not sense the larger public interest they are supposed to serve.

Police are supposed to make arrests and "bring criminals to justice." The juris-prudence that says they must make their catch in certain ways only is dismissed as a technicality. The same police department in Minneapolis that conducted the raid on Dr. Lykken's home interrogated a college graduate who sought a job on the force and who had received a grade of 96 on the written civil service examination with such questions as "What do you think of Margaret Mead?" Not surprisingly, he failed the oral examination and was put on probationary status in a suburban department. The fear of educated policemen is a significant deterrent to the staffing of a professional force.

The lack of professionalism is widespread. The lower substratum of judges is almost uniformly inferior. There never has been a professional civil service class in the United States from which could be drawn the thousands of officials who serve in policy-making positions. Instead of men and women who put the public interest first, federal agencies are frequently staffed with political hacks.

Even when top jobs go to extremely able people, the danger of conflict of interest is always present. Traditionally, conflict of interest has meant a conflict between private interest and public trust. Of late, the term has come to mean in addition "confluence of interest"; thus, retired military officers work for defense contractors and tax lawyers get important posts within the Internal Revenue Service, not because they have bribed someone or worked out compelling financial arrangements that can be augmented by official positions, but because the old and new jobs are complementary and call on the same body of knowledge and experience.

The "conflict of interest" is often simply a shared mutual interest. The mutual-ity of interest means, however, that private industry can seduce the civil servant to return to the fold; since partisan politics dominates the selection process, the public servant becomes expert in one substantive area but rarely in the art of government. The lawyer or businessman does not go from one agency to another but from private industry to government and back to the same industry. The implications of such a system are well known: no person who has a stake in a particular industry is likely to devote his entire energies to devising rules that may decrease that industry's profitability.

Even in the few areas of American Government where a career class has de-veloped—such as in the military—the extent of professionalism leaves much to be desired. A Coast Guard Rear Admiral, who presumably received training in the things that can happen to, on, or near the American coasts, apparently was never told about the rules governing defectors—or else he forgot. The few officials on duty in the State Department were similarly unresponsive. And after the Mylai exposure, the Army began beefing up its training sessions on the laws of war—in the belief that the learning was relevant and maybe officers-to-be and soldiers would learn it.

LACK OF RESOURCES. In any human "system" there are always more jobs to be done than time and resources will permit. The "Noble Experiment" of Prohibition was a failure because no sound enforcement program was ever devised. Ramsey Clark relates that for a good part of the 1960's only two narcotics inspectors were responsible for patrolling the entire United States-Mexico border. Inspection programs under the Walsh-Healy Act, which is supposed to protect the safety of workers in factories with federal contracts, is so poorly funded that inspectors cannot hope to examine more than two or three percent of the thousands of federal contractors covered. The United States Geological Survey, which has jurisdiction to police the oil drilling industry, has seventeen inspectors who watch over forty-five hundred oil wells. The Federal Renegotiation Board, responsible for overseeing more than $60 billion worth of government contracts, has a staff of fewer than two hundred people; according to Vice Admiral Hyman Rickover, who has documented its failures in protecting the taxpayer, the Board "is about as effective as putting a Band-aid on cancer."

The Office of Corporation Counsel in Washington is so understaffed that its former chief reported to a City Council budget hearing that "literally no enforcement of the housing code and tax laws could be carried out. Former Corporation Counsel Charles T. Duncan noted in his report that three-quarters of his enforcement division's time was devoted to prosecuting traffic offenses, which require little effort or energy to prosecute—with a like effect on the offenses. He said that "assistants do not have adequate time to prepare for trial or research points of law. . . . Enforcement of various regulations necessarily is haphazard and takes place, if at all, on a time-available basis. There is literally no enforcement of the regulations relating to fair housing and fair employment simply because staff is not available to engage in the extensive preparation which those cases require."

The problem there, as elsewhere, is a severe shortage of money. There are so many laws in the United States and so many ways to avoid them that adequate enforcement funding might take the entire budget. Of course, if the federal Government, not to mention every other government, ever became serious about enforcing laws, the culture of industrial lawbreaking, at least, might be changed.

The lack of money is reflected in other kinds of lawbreaking as well. Perhaps the best example is the constant and nationwide attempt to cut welfare expenditures, legally or not. Full enforcement of the welfare laws, it has been estimated, would double the number of people on welfare and would require an increase in the payments to many people now on the rolls. The incentive to break the law in order to hold down the budget is evident.

THE INOPERATIVE PERSONAL BELIEF SYNDROME. A perversity of the human spirit permits many people to avoid practicing what they preach. Many rail against vice but commit immoral and evil acts, like the politician who frequents private gambling clubs but calls on the police to stop his poorer neighbors from rolling dice in the streets.

The discrepancy between practice and belief is not always easily explained. Sometimes the discrepancy springs from ignorance; Havelock Ellis told the story of the prim lady who for years inveighed against certain private practices of adolescents only to discover in one horrifying moment that she was no stranger to the secret sin herself. Ellis's example is an extreme one, but the Victorian mood that produced it has tenacious roots and its continued growth gives the Government great opportunity to break the law.

Thurmond Arnold put it best when he wrote in 1935 that "most unenforced criminal laws survive in order to satisfy moral objections to established modes of conduct. They are unenforced because we want to continue our conduct, and unrepealed because we want to preserve our morals."

This contradiction between behavior and expressed belief may be called the "inoperative personal belief syndrome," because the belief, though expressed, does not operate to restrain its holder. The cause of the syndrome is multifaceted. Part of the cause lies in the differing moral beliefs of the community. Some people honestly believe that prostitution, vagrancy, gambling, and other vices are immoral. Others are not so persuaded or do not care. Another part lies in the weakness of the human flesh and spirit (else there would be little use for moral codes).

Many people, therefore, do what they know to be wrong, immoral, or dissolute. The politician, who must get himself elected at regular intervals, can rarely discuss openly and honestly his personal beliefs, for popular beliefs in matters of vice and immorality seem to exist, ghostlike, separate and apart from the men and women who espouse them. Legislators must refer to this assumed moral standard, which endures because each person thinks the other person will refer to it. Though no one may really believe in the necessity for a given rule, the belief that another may believe it reinforces it. This can be expressed mathematically by the equation: $0 + 0 = 2$.

What gets enacted by legislators as a result of this syndrome is a set of laws that characterizes as criminal many popular forms of behavior. To protect the legislators themselves, the laws give the police and other law enforcement officials the widest latitude in interpreting the criminal codes. People without influence can be arrested for a variety of petty or harmless offenses; the police often use their discretionary power to enforce these laws in a grossly discriminatory way.

Vice laws invite discrimination. Police often makes arrests in ghetto areas for vague offenses such as "failure to obey a police officer's order to move on" and for using the same profane language toward a police officer that police officers use among themselves back at the precinct.

Police make gambling raids in some areas of town and leave others wide open. In one flagrant instance, police in Pasadena, California, conducted a series of gambling raids in the black ghetto. In 1957, of 292 people arrested for gambling, only 16 were white. Of 91 arrested in 1958, only 9 were white. In 1959, no whites were arrested at all, despite the fact that the police had actually found some whites engaged in illicit gambling. The police had special patrols in black neighborhoods but none in white ones. The Pasadena Chief of Police belong to an Elks Club that maintained a semisecret card room in which a "key card" was necessary to gain entrance; two other private clubs also had gambling facilities. At a gambling trial of blacks picked up in a raid, the defendants sought to introduce evidence of these facts to show a pattern of discriminatory enforcement. The "keeper" of the card room refused to testify on the grounds that he might incriminate himself.

Another type of law supported by the inoperative personal belief syndrome is the Sunday closing law. Enacted in a more religious time and upheld as recently as 1961 by the Supreme Court, the Sunday closing laws are nothing more than an invitation to corruption. It has been estimated that to forestall prosecutions police in New York City take more than $6,200,000 a year in bribes from ten thousand Puerto Rican shops. Police graft extracted from delicatessens and other shops open on Sunday in New York is reported to be equally widespread.

Evidence of this kind of corruption is exceedingly elusive and difficult to gather; one concrete case of a two-dollar payoff received by a policeman from a Brooklyn grocery store owner was documented by Detective Frank Serpico, who made a tape recording of a conversation in which the bribe-taker admitted the act to another policeman. The grocery store owner was Serpico's brother; the policeman taking the money was dismissed from the force.

Police latitude in enforcing unenforceable law is often explicitly approved by the courts. The Arkansas Supreme Court once upheld the police practice of prosecuting only grocery stores under the Sunday closing laws. Drug stores, hotels, filling stations, restaurants, funeral homes, bakeries, tourist courts, bus stations, city park concessions, and sporting goods stores operated on Sunday without arrests or prosecutions. In spite of the fairly clear evidence of discrimination here, the Arkansas court affirmed a directed verdict of guilty. The court found the constitutionality of the discriminatory practice in the answer to the question: "If the state statute applied by its terms to grocery stores alone, would it be valid?" The answer to that question, the court said, was clearly in the affirmative, since the legislature is empowered to make classifications in its criminal law. Just so, but traditionally that power is presumed to be in the legislature alone; by its decision the Arkansas Supreme Court permitted the police themselves to make the criminal law of the state.

The use of these laws does not prevent white-collar and Government officials from engaging in the same activities. The common streetwalker is often arrested, but the expensive call girl who may spend a few days with a Congressman or high official on a yacht or in a private suite is rarely charged. The police did not devote an inordinate amount of attention to social drinking by influential people during Prohibition, nor does respectable gambling run much risk of finding itself abated.

The morals statutes, illness statutes (such as those condemning alcoholism or drug addiction), and nuisance laws (vagrancy, loitering, and others) have been said to represent the practice of "overcriminalization" prevalent in American society, but they are not the only manifestation of the inoperative personal belief syndrome. The widespread disregard of Supreme Court decisions against prayers in public schools represents a different aspect of the syndrome. Teachers and administrators, as well as private citizens, have ignored the Court's decisions. Few of the parents who protest the loudest believe in the efficacy of morning prayer; otherwise prayers at the breakfast table would serve as well as public requests for absolution one hour later. Moreover, the parents undercut their own position by admitting the blandest and most nondenominational prayers would satisfy them. Nevertheless, they cannot admit to friends and neighbors (and perhaps to themselves) that their heated protests against the Supreme Court spring more from a desire to look respectable in the eyes of the community than a heartfelt and devout wish that their children learn the lesson of personal and daily supplication to that mysterious (but nondenominational) omnipotence that rules us all.*

CRISIS. The Government's perception that an incident or problem has reached a crisis and cannot be handled routinely may determine whether or not the Government will break the law. Official conduct that would not be contemplated in the absence of an emergency is often felt to be compelled when a crisis is at hand. The more politicized the issue the more likely that the Government will interpret the situation as a crisis requiring strong measures that may overstep the bounds of law. Sometimes the overstepping is deliberate and sometimes it is the inevitable result of the lack of time to ponder the best course.

The "necessity" that attends any crisis can naturally be overworked. "Military necessity" is a catch phrase that permits nations to avoid calumny (they think) or legal responsibility for acts that would otherwise be war crimes; similarly, the Government has argued, unsuccessfully, that domestic security permits it to adopt measures that would be unthinkable in the absence of a crisis. The threat of war or its acutality is the most frequently heard excuse for extensions of

---

*This is not to argue that lawbreaking caused by the overcriminalization statutes is the same as that caused by the Supreme Court's prayer decisions. The first type of law creates black markets and establishes an enormous potential for public corruption; the second type of law does not create malfeasance, at least overtly. The first type of law is maintained and supported by the inoperative belief syndrome; the second type is violated because of that syndrome. But in both situations, the syndrome is responsible for lawbreaking by public officials.

governmental power. President Roosevelt in 1942 invoked the war power to "suspend" certain laws, and he herded Japanese-Americans into concentration camps and got away with it. President Truman seized the steel mills pursuant to the same claim. President Roosevelt permitted the writ of habeas corpus to be suspended during World War II (although the Supreme Court ruled after the war that the suspension was illegal).

The cold war has produced other kinds of crisis—real or imagined—and the argument for unauthorized wiretapping and other spying stems from the same theory. Whether the crisis is rhetoric or reality is usually difficult to discern and the bipartisan spirit that usually hovers over issues of war and peace quite frequently permits the Government to do what it wants.

Crisis is not perceived alone in the eyes of the Government. The ultimate fact for America is that the Government is sustained by the beliefs of the population at large. And the conclusion is inescapable, therefore, that the Government often breaks the law simply because the people want and expect it to do so. The crisis of crime in the late 'Sixties was clearly a real fear in the minds of a substantial number of the population. Politicians did not invent the crisis, but they inevitably played upon it. The off-duty policemen who attacked black citizens in a New York courthouse were doubtless responding as a good portion of the electorate would have had them respond—somehow their action was helping counter "crime in the streets." When a fearful but dominant majority wants action, the lawless solution is usually the quickest.

ABSURDITY OF THE LAWS.   One short answer to the why of some Government lawbreaking is that some of the laws officials are bidden to obey are manifestly absurd. In almost every political jurisdiction district attorneys are commanded by law to prosecute every infraction of the law ("The district attorney *shall* prosecute . . ."). But even if it were possible, why would the police want to arrest every jaywalker when it is far safer, in most cities, to cross the street in the middle of an empty block than at a crowded and irrational intersection? Why should the police try to enforce laws prohibiting the sale of contraceptive devices? Why should they arrest people on the streets, otherwise quiet, who don't "appear" to have "gainful employment"? Many of these laws present so many administrative headaches that the police need no excuse to ignore them.

The 1970 Policeman of the Year, Sgt. Paul E. Fabian of Rotterdam, New York, was named jointly by the International Association of Police Chiefs and *Parade* Magazine for his effective fight against drug addiction. His method was simple: instead of arresting suspects, he pledged them immunity from prosecution if they promised to do nothing more than talk to him honestly about their problems and perhaps tell the names of their pushers. According to a news account: "the sergeant, along with his chief, Joseph S. Dominelli, and the Schenectady County District Attorney, Howard A. Levine, readily admits that his informal administration of immunity is both unusual and illegal. But all of them agree that it has produced remarkable success in keeping a growing narcotics problem in Rotterdam from turning into an epidemic."

If at the stationhouse, so too—perhaps—at the White House. From the perspective of the Presidency, Congress enacts many downright foolish laws the country would be far better off without. If he can, the President will veto them. Lamentably, however, the Constitution provides him with no item veto, and Congress has the unfortunate habit of joining in one single bill many unrelated items—some worthy, some laughable or harmful. If he does not want the latter he cannot afford to veto the former. What can he do? Sign the bill and refuse to spend money on a wasteful weapons system the country does not need?—that is sometimes the only possible political response to an absurd and unnecessary law.

Sometimes, that is, the matter is too clear for doubt, and if it bothers the purist, that is the purist's problem. So says the Government.

Effects

The general effects of Government lawlessness are obvious: Government lawlessness, as Justice Brandeis said, breeds contempt for law; it creates gross injustice in particular cases; it is responsible for enormous monetary expense, both in the waste of taxpayers' dollars and in the failure to redress the overwhelming distortions that private business introduces into the "feee market"; it brings further crime and violence in its wake; and, finally, it may lead, paradoxically, both to dictatorship and anarchy.

Contempt for law is written in the acts of those who disobey it. When people see that Government officials who break the law are treated leniently—and the higher the rank the more lenient the treatment—they become skeptical of the belief that respect for law is of vital importance to a free society. When a two-star general loses one star but is not court-martialed for his role in covering up grievous American war crimes, but junior officers and enlisted men are subjected to the possibility of the death penalty, the prospect of law seems nothing but the prospect of brute force. When a Congressman convicted of crimes is given a light sentence but possessors of marijuana draw years in jail;* when police officers are rarely charged and even more rarely convicted for homicide, harassment, and corruption; when those who commit crimes against members of minorities are not even indicted; when people are fired from Government jobs

---

*In 1970, a philosophy professor, to protest the war, filed a false claim of twenty exemptions on his income tax return. The Government brought a criminal suit (it could have instituted a civil case to recover the taxes owed), and the protester was sentenced to a year in jail. A year later, former Congressman (and a past national commander of the American Legion) Martin B. McKneally of Newburgh, New York, pleaded guilty to a charge of filing no return in 1965. In return for the plea, the Government dropped charges of failing to report a total of $54,000 in 1964, 1966, and 1967. His one-year sentence was *suspended*, though he was fined $5,000.

for telling the truth on behalf of the taxpayer; when prosecutors fabricate evidence to maintain their own reputations; when judges violate law to teach men humbled before them to respect it; when legislators ignore constitutional requirements and when they engage in the most obvious conflicts of interest—then legal institutions are demeaned and undercut. The incentive to obey the law is reduced to a game of "doing whatever you can as long as you can get away with it" and we return in no small measure to the natural state that Thomas Hobbes saw for humankind: "solitary, poor, nasty, brutish, and short."

Since a democracy is premised on a series of governmental checks and balances, the lawbreaking of one branch of the Government may be expected to produce a reaction from another. The open violation by state governments of constitutional policies against racial segregation has led directly to intimate federal supervision over large areas of what was once considered the province of state legislatures. The open display of contempt by state legislatures toward their own constitutions has led to direct judicial supervision of their apportionment process. The sustained example of police lawlessness in certain areas of the criminal process has likewise brought stern rebuke from the courts.

But the courts are not structured or intended to do the jobs of other organs of Government. Necessarily, therefore, the attempt by courts to control other governmental lawbreaking will itself be an overreaction, in turn requiring a response from the agencies they are attempting to control. The curious spectacle of one branch of Government hurling accusations of wrongdoing at another can only confuse the citizen and bring the law into further disrepute. Moreover, it can often lead to ludicrous results; for instance, President Nixon first campaigned against judicial interference in the criminal process, raising the hopes of the police that he would return the nation to their nostalgic vision of its (misremembered) former quiescence, but he later declared that he would not move to end de facto segregation because the courts had not yet required him to do so.

Nothing need be added here about individual injustices caused by Government lawlessness. The effects are explicit in all the examples presented in these pages, and it may be admitted in passing that the chapter titles in this book are obviously artificial: an injustice to one person is a grave potential threat to all of us. Similarly, the high cost to everyone of Government crimes needs no further elaboration.

Government lawlessness can breed hostility that turns to violence. A Government that refuses to enforce its proscriptions and that violates its own prescriptions cannot expect to remain unscathed; a society that permits its Government to break the law cannot expect to remain unharmed. Civil disobedience is almost a corollary to Government illegality, and criminal disobedience is certain, for the art of skillful retaliation is subtle and rage can be expressed best by hostility. As the authors of a study of New York's failure to enforce its antidiscrimination policies concluded:

Thus far, the only progress that has been made in the hiring of blacks in the construction trades has been as the result of confrontation and nearly open conflict. Not until students at the State University of Buffalo picketed the campus was construction there halted, and effort to achieve improvement begun. Now, even as confrontation has eased, the state has begun to delay and hamstring local efforts to hire the unemployed for state-financed construction there. A high official of the State Division of Human Rights put it to us succinctly: "The only time the Division can act," he said, "is when pressure is brought from outside." Thus the entire policy of the state is directed at inviting confrontation by not acting in its absence; and further, encouraging confrontation by responding to the pressure it brings. The result is to invite in New York and Buffalo, in Albany and elsewhere across the state precisely that kind of racial confrontation which has so severely divided this country and this state already. It is a prescription for disaster.

That Government lawlessness can lead to a dictatorship is almost a truism. A classic statement of the proposition that the law can be ignored when greater purposes are to be served—that the Government ought to engage in civil or criminal disobedience—was Congressman F. Edward Hebert's celebrated 1967 advice to the federal Government that it ignore the First Amendment and induct vocal antiwar demonstrators into the Army. Said Hebert: "Let's forget the First Amendment. . . . I know this [prosecution] would be rescinded by the Supreme Court but at least the effort should be made. It would show the American people that the Justice Department and Congress were trying to clean up this rat-infested area." In response to a flurry of criticism, Congressman Hebert a few days later provided a gloss on his remarks: "It's not that I love the First Amendment less; it's that I love my country more." This was candid advocacy of the "chilling effect": damn the law, prosecute anyway.

Human rights are fragile and abstract notions. When disregarded or toyed with they have a tendency to shatter or dissolve. The logical extension of Hebert's assertion that governmental lawlessness is occasionally proper is to put everyone in jail and let the courts decide who should not be there.

The vesting of broad discretionary powers in all public officials leads to the possibility of dictatorship. It is a standard rule of constitutional law that vague statutes—e.g., "disloyalty to the state," or "immoral behavior"—cannot be used as the basis for criminal sanctions. But the evil is the same if a panoply of laws permits the police to pick and choose the laws they want to enforce and the people against whom they wish to enforce them.

Finally, Government lawlessness may lead even to anarchy. When the bureaucracy avoids individual responsibility by diffusing all responsibility throughout a bloated hierarchy, the lack of accountability is precisely the same anarchy feared in the private sector. Anarchy is chaos or the lack of order; it presupposes no restraints, force, or regulation. Precisely this situation may occur in bureaucracies operating under regulations that permit them to go in both directions at once or to ignore their legal responsibilities altogether. And when that happens often enough, we may reasonably expect that crime, inflation, unemployment, poverty, war, pollution, environmental decay, racism, consumer fraud, and monopoly will result.